I07929B2

IMAGES
of America

AMERICAN INDIANS IN MILWAUKEE

On the Cover: Pictured is the Consolidated Tribes of American Indians dance group in 1948. They are, from left to right, (first row) Opal Skenandore, Doris Steffes, Shirley Steffes, Myron Skenandore, and Joseph Webster; (second row) Alpheus Smith, James Webster, Frank Smart, and Henry Jacko; (third row) Mrs. Henry Jacko, Delia Smith, Francis Webster, Kenneth Powless, Ronald Reil, Francis Coleman, and Eugene Silas. (Photograph by Russ Andrews; courtesy of Opal Skenandore.)

IMAGES
of America

AMERICAN INDIANS IN MILWAUKEE

Antonio J. Doxtator and Renee J. Zakhar

ARCADIA
PUBLISHING

ISBN 978-0-7385-8258-0

Published by Arcadia Publishing
Charleston, South Carolina

Printed in the United States of America

Library of Congress Control Number: 2011924852

For all general information, please contact Arcadia Publishing:
Telephone 843-853-2070
Fax 843-853-0044
E-mail sales@arcadiapublishing.com
For customer service and orders:
Toll-Free 1-888-313-2665

Visit us on the Internet at www.arcadiapublishing.com

To the members of the American Indian community of Milwaukee, who inspired this book

Contents

ACKNOWLEDGMENTS

We want to express appreciation to the Milwaukee Indian community for allowing us to use their images and private photographs. The authors wish to thank their family and friends—without their encouragement, information, and financial support, this book would not be possible. Renee Zakhar would also like to thank the Academic Opportunity Program at UW-Milwaukee for fellowship support. We are especially indebted to those who shared their photographs, especially Opal Skenandore, Diane Amour, Diane Porter, Kitty Hill and Donna Skenadore, Drew LaBelle, Dona Yahola, and the Doxtator and Zakhar families. Several photographers gave us permission to reprint their work, including Empire Studios, Todd Dacquisto, Peter Graves, Barbara Jakopac, Nicholas Patrinos Jr., and Siobhan Marks. Susan Otto of the Milwaukee Public Museum, Mark G. Thiel, Melissa Sweetser of Marquette University, and Ellen Engseth, Brad Houston of UWM Archives, and Rose Fortier of the Milwaukee Public Library went out of their way to go through their files to track down images and information. Also, Ron Smith and Alan King of the *Milwaukee Journal Sentinel* helped us gain access to the newspaper's archives. Genevieve G. McBride allowed us to use her concept of Josette Juneau as Milwaukee's "founding mother." Finally, we wish to thank Jeff Ruetsche, our editor at Arcadia Publishing, for his assistance. All efforts have been made to attribute photographers and individuals correctly. Anyone with knowledge of ownership, mistakes, or omissions, let us know and it will be corrected in future printings.

INTRODUCTION

Dancing, swirling native people in costume is how an Indian community is often photographed. It would have been easy to present photographs for their colorful nature. Instead, we have gathered photographs that show the political, social, and cultural history of American Indians in Milwaukee.

Indian people have always lived in the area now known as Milwaukee. Our narrative begins in the mid-1700s with a cluster of fairly autonomous villages along the lakeshore of Potawatomi, Ho-Chunk, and Menominee people mixed with significant minorities of Ottawa, Ojibwa, and Sauk. This mix can confuse people today who tend to think of social groups in a racial or nationalistic manner, but the way of life then was centered on family and clan obligations and not just tribal relationships. Intermarriage reinforced and maintained these family ties. French fur traders flowing down from Canada followed this pattern by marrying into Indian families, and those relationships furthered their own business interests. Josette Juneau was part of this web as the third generation of her Menominee family to marry a French trader. She married Solomon Laurent Juneau, who is considered the founder of Milwaukee. The couple assumed one of her father's well-established trading posts along the western shore of Lake Michigan. Josette took on the responsibility of running it, as her husband often traveled for business.

By the mid-1800s, Indian people were forcibly removed from Milwaukee by federal policy, and although it is likely there has always been some kind of Indian population in the city, there is very little record of permanent settlement until the 1930s. Prior to then, Indian people did come back to perform in pageants, shows, and Indian village recreations at the state fair and along the lakefront. Their primary liaison was the Milwaukee Public Museum and the director, Samuel A. Barrett. In 1926, Barrett arranged to have a village constructed for the opening of the Lincoln Memorial Drive and Bridge, and villages were set up for several years after with different tribes taking turns at hosting their culture at the Milwaukee Mid-Summer Festival. A group from the Lac Courte Oreilles band, for instance, traveled by truck from their homes to a train with a stop in Chicago, finally arriving in Milwaukee with everything they needed to construct a village and live within it for five days.

By the 1930s, the Indian population in Milwaukee increased substantially, and about 300 individuals are recorded living primarily in the downtown area. Most of them were Oneida, who came to the state from their reservation in New York in stages beginning around 1822. There was enough of an Indian presence in Milwaukee to inspire a formal organization of 200 members called the Council Fire of American Indians with three Oneida women as officers in 1929. Another organization formed in 1937, the Consolidated Tribes of American Indians. The Indian people that belonged to these organizations did not recreate villages, but they did dress in general forms of native-inspired outfits and initiated many sports teams, a women's guild, and music socials.

After World War II, Indian people began to move to the city and settle in ever larger numbers through today, echoing the general American pattern of urban migration. From the 1950s through the 1970s, things changed substantially as Milwaukee Indians—especially urban Indians—joined others in using protest as a way to meet their goals. But their goals were unique compared to other groups in that they chose to protest for sovereignty and autonomy rather than inclusion and equality. Increasingly, they took control of their performances and powwows, and they initiated new organizations, such as the American Indian Information and Action Group and the local chapter of the National Indian Youth Council, signaling a new, more-challenging attitude. These new organizations were more political than cultural, and members did not perform other than through protest or confrontation.

Several long-lasting programs came out of this new attitude. The Indian Community School partnered with the Forest County Potawatomi for a joint venture in gaming. The school gained secure funding, and the Potawatomi regained historical land now held in trust in the Menomonee Valley. The Milwaukee Area Technical College (MATC) and the University of Wisconsin–Milwaukee (UWM) started Native American student and student-assistance groups. They focused on developing classes with a Native focus, launching language efforts, speakers' bureaus, and conferences, and establishing their own powwows.

Between the 1980s and today, American Indian organizations have become more specialized. This has had the effect of increasing participation of Indian people seeking not just culture or political satisfaction but tribal identification and knowledge, but it has also drained the participation of intertribal organizations. The Oneida and the Ho-Chunk opened branch offices in Milwaukee. The Catholic church established an interdenominational center that led to Lutheran and Catholic churches to meet the needs of urban Indian people. Indian Summer Festival launched in 1987 and quickly became the most popular intertribal venue for Indians in the region.

Going forward, the Forest County Potawatomi have renewed their commitment to provide an intertribal Center in Milwaukee. New Indian organizations and activities such as an Indian chamber of commerce, hymn-singing, language classes, drumming practice, and film and art projects continue to show the innovation and dedication of Indians in Milwaukee to the spiritual, cultural, and social well-being of their community.

One

The Gathering Place

The history of any city in America is steeped in Indian history, and Milwaukee is no exception. The pattern of urban settlement is similar as well: Indian autonomy, Indian removal, an invitation to come back and recreate a city's imagined romantic past, and finally, Indian resettlement under new conditions.

The roots of Milwaukee as a city are found in its unique spot as a convergence of waterways of the Great Lakes that made it attractive to Indians and, later, Europeans. What made Milwaukee unique for Indians compared to other water highway regions was its relative isolation from European interests in Green Bay or Chicago. Around the time of the American Revolution, Milwaukee was a gathering place, a cluster of the five relatively autonomous villages of Potawatomi, Menominee, and Ho-Chunk who pursued their own interests somewhat independent of European designs. Canadian French trader Jacques Vieau staked a claim in Milwaukee, marrying a daughter of an Indian leader and establishing a robust trading post by 1795. Vieau's daughter Josette married his clerk Solomon Juneau and by 1825, they took over her father's post and helped build the character and foundation of Milwaukee.

Federal policy of forced Indian removal in the 1830s literally drove Indian people from Milwaukee. Starting around 1900, Indians were invited back to work, recreating Indian villages and performing in elaborate pageants at local theaters, the state fair, and Milwaukee's lakefront. For Milwaukeeans, Indians in the city contrasted urban progress and reenacted the romanticized, primordial past of the region. For Wisconsin Indian people, it was an opportunity to make a living.

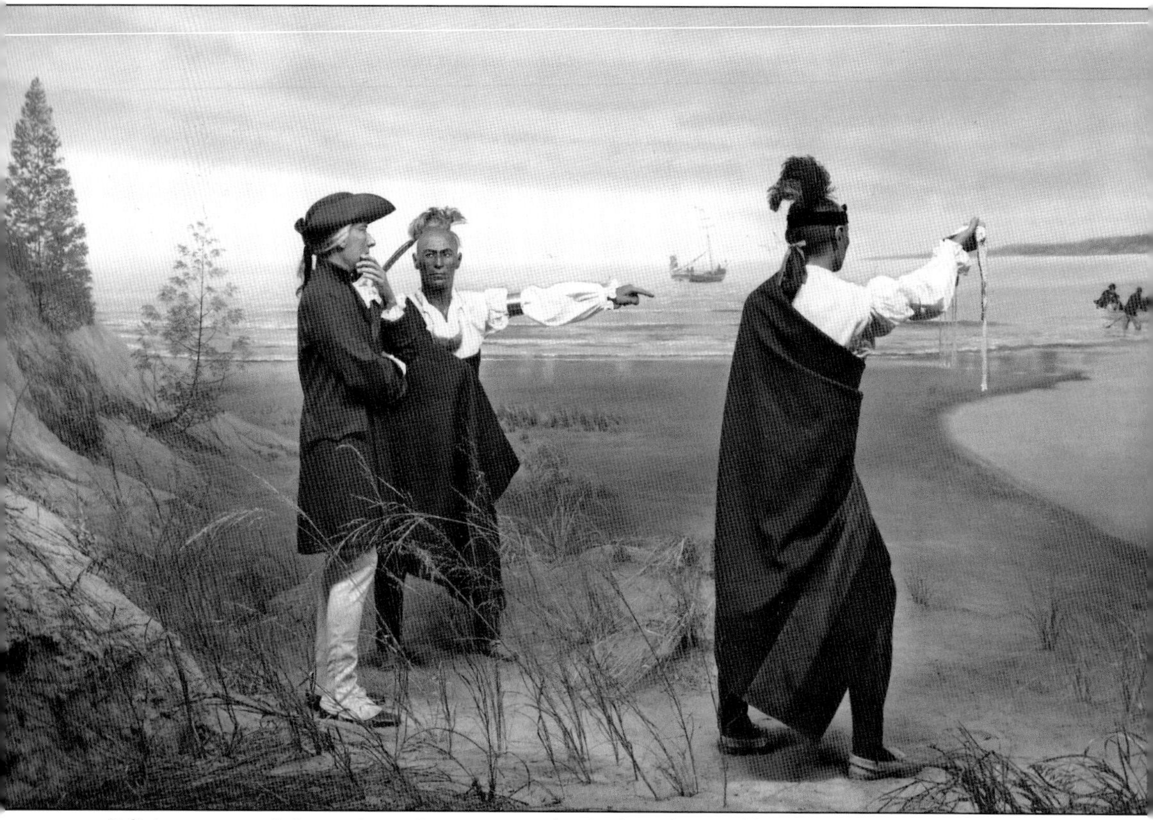

Felicity is one of the earliest dioramas in the Milwaukee Public Museum. At the time of the Revolutionary War, the Milwaukee region was home to about five autonomous Indian villages of Potawatomi, Menominee, and Ho-Chunk, and within each village were significant minorities of the Ottawa, Ojibwa, and Sauk tribes. One of the Milwaukee Potawatomi's most influential chiefs was Siggenauk, or Blackbird, who made alliances with Americans to counter British desires for the area. In the 1780s, the ship *Felicity* was deployed to patrol the Great Lakes to persuade area Indians of British strength. In a likely interpretation, a British officer of the *Felicity* and others stand facing and pointing south towards principal Potawatomi villages that Siggenauk led. One source has said the British planned to use the ship's patrol to capture the defiant chief either by force or by bribing other Indians and having him turned over to British authorities. But the plan failed and the British were never able to get a strong hold on the Milwaukee area, easing the path for American dominance. (Courtesy of the Milwaukee Public Museum.)

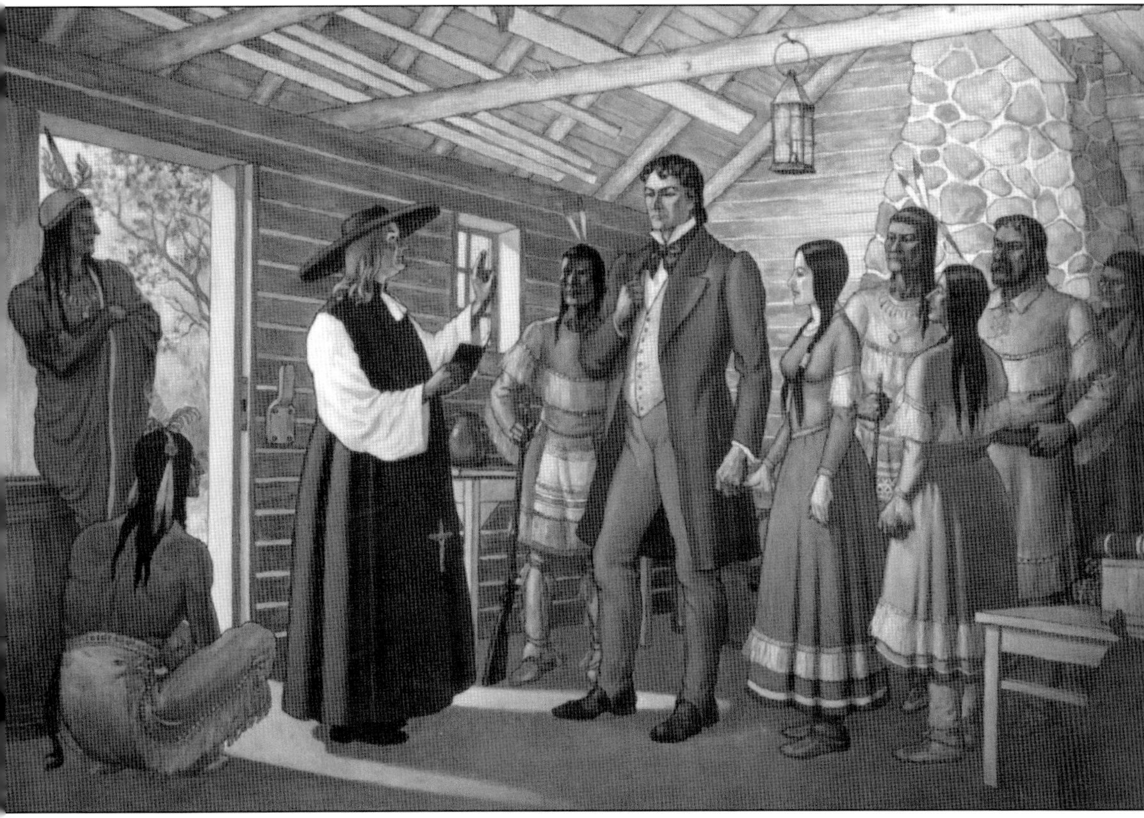

Historian Genevieve McBride has referred to Josette Vieau Juneau as the founding mother of Milwaukee. Without disputing Solomon Juneau's influence as founder of Milwaukee, Josette and her family are equal in reflecting the growth and character of the city. Josette's father, Jacques Vieau, was already an established fur trader in the region when he made a beneficial match with Angelique le Roy, whose maternal grandfather was an important Menominee tribal leader with strong ties to the Potawatomi. Josette was likely born of another woman but lived with her father. Vieau established and maintained trading posts along the west shore of Lake Michigan that eventually developed into Euro-American towns. As the fanciful painting above illustrates, Josette married Juneau, and they moved to Milwaukee to fully assume Vieau's post by 1825. (Courtesy of the Milwaukee County Historical Society.)

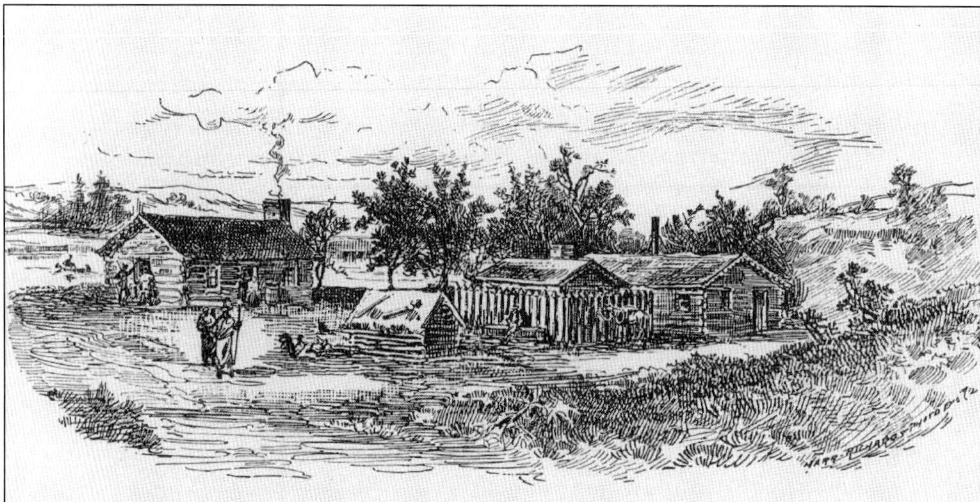

SOLOMON JUNEAU'S LOG DWELLING AND STOREHOUSE.

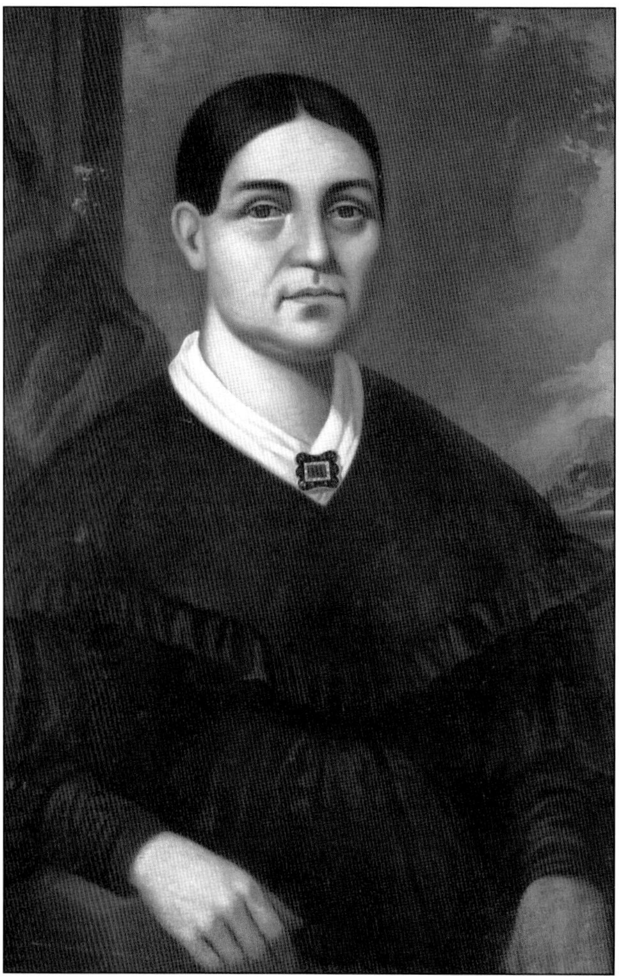

The Juneaus' post overlooked the Menomenee Valley. Like most French traders, Solomon Juneau was highly mobile, traveling to secure goods. It fell to Josette (and her children) to run her husband's store, stockade, and home while giving birth to his 17 children. (Courtesy of the Milwaukee County Historical Society.)

By most accounts, Josette Juneau was a quiet, devoutly Catholic woman who was popular in the city and with Indian people. Charles Milwaukee Sivyer is quoted as saying, "Solomon Juneau has been lauded to the skies and he is richly deserving of it all. But Solomon Juneau was not alone. He had a helpmate, a loving, loyal wife, and a brave woman. Had she the education of a white woman, she would have shone as brightly as any of her white sisters. Why all these orators don't give that good woman more praise I don't know. Why, the last words of Solomon Juneau were 'Dear wife, I come to you.'" (Courtesy of the Milwaukee Public Museum.)

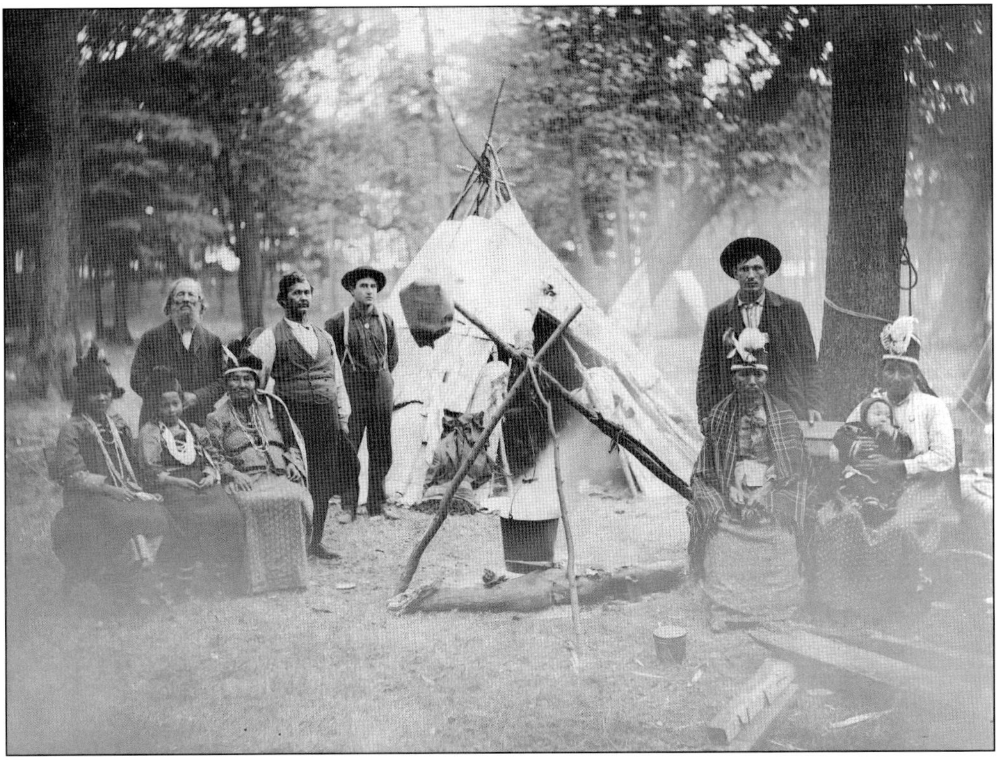

In 1906, members of the Menominee Nation constructed an Indian village on the fairgrounds in West Allis within a few hundred feet to the entrance of the fair. The short hair and modern clothes of this group may have surprised fair attendees. Indian villages remain a popular event in urban centers to this day. (Courtesy of the Historic Photo Collection/Milwaukee Public Library.)

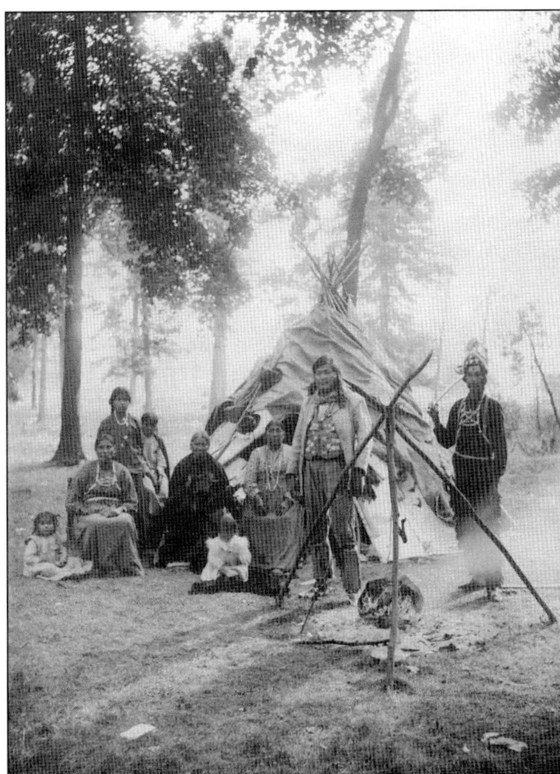

In the early 1800s, Indians were officially removed from Milwaukee by federal policy. However, they were invited back to do the one thing city residents continued to enjoy from them: performances and recreations of Indian villages, like this one at the Wisconsin State Fair in West Allis in 1904. Charles Headflyer, a member of the Lac Courte Oreilles band of Ojibwa, is standing in the center. (Courtesy of the Historic Photo Collection/Milwaukee Public Library.)

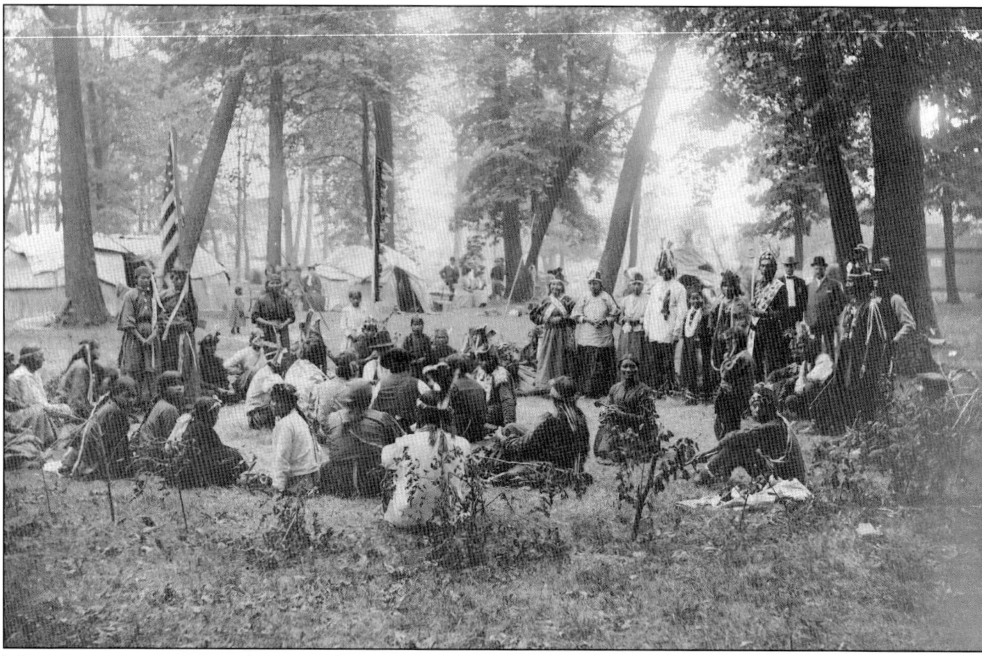

The inscription of this photograph is "Indian Pow-Wow" from the 1906 fair at the Wisconsin State Fairgrounds in West Allis. The Menominee group surrounded a drum and wore more traditional turbans and clothing for their performance in front of an audience. (Courtesy of the Historic Photo Collection/Milwaukee Public Library.)

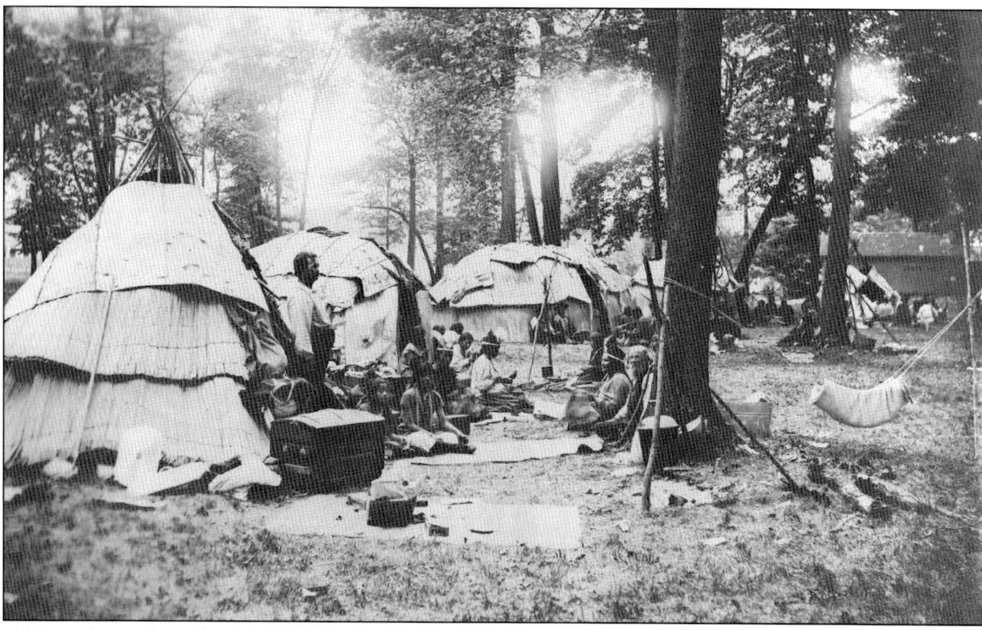

Although neither the date nor group is identified in this photograph, the traditional wigwam-style housing and hammock for a baby implies these are Woodland Indians of Wisconsin, likely Ojibwa. The natural settings Indians are presented in through these Indian villages are designed to demonstrate the progress of a city from a more primitive locality to a modern metropolis. (Courtesy of the Historic Photo Collection/Milwaukee Public Library.)

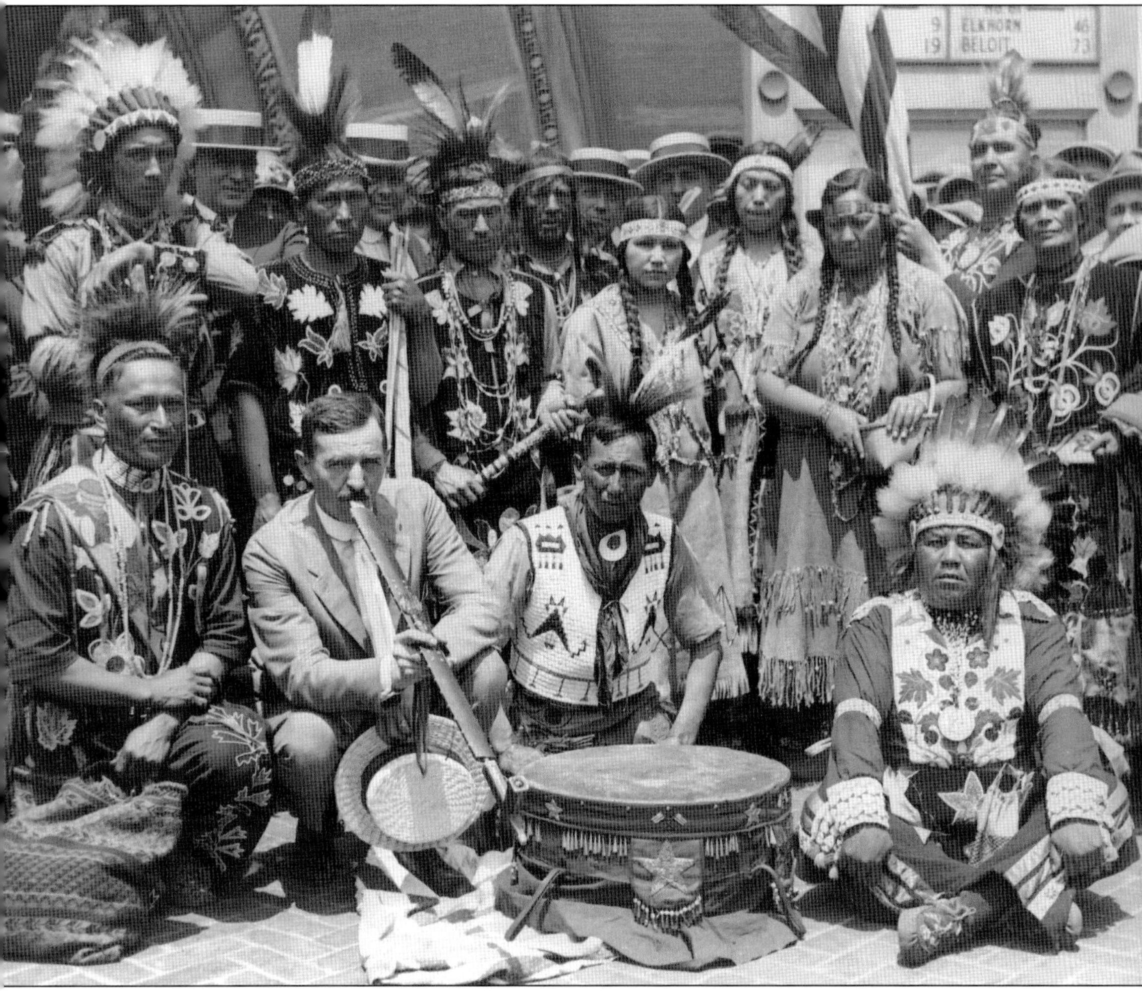

Pageants featuring American Indians were common after the early 1900s, when their extinction was thought to be eminent. Milwaukee held its share, such as a month of performances from Wisconsin Dells featuring native sopranos, harp players, and quartets. This photograph from 1925 shows Mayor Daniel Hoan meeting a group of Ojibwa that came to promote a pageant in Bayfield, Wisconsin, with a show at Saxe's Strand Theatre. Although the names of the Indians were recorded in a *Milwaukee Journal* article as Chief White Frog and Jocco of the Apostle Indians, other articles and information from Bayfield and tribal roles identify the leads as James White Jr., born in 1884 on the Bad River reservation, and his daughter Rena White, born in 1905 and educated at Haskell in Lawrence, Kansas. Jocco is Henry Jacko, also of the Bad River band, born in 1900. Many of the other players were educated in the Tomah, Flandreau, or Carlisle boarding schools for Indian youths. (Courtesy of the Historic Photo Collection/Milwaukee Public Library.)

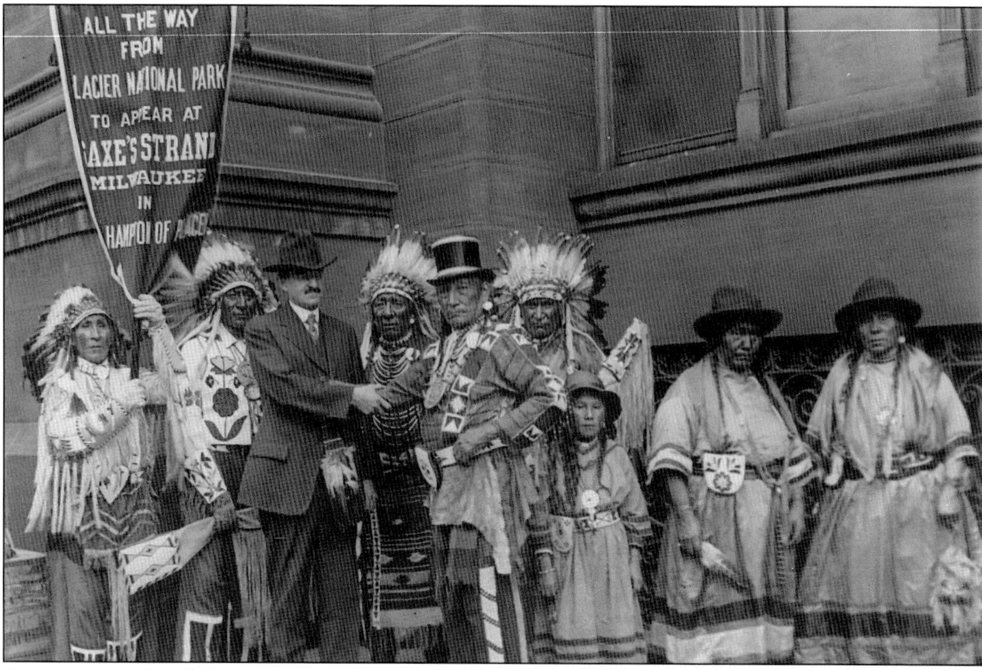

Organizers in Bayfield, Wisconsin, hoped to dazzle and procure investment from local Milwaukee businessmen with their plans for a romantic Indian event they believed would draw 2,000 Indians and become one of Wisconsin's largest events. The banner in the photograph indicating this group came from Glacier National Park may be true as Indian performers then, as today, come long distances to work. (Courtesy of the Historic Photo Collection/Milwaukee Public Library.)

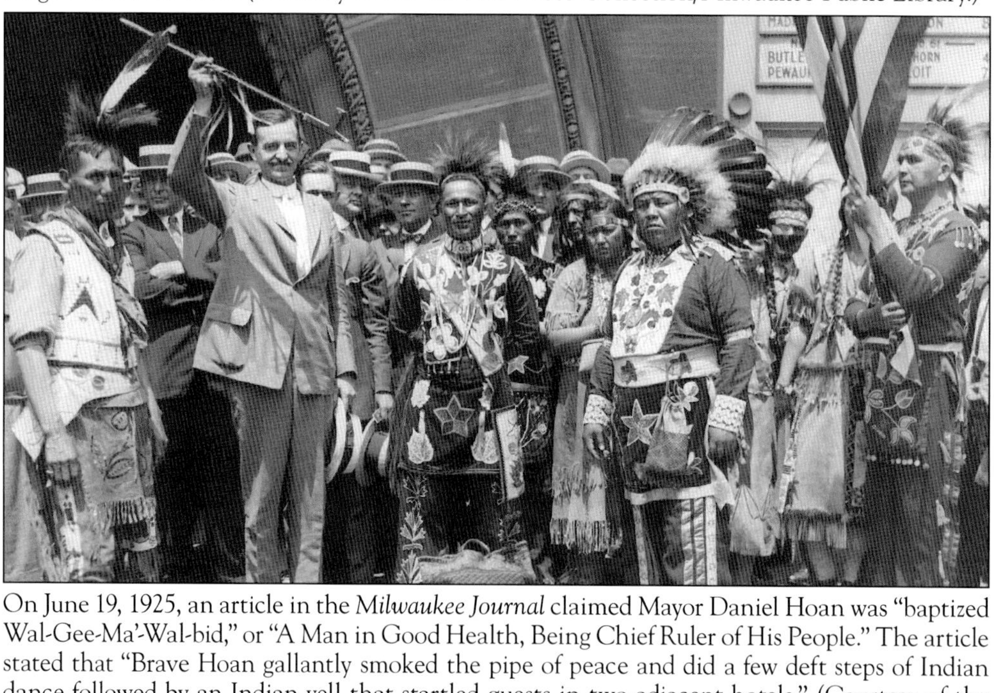

On June 19, 1925, an article in the *Milwaukee Journal* claimed Mayor Daniel Hoan was "baptized Wal-Gee-Ma'-Wal-bid," or "A Man in Good Health, Being Chief Ruler of His People." The article stated that "Brave Hoan gallantly smoked the pipe of peace and did a few deft steps of Indian dance followed by an Indian yell that startled guests in two adjacent hotels." (Courtesy of the Historic Photo Collection/Milwaukee Public Library.)

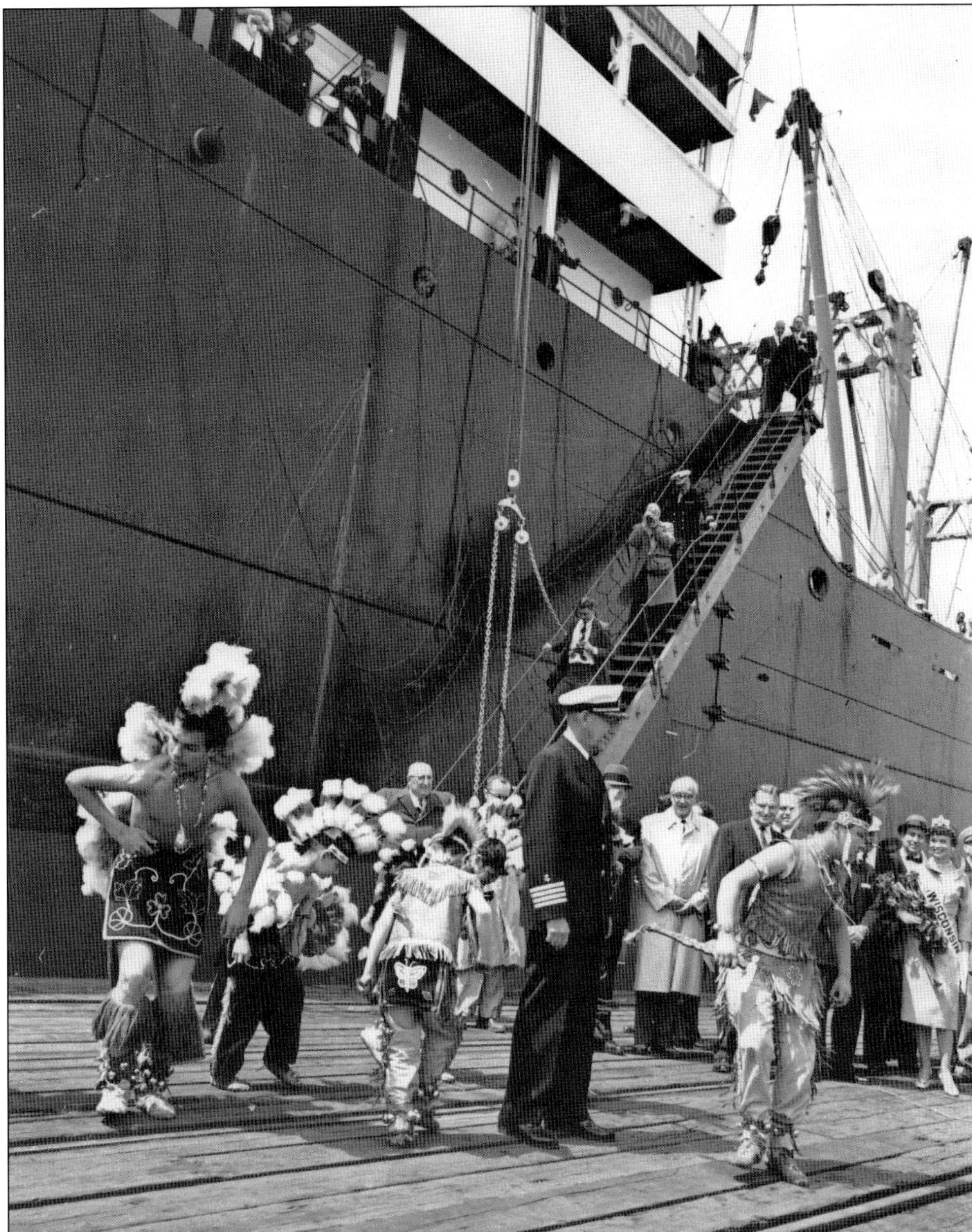

In this image, members of the Milwaukee Consolidated Tribes of American Indians dance during the opening celebration around former mayor Daniel Hoan on May 2, 1959. After generations of effort, the *Santa Regina* steamed in to the Milwaukee harbor, now part of the St. Lawrence Seaway. Hoan was part of the welcoming committee, as was Mayor Frank P. Zielder and Edmond Fitzgerald, then-president of the Northwestern Insurance Company. (Courtesy of the Historic Photo Collection/Milwaukee Public Library.)

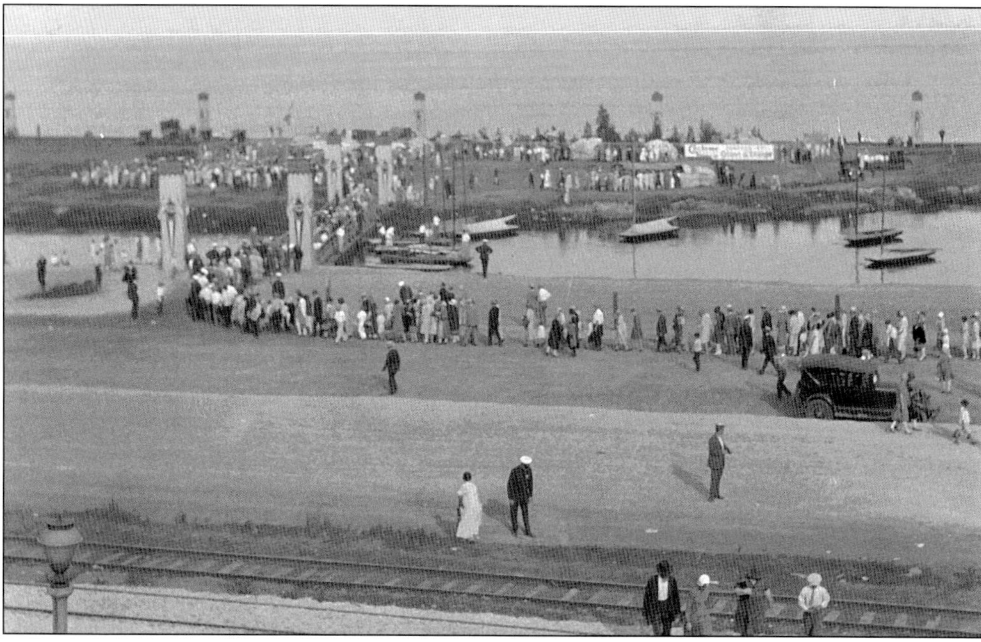

An Indian village was built at Milwaukee's lakefront to celebrate the opening of the Lincoln Memorial Drive and Bridge from August 6–8 in 1926. Members of the Lac Courte Oreilles band of Ojibwa and the city of Milwaukee built the village on an island just off of Juneau Park's lagoon. (Courtesy of the Milwaukee Public Museum.)

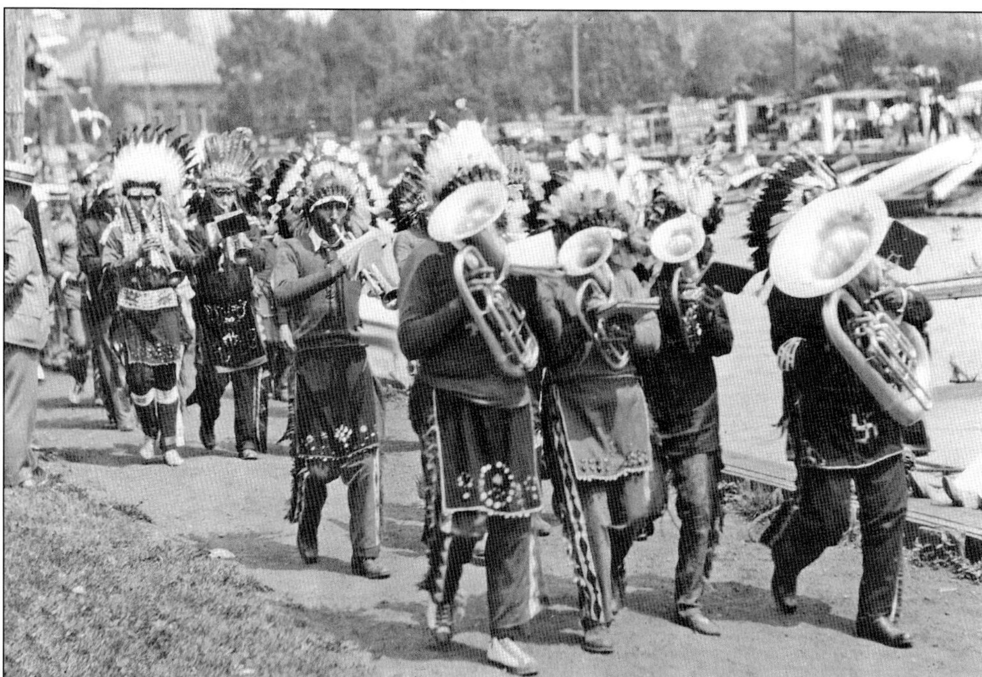

In 1926, an Indian band took part in the 10-mile parade that was the highlight of the Court of Neptune pageant, commemorating the opening of the Lincoln Memorial Bridge, the predecessor to the Daniel Hoan Bridge, which eventually replaced it. (Courtesy of the Milwaukee Public Museum.)

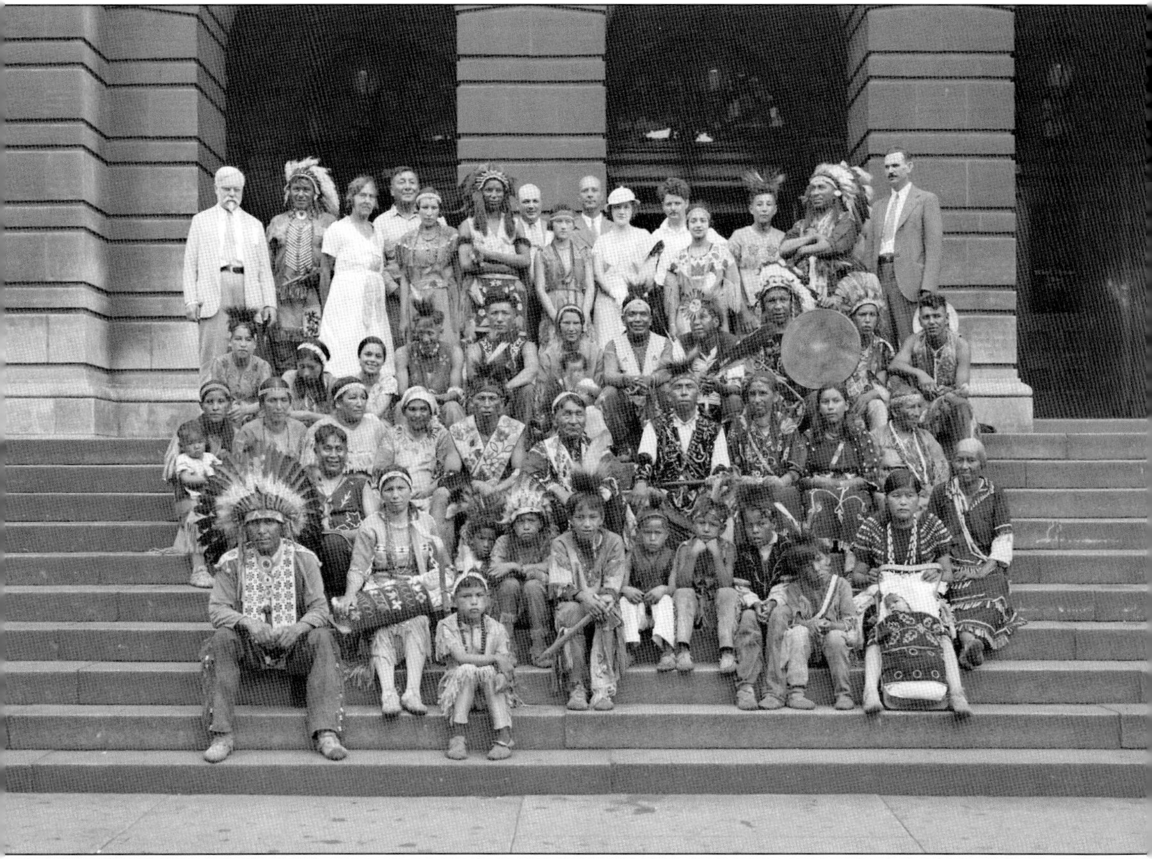

Members of the Lac Courte Oreilles band of Ojibwa pose on the Milwaukee Public Library stairs in 1933. Milwaukee mayor Daniel Hoan issued a formal proclamation for Milwaukee Homecoming Week in mid-July. The city officially gave workers a half-holiday on Wednesday and Thursday of that week and encouraged business owners to release their employees in order to take part in the festivities. Events took place all around the city at churches and playgrounds, along with visits to breweries and industrial plants, and a parade down Wisconsin Avenue. At the lakefront, an Indian village was constructed following the tradition of Indian villages built at the Wisconsin State Fair Park in the early part of the century, presumably to reconstruct what the city looked like before the first white man came to the area and, as Hoan wrote in 1933, to show Milwaukee's progress from "an Indian trading post to a great metropolis." (Courtesy of the Milwaukee Public Museum.)

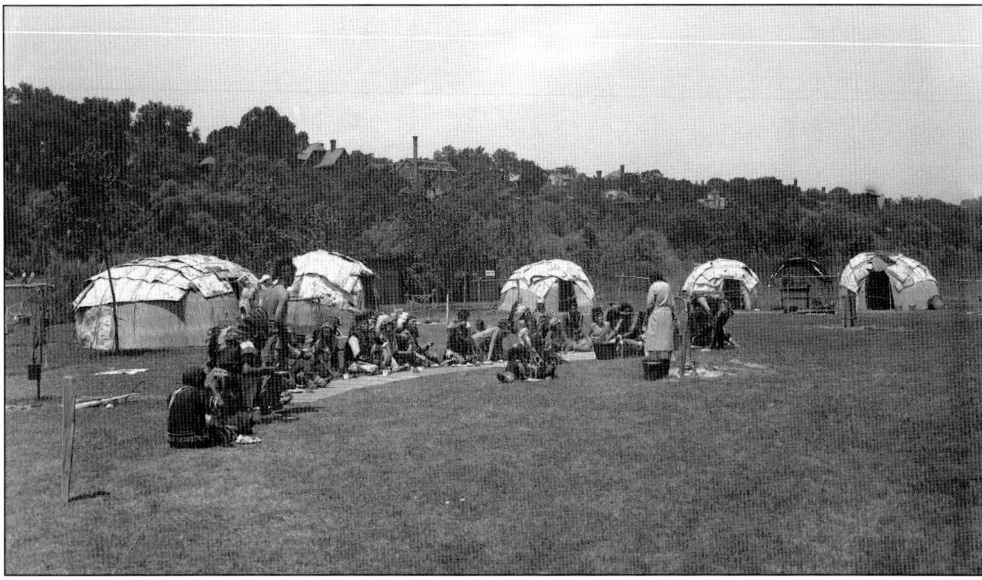

A Works Progress Administration project team assembled and labeled more than 1,000 photographs recording the partnership between the Milwaukee Public Museum and Wisconsin Indian tribes to construct Indian villages at the lakefront. This 1933 photograph show the site near the lagoon in the village's Juneau Park. (Courtesy of the Milwaukee Public Museum.)

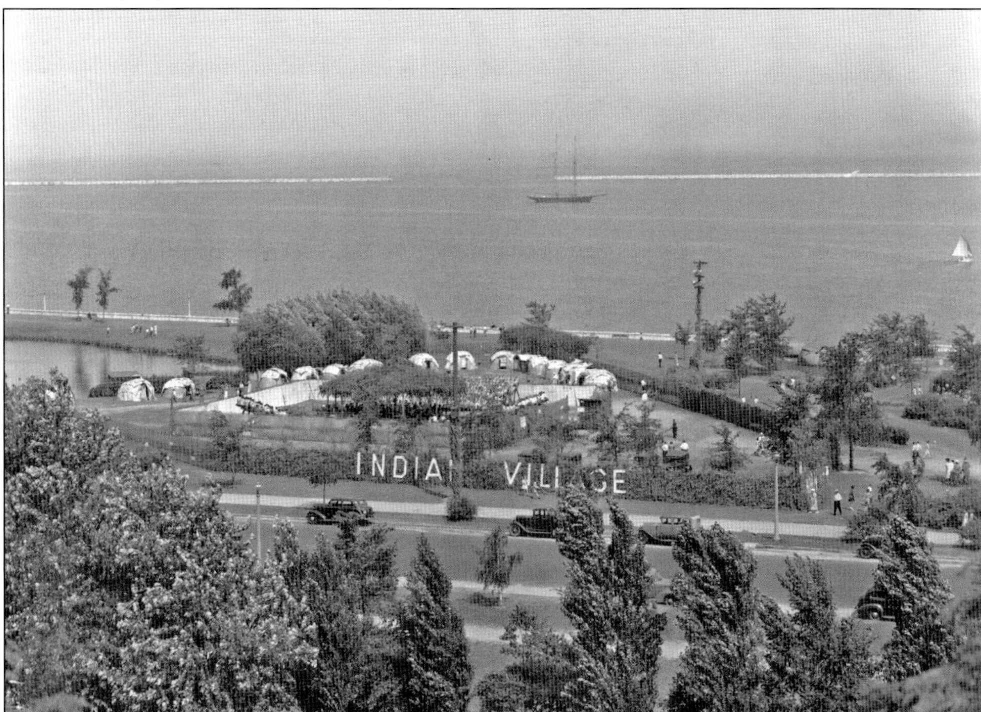

The Ojibwa and the Milwaukee Public Museum continued their partnership in the years 1933, 1934, 1936, and 1937. It was recommended that the Indian village be moved to the eastern shore of the lagoon to boost attendance, and this picture shows it reestablished on that side in 1936. (Courtesy of the Milwaukee Public Museum.)

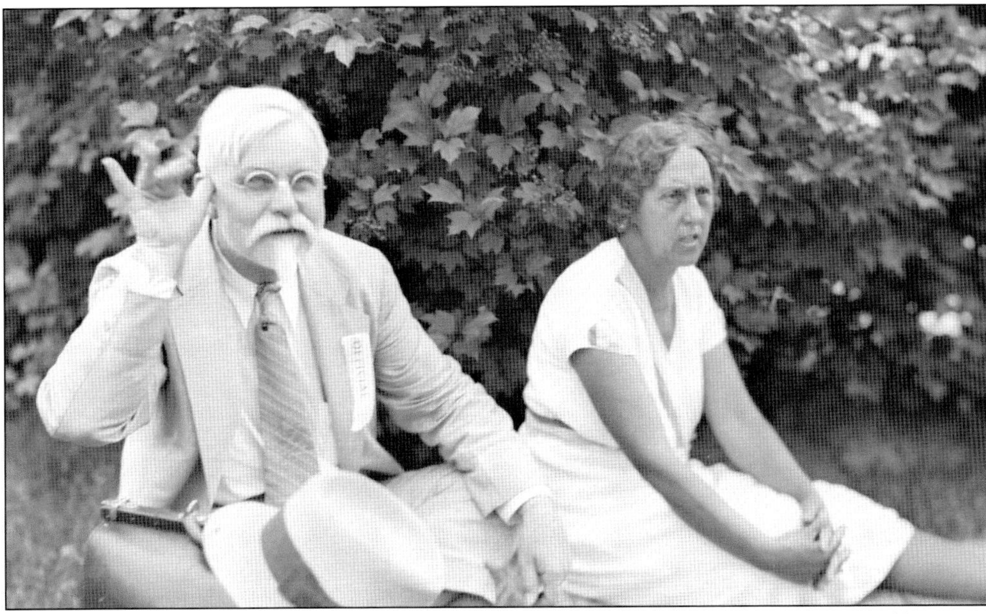

The director of the Milwaukee Public Museum, Dr. Samuel A. Barrett (left), was appointed by Mayor Daniel Hoan to head the Committee of the Indian Village. Barrett contracted with Mayme Perkins of the Lac Courte Oreilles band of Ojibwa (right) to arrange for the families who would construct homes and live and dance within the village site. (Courtesy of the Milwaukee Public Museum.)

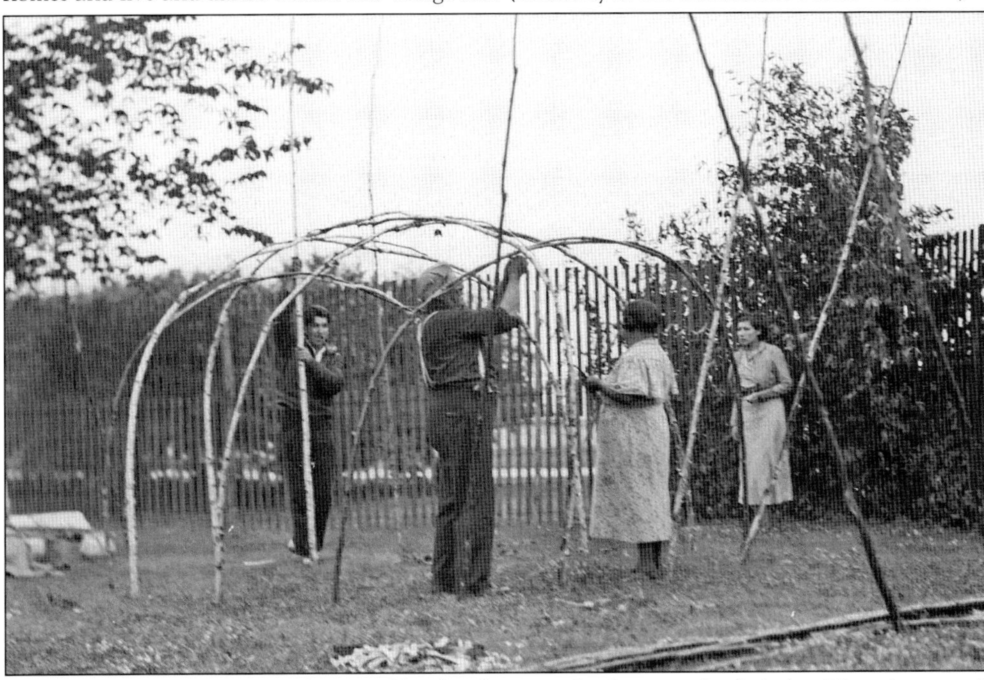

In the image above, Louis Corbine and his family set up the framework of a lodge. This photograph is typical of those that show the Lac Courte Oreilles band of Ojibwa assembling authentic birch-bark-and-mat wigwams in 1933 for 10 different families that came by truck, then train, before making a stop at Chicago. The visitors carried enough material, equipment, and regalia for 32 adults, seven children, and four babies. (Courtesy of the Milwaukee Public Museum.)

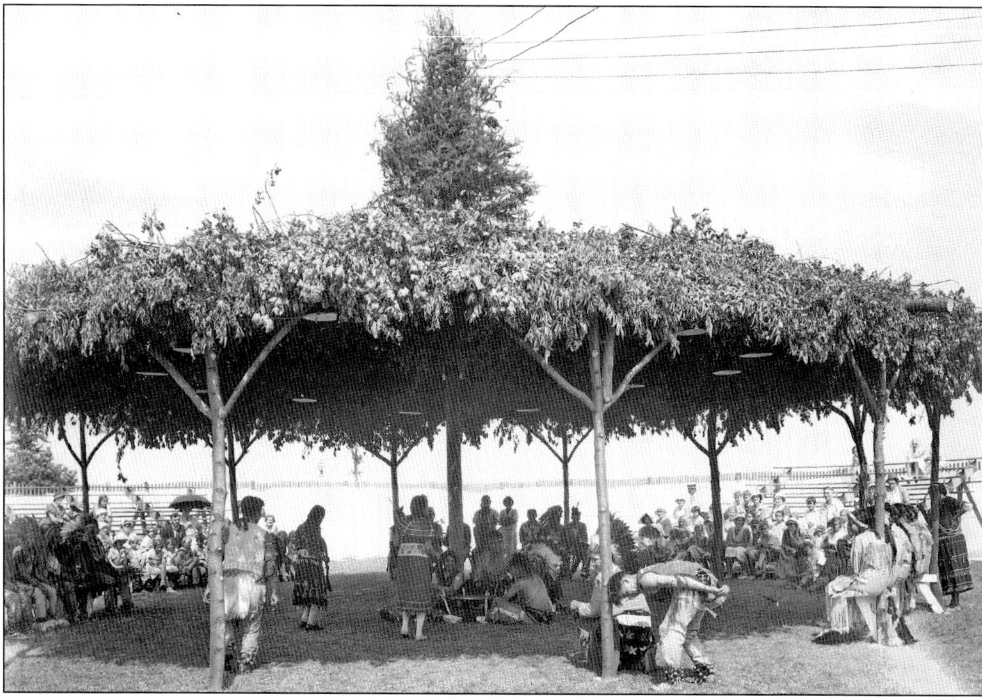

The Milwaukee Public Museum arranged to build a large pole and canvas, brush-covered arbor that was lighted from within and surrounded by plank bleacher-seating for spectators. The arbor protected the dancers and allowed for night performances. Tickets to watch the dancers in 1933 were 25¢ for adults and 10¢ for children. (Courtesy of the Milwaukee Public Museum.)

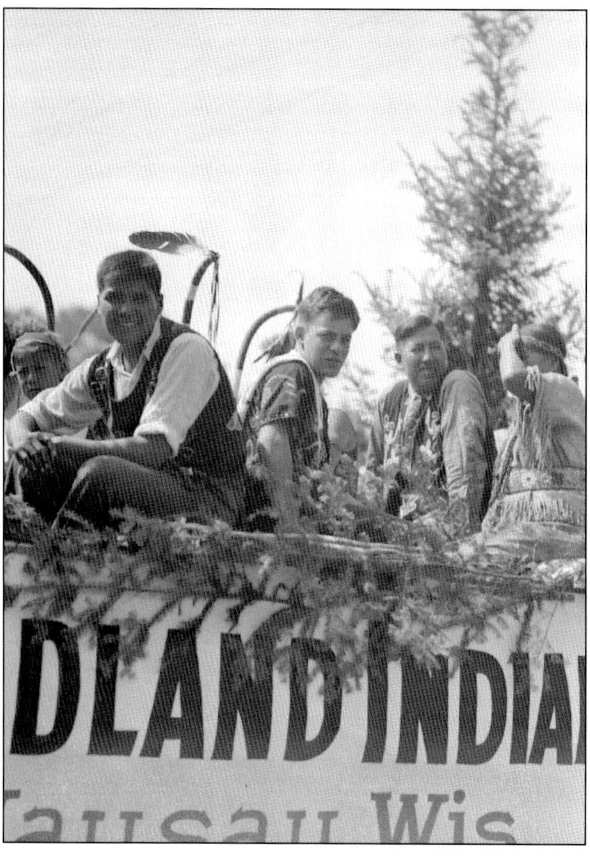

Seen in this 1938 photograph, Alphus and Ophelia Long-Ho-Chunk of Schofield, Wisconsin, sit atop a float in a parade heading down Wisconsin Avenue. Indian performers' wages were standard per day, regardless of the activity. Adult dancers were paid $2 per day while females and artisans received $1, and children made 50¢. Babies received nothing. (Courtesy of the Milwaukee Public Museum.)

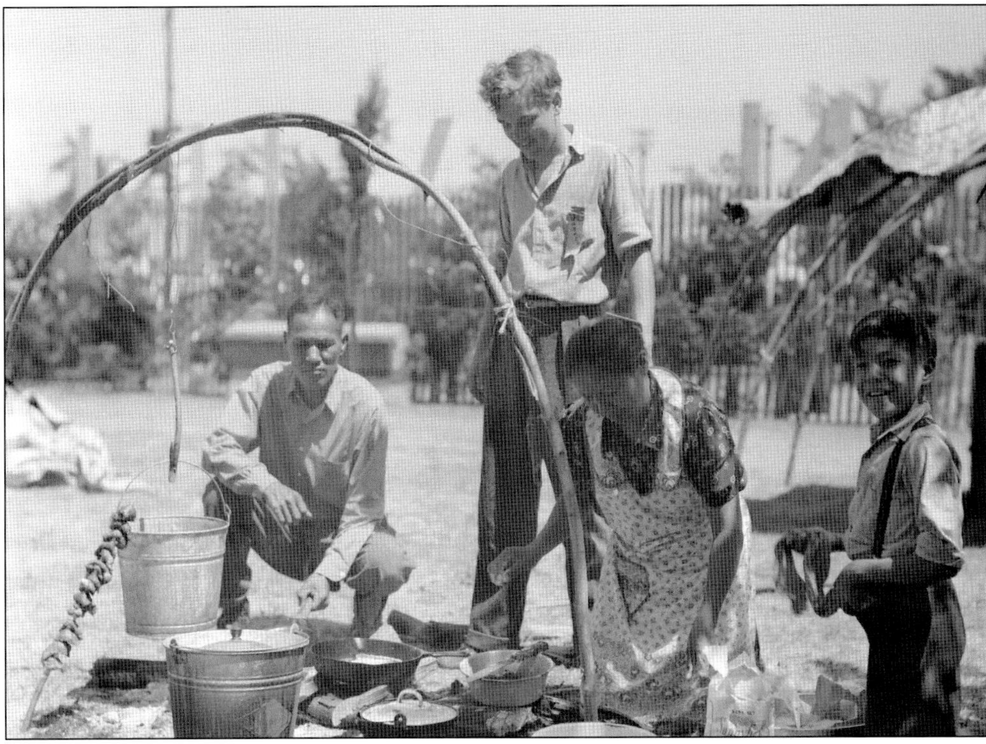

Families lived and performed on the village grounds. Fresh goods were brought in daily for families to prepare for their own meals and larger ceremonial ones with local dignitaries. In this 1939 photograph, Wisconsin Ho-Chunk prepare and eat dinner. From left to right are Chief Hanaka, Jack Heibler (museum staff), White Bear, Mrs. Leonard Hopinka, and Chauncy Hopkin during a break. (Courtesy of the Milwaukee Public Museum.)

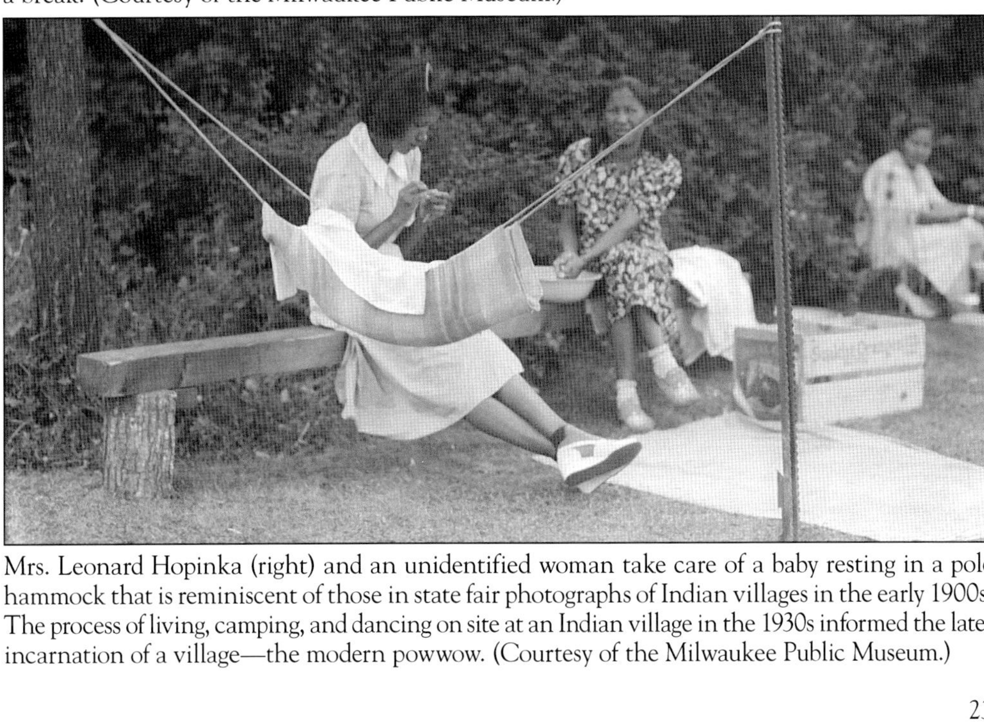

Mrs. Leonard Hopinka (right) and an unidentified woman take care of a baby resting in a pole hammock that is reminiscent of those in state fair photographs of Indian villages in the early 1900s. The process of living, camping, and dancing on site at an Indian village in the 1930s informed the later incarnation of a village—the modern powwow. (Courtesy of the Milwaukee Public Museum.)

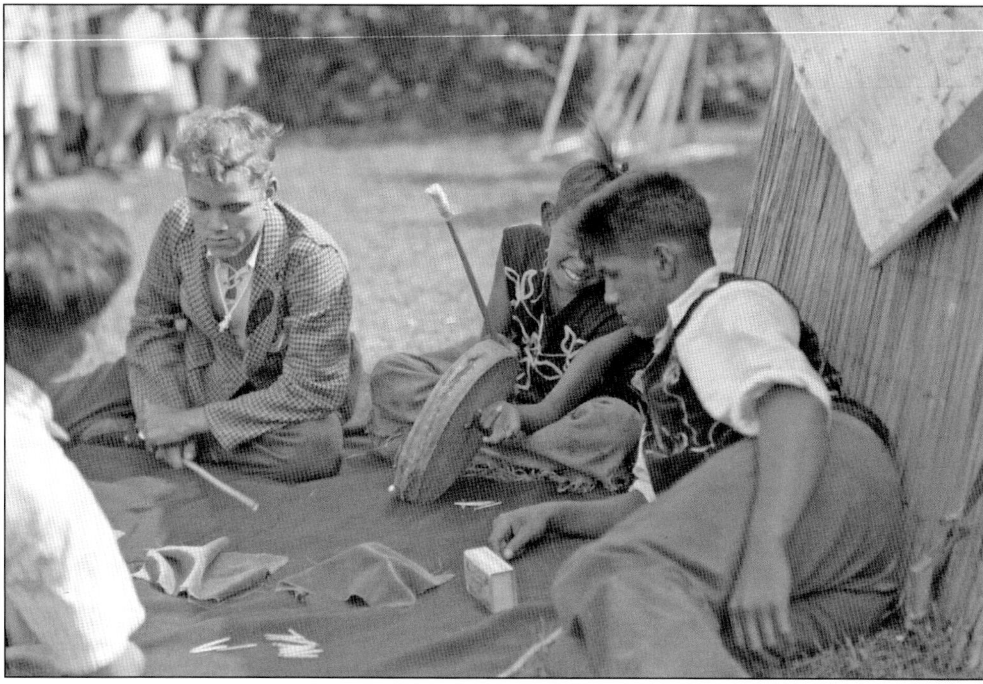

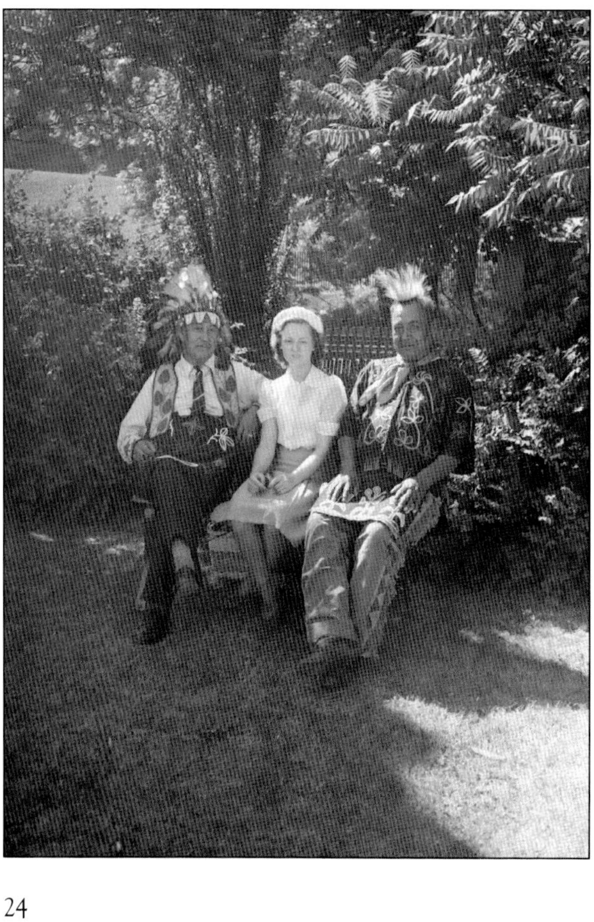

Behind the scenes, life for those in Indian villages was more than a spectacle for audiences. Young people, in particular, found common interests. Here, Ho-Chunk boys show a young man how to play the moccasin game behind a wigwam during a break from work. (Courtesy of the Milwaukee Public Museum.)

In this image, from left to right, are Dr. Homer Kindness, Helen Kovack, and Nathaniel Decorah. Kindness was a noted Indian of the time that traveled around Wisconsin and helped many other Indian people. His doctor moniker may have come from helping others or from his relatives and ancestors, who also went by "doctor." Although Kindness lived in the Ho-Chunk area at the time this photograph was taken, his lineage includes both Oneida and Brotherton lines. (Courtesy of the Milwaukee Public Museum.)

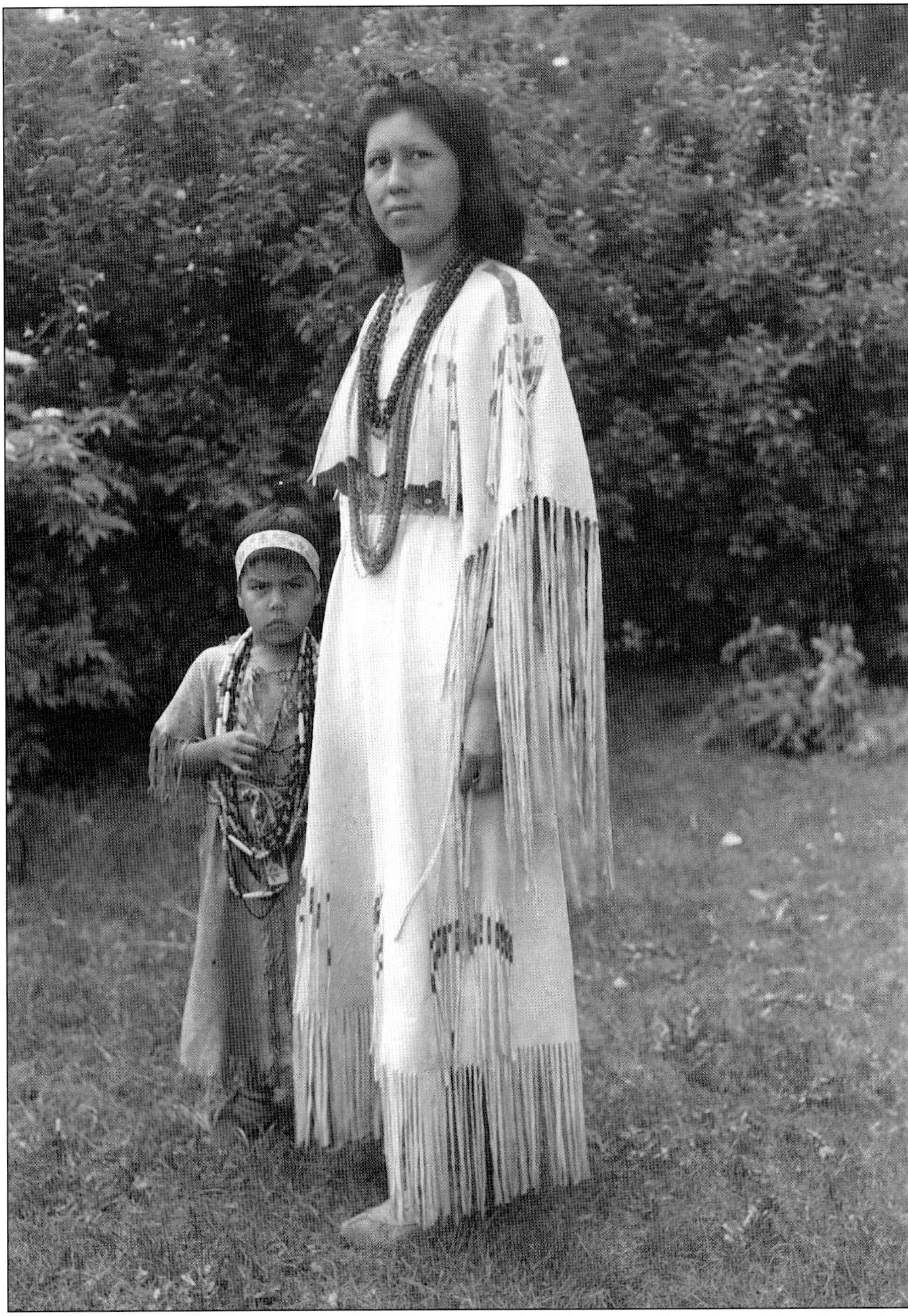

In this 1940 photograph, Vera Kitchegume-Potawatomi (right) poses with Rebecca Young's daughter Delores Young from Tripoli, Wisconsin. Kitchegume-Potawatomi is the older sister of Thomas Kitchkume Jr., who moved to Milwaukee in 1947 and became a leader and traditional elder in the Milwaukee Indian community for many years. (Courtesy of the Milwaukee Public Museum.)

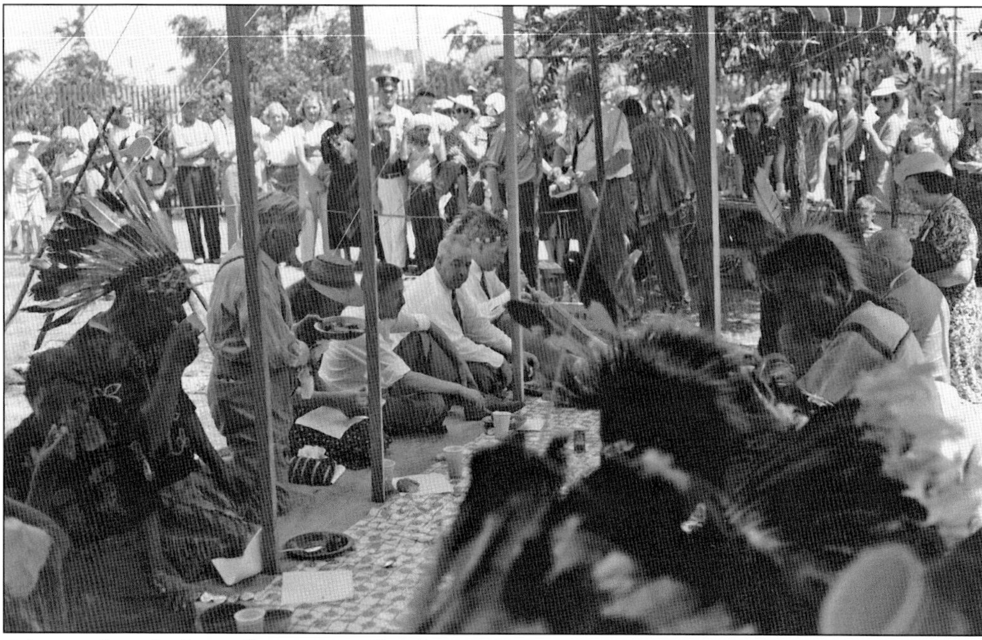

Often at these Indian villages, city officials were honorarily adopted into tribes, with a ceremonial dinner and presentation of regalia accompanying the event. In 1940, the Potawatomi prepared a meal for Mayor Carl F. Zeidler, pictured fifth from the left. Dr. Samuel Barrett is pictured third from the left, and Dr. Ira Edwards, head of the anthropology-history division, and W.C. McKern, head of the geology department, are also in the photograph. (Courtesy of the Milwaukee Public Museum.)

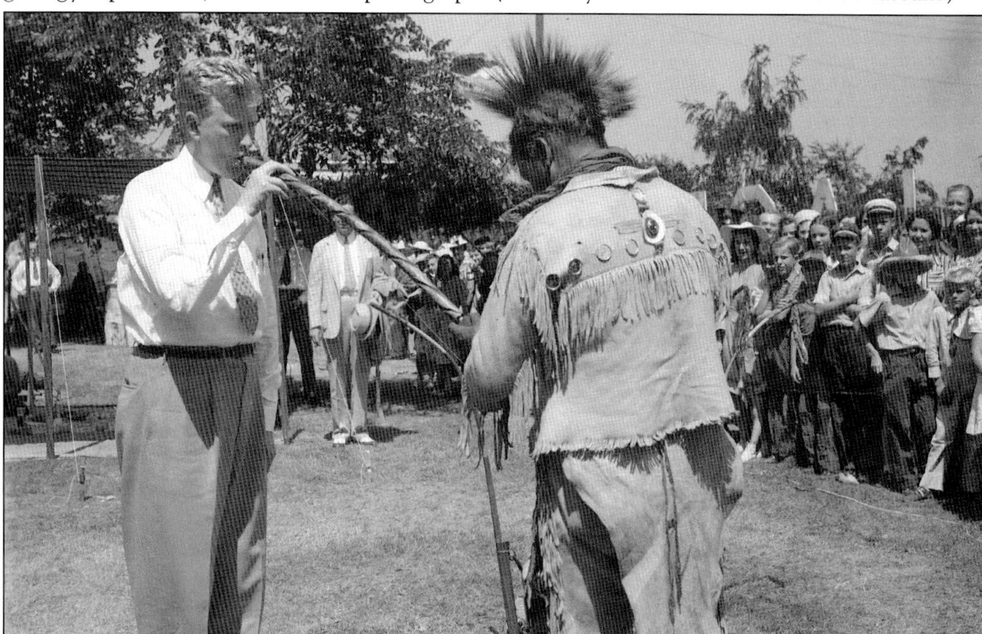

In this 1940 photograph, newly elected Milwaukee mayor Carl F. Zeidler participates in a ceremony with Potawatomi Indians. He smokes the pipe offered by John Link before an audience during the opening day of the village. (Courtesy of the Milwaukee Public Museum.)

Two

Indians Return to the City

After the Indian removal from the city of Milwaukee in the 1830s, there was no sizeable American Indian population in the city until the 1920s. Having been forced onto lands in northern Wisconsin or relocated west of the Mississippi, Indians struggled out a meager existence on isolated reservations. Their main occupations were in the farming and timber sales industries.

The 11 federally recognized tribal nations located within Wisconsin borders all had various reasons and time periods when they arrived in Milwaukee. The Oneida, located near Green Bay, were among the first to arrive in the city in the early 1900s. Oneidas were only 100 miles away from Milwaukee, making them the closest in proximity of all the tribes. They were also the tribe most used to dealing with the city, as they were only a few miles from the city of Green Bay. Americans Indians were drawn to Milwaukee during World War II because of the defense work available at the time, as well as heavy industry employment.

In 1953, there were 1,000 Indians residing in Milwaukee, consisting of 306 Indian households, and 190 of those Indian households were Oneida. Other tribes began arriving in numbers, including the various bands of Ojibwa, Menominee, Stockbridge-Munsee, Potawatomi, and Ho-Chunk, along with tribal members from reservations in other states.

During the years between 1952 and 1955, forty-four Indian families came to Milwaukee through the relocation services of the Bureau of Indian Affairs. The Travelers Aid Society of Milwaukee served as a field relocation office. In 1960, there were 2,984 total American Indians with 996 males and 1,988 females residing in metropolitan Milwaukee. Urban Indians first settled mainly on the near north side and near south side of the city.

Due to all the American Indians in Milwaukee in the 1930s, intertribal Indian groups were established, starting with the Consolidated Tribe of American Indians. It was a way to promote fellowship and tribal unity amidst the discrimination and alienation many felt in the city. Indian people learned each other's songs and dances and looked for commonalities in their strange new homes.

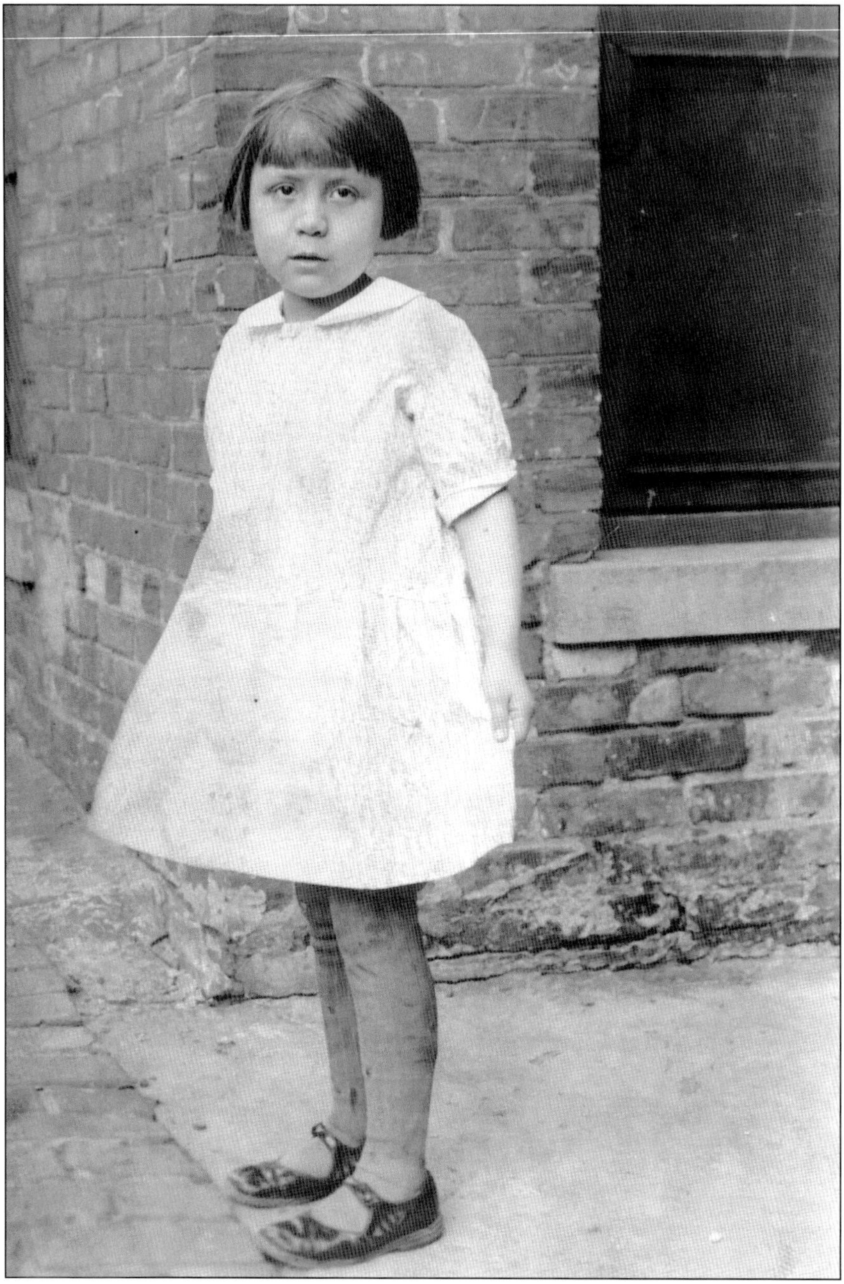

The identity of this little girl is unknown, but she is likely an Oneida living in Milwaukee in the late 1920s. Despite removal, Indian people never fully left Milwaukee, but permanent urban settlement did not increase measurably until the 1930s when many moved here for work. Two-thirds of the 300 Indian people in the 1930 census in Milwaukee were Oneida. Oneidas often lived in close range of each other in enclaves, and many families had Indian borders. Oneidas held fairly good employment; a number of them worked as laborers at the gas company. Interviews conducted by Robert Ritzenthaler at the Milwaukee Public Museum in the 1950s reveal that the move worked out for many of them as the Oneida interviewees maintained long-term employment. (Courtesy of Opal Skenandore.)

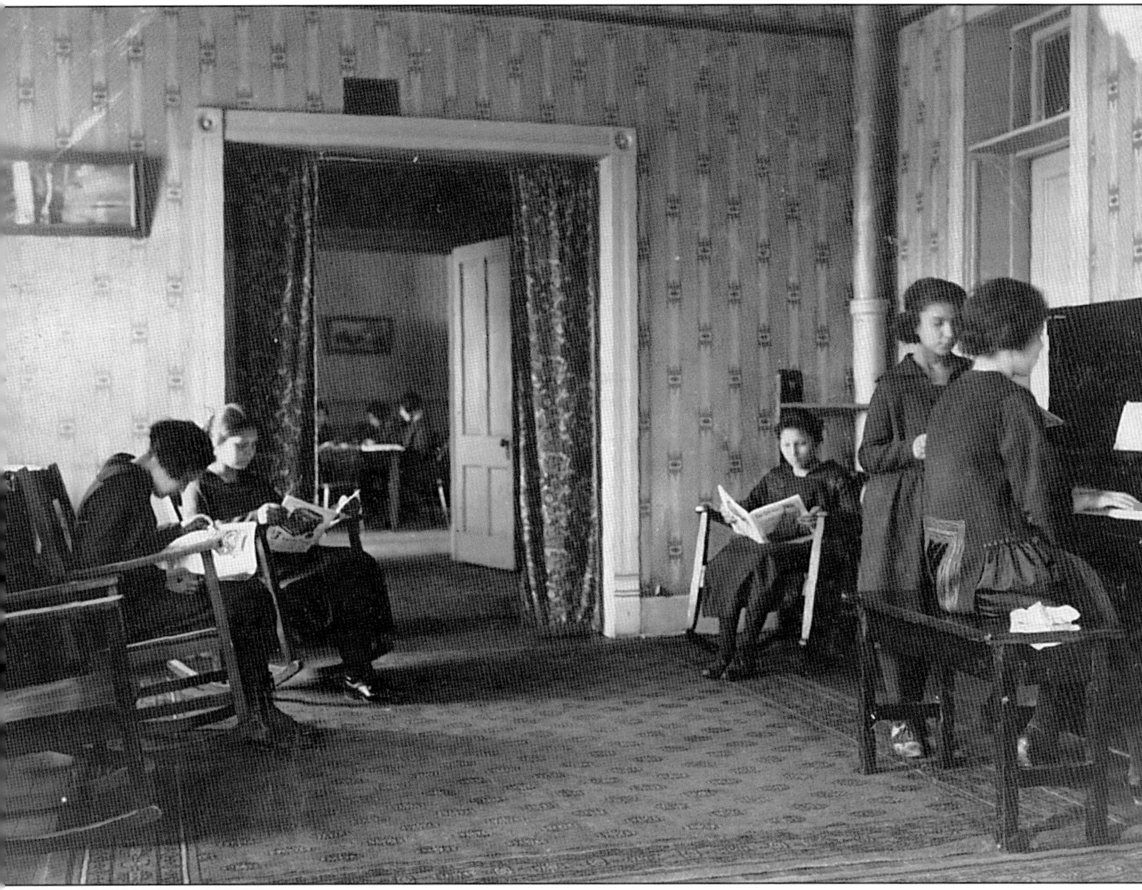

Above is the Flandreau Boarding School for Indian children around 1917 or 1918. Opal Skenandore's adoptive mother and father, Julius and Susan Summers, both went to Flandreau. They met later in Milwaukee and married. Mrs. Summers graduated from Flandreau and returned to work at the school and was assigned a dorm. She wanted to comfort native children, as she thought they did not receive much at the school. (Courtesy of Opal Skenandore.)

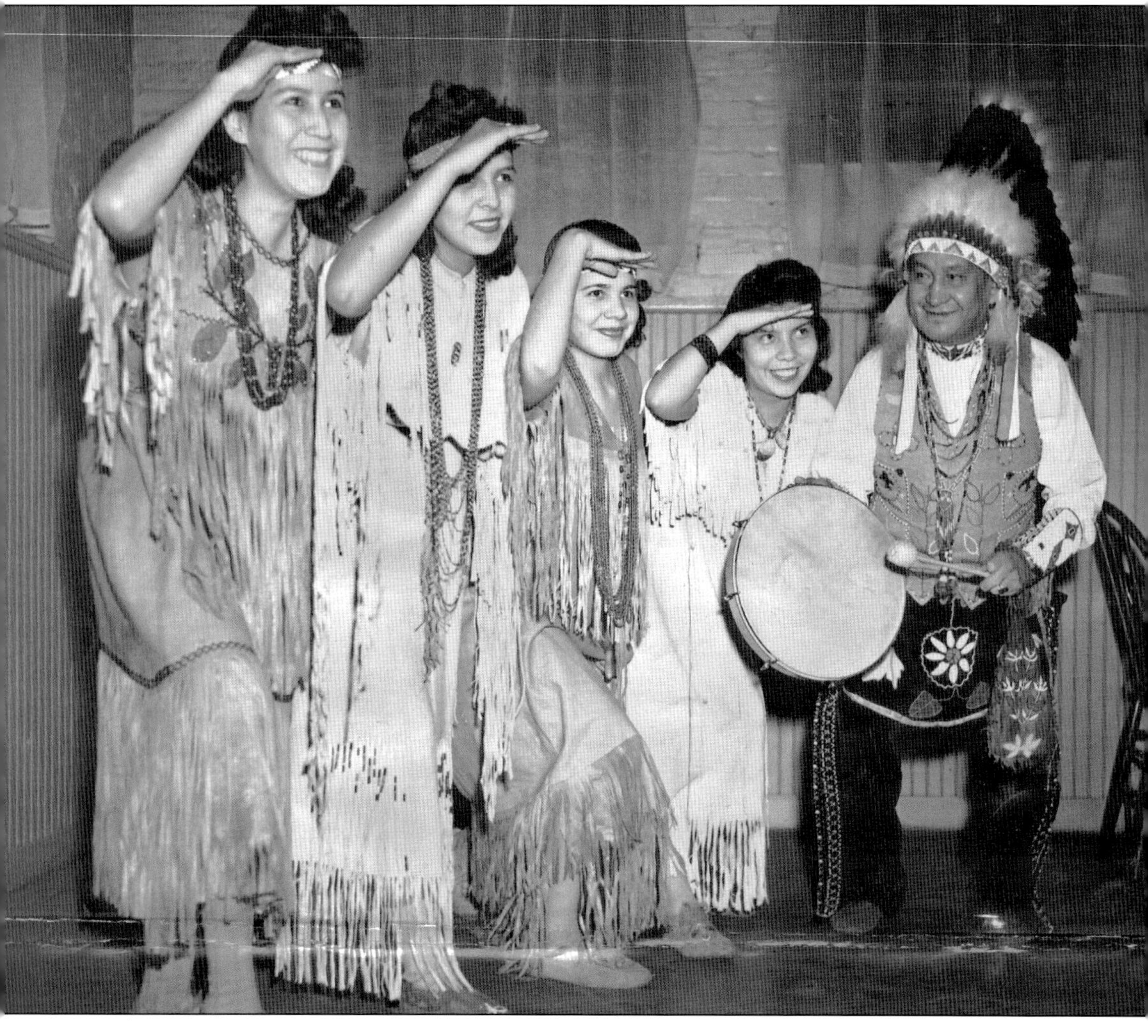

The Consolidated Tribes of American Indians dancers do an Indian-related gesture in this early-1940s photograph. The dancers are, from left to right, Vera ?, unidentified, Esther Steffes, Ethel Summers, and Chief Whitefeather with the drum. The dancers wear Plains Indians buckskin outfits and Chief Whitefeather wears a war bonnet. Alpheus Smith and 12 other local Indians founded the Consolidated Tribes of American Indians in 1937. (Courtesy of Opal Skenandore.)

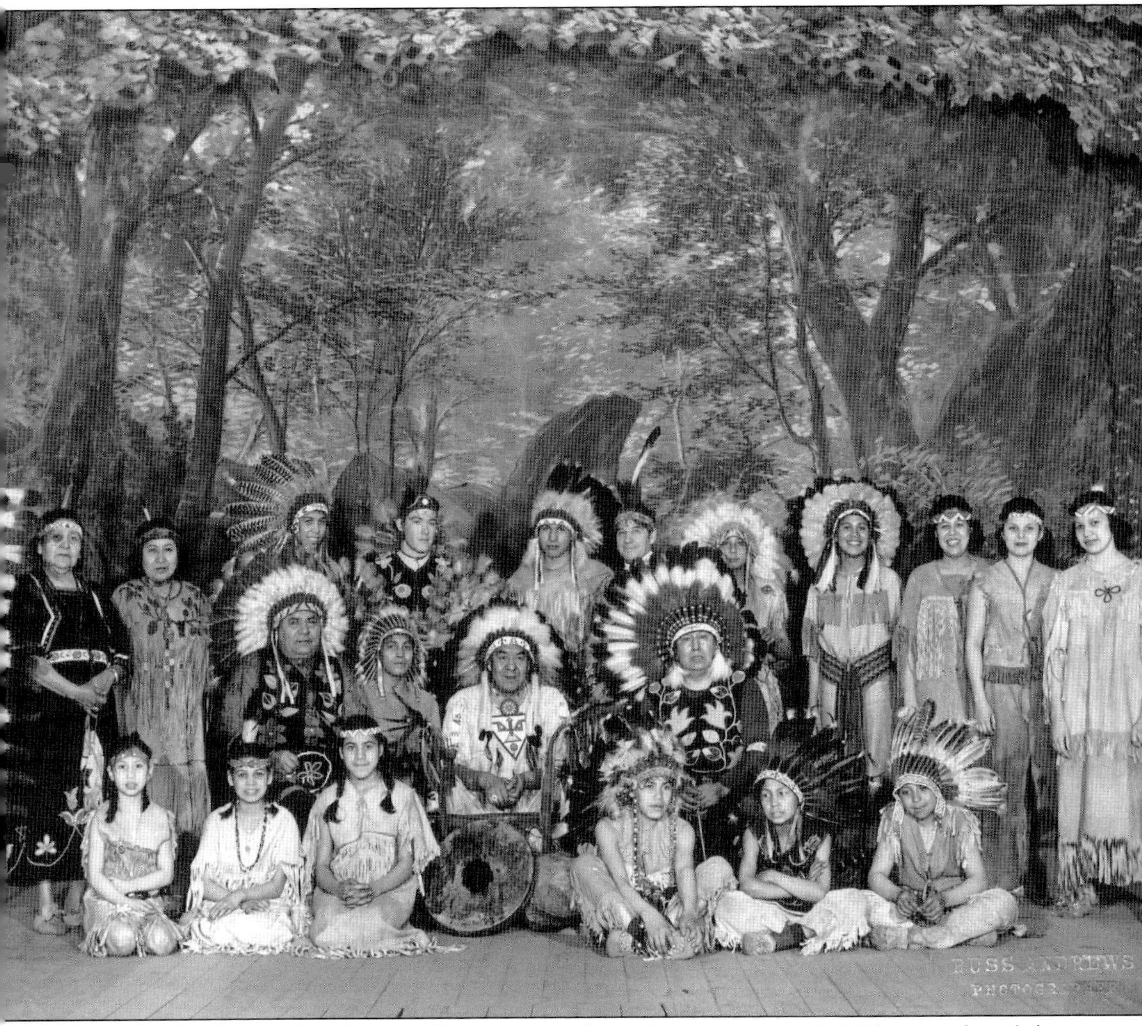

Pictured is the Consolidated Tribes of American Indians dance group in 1948. They are, from left to right, (first row) Opal Skenandore, Doris Steffes, Shirley Steffes, Myron Skenandore, Joseph Webster, and Dewey Silas Jr.; (second row) Alpheus Smith, James Webster, Frank Smart, and Henry Jacko; (third row) Mrs. Henry Jacko, Delia Smith, Francis Webster, Kenneth Powless, Ronald Reil, Francis Coleman, Eugene Silas, Kenneth Skenandore, Donna Skenandore, Shannon DeNomie, and Delores Steffers. (Photograph by Russ Andrews; courtesy of Opal Skenandore.)

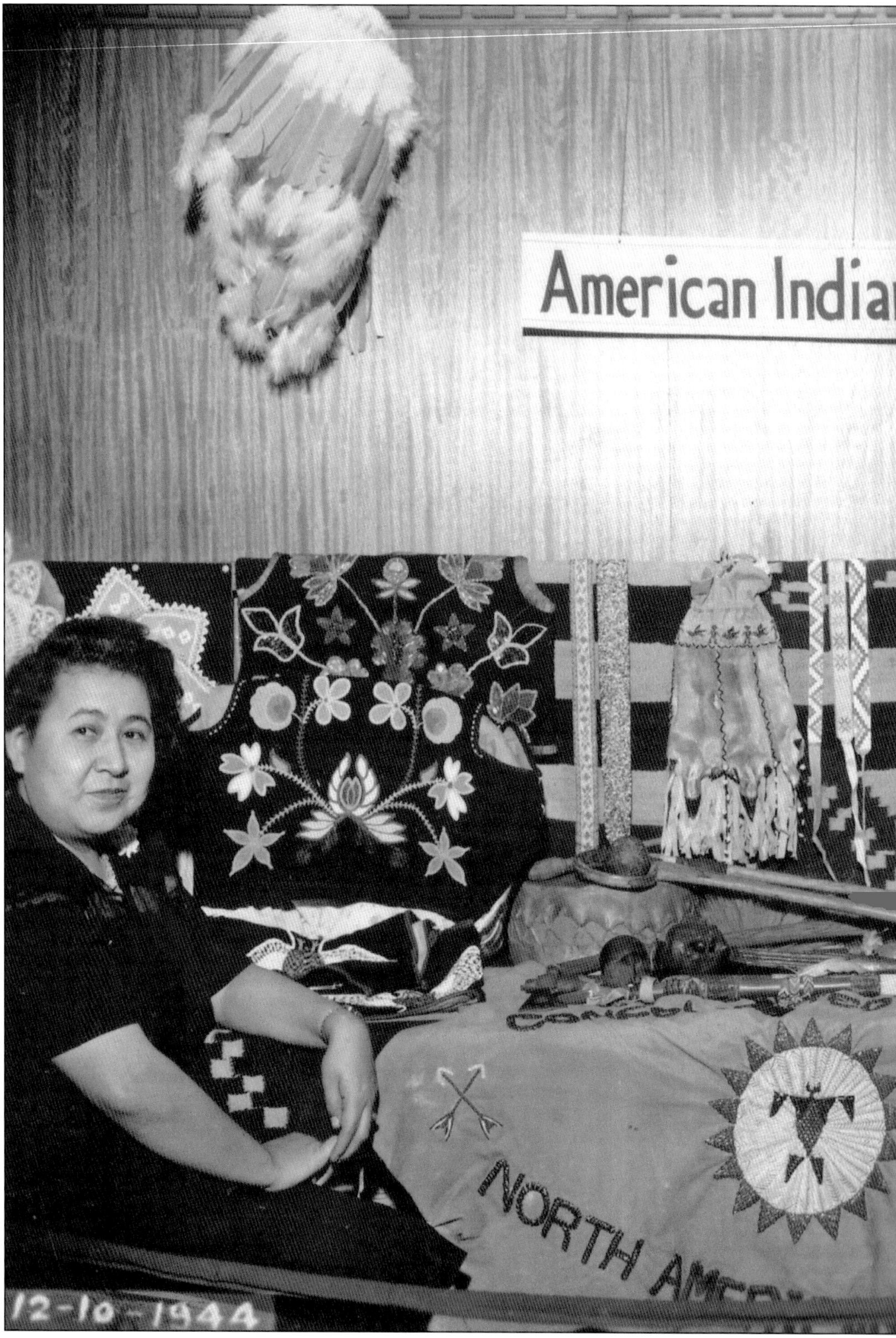
American India
NORTH AMER
12-10-1944

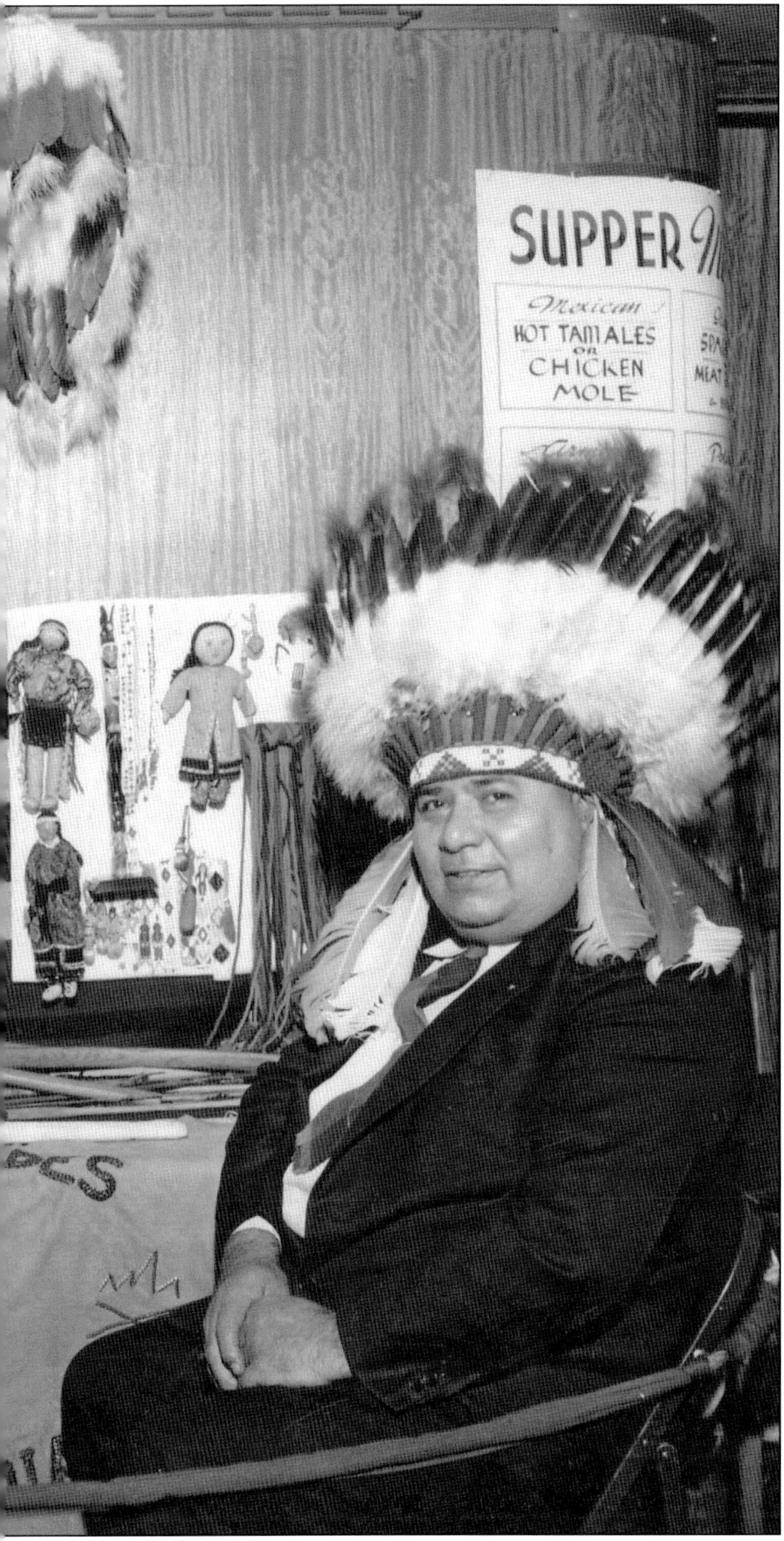

Alpheus and Delia Smith are pictured at a Consolidated Tribes of American Indians event on December 10, 1944. Alpheus, Oneida, was born on the Oneida reservation, and his wife, Delia (Webster) Smith, was born on the Lac Du Flambeau reservation. Alpheus attended the Tomah Indian School and the Carlisle Institute in Pennsylvania. The couple moved to Milwaukee in 1927. He worked as a machine operator for the International Harvester Company in Milwaukee from 1929 until his retirement in 1963. After his retirement, he moved the Lac Du Flambeau reservation until his death from leukemia on March 19, 1969. As a founder of the Consolidated Tribes of American Indians, Alpheus served nine terms as chairman of the group. (Courtesy of Opal Skenandore.)

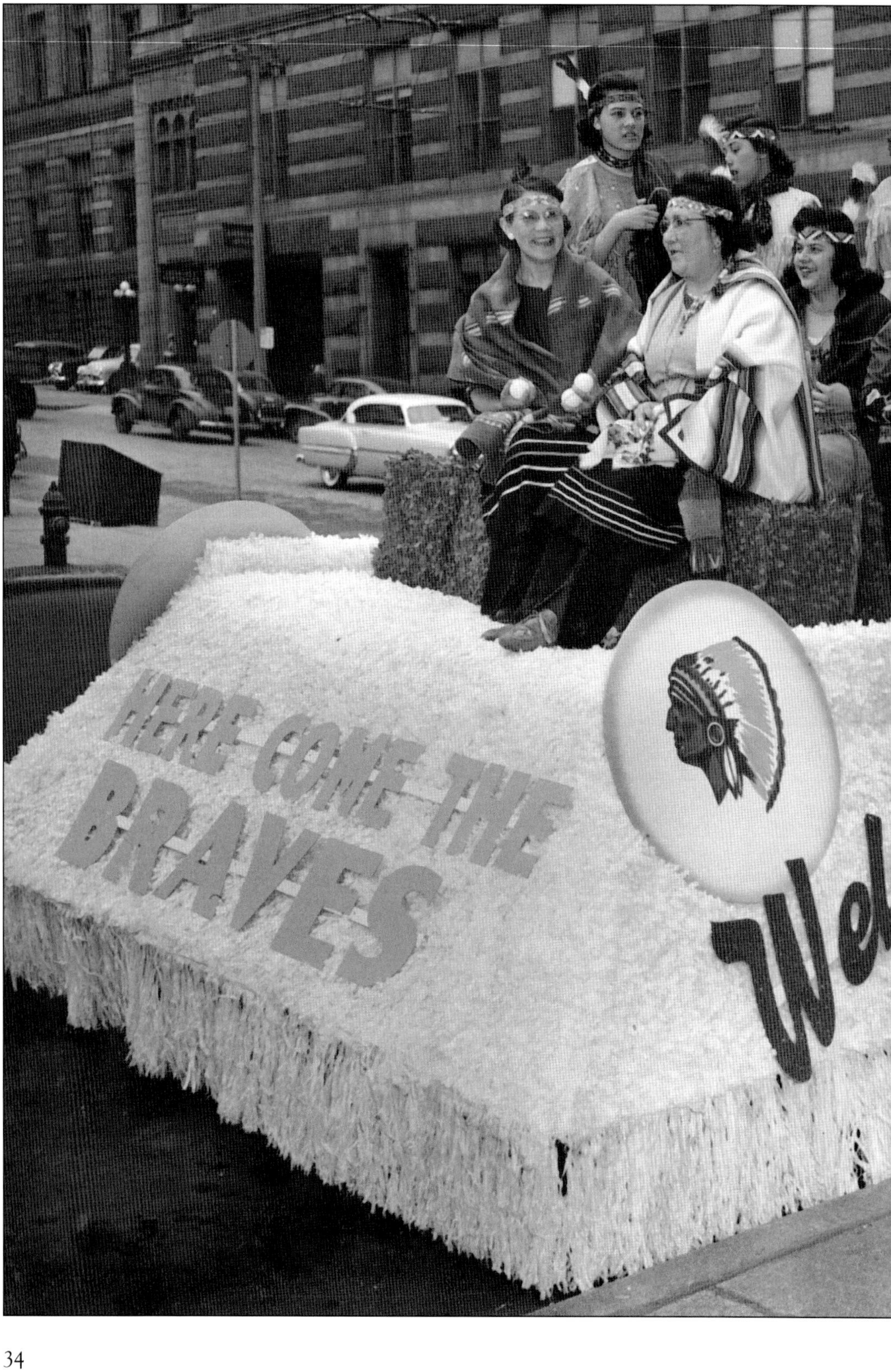
HERE COME THE
BRAVES

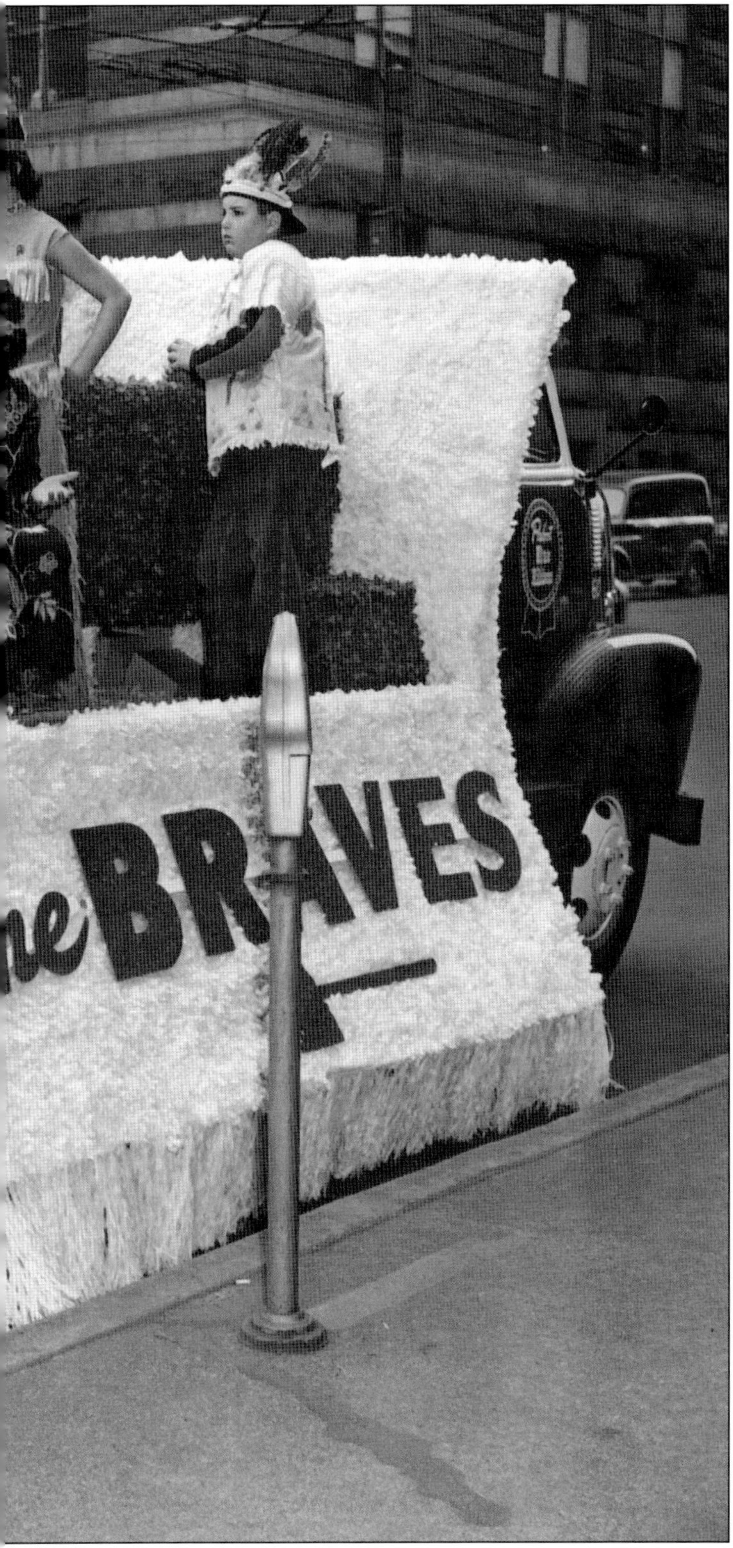

The Consolidated Tribes of American Indians rode atop a float in a homecoming parade for the Milwaukee Braves baseball team on April 8, 1953. From left to right are (first row; sitting) Ruth Baird and Estelle Webster; (second row; sitting) Susan Summers and an unidentified girl; (third row; standing) Doris Steffes, Marlene Silas, unidentified, Opal Skenandore, and an unidentified boy. (Courtesy of Opal Skenandore.)

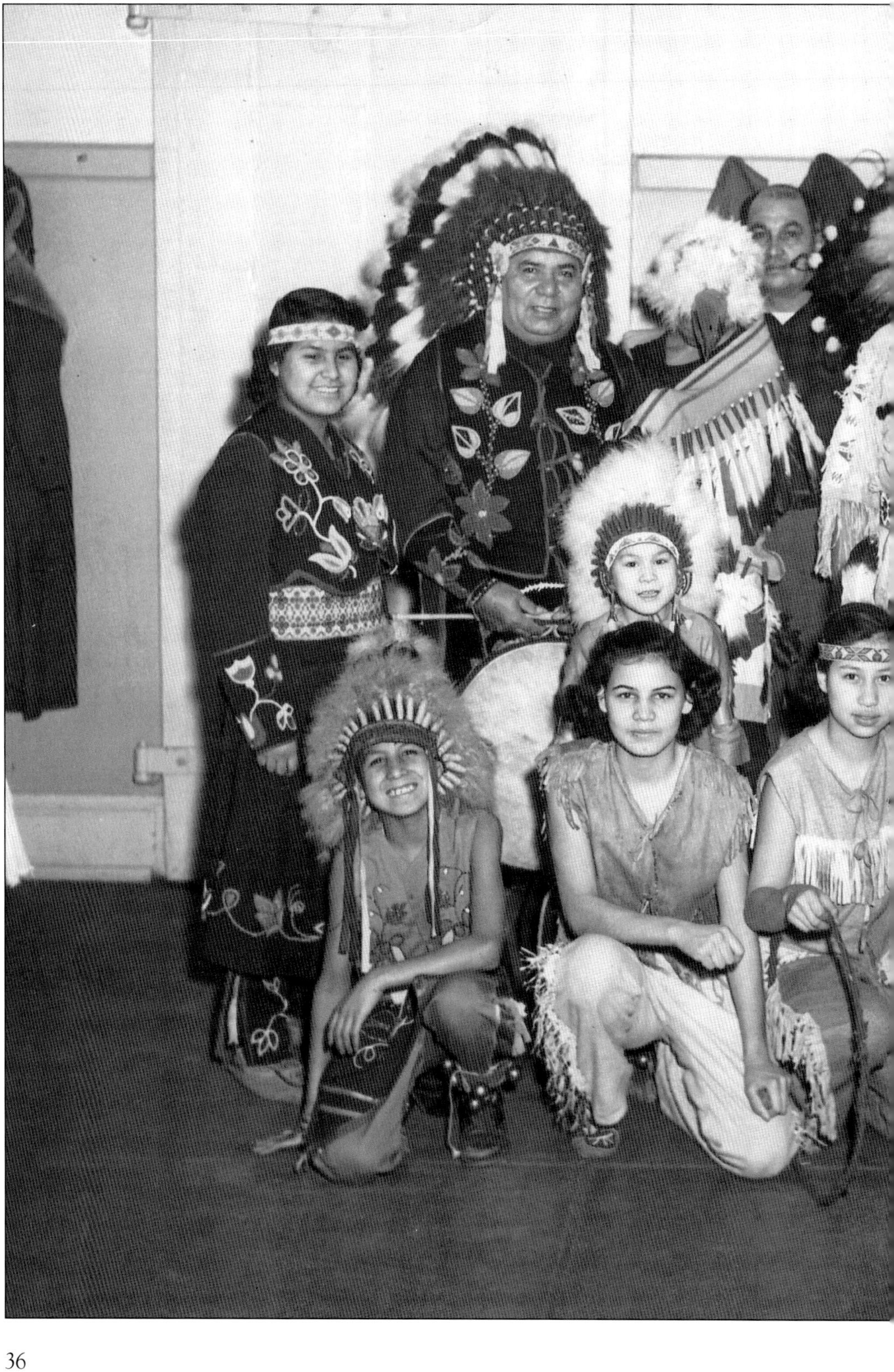

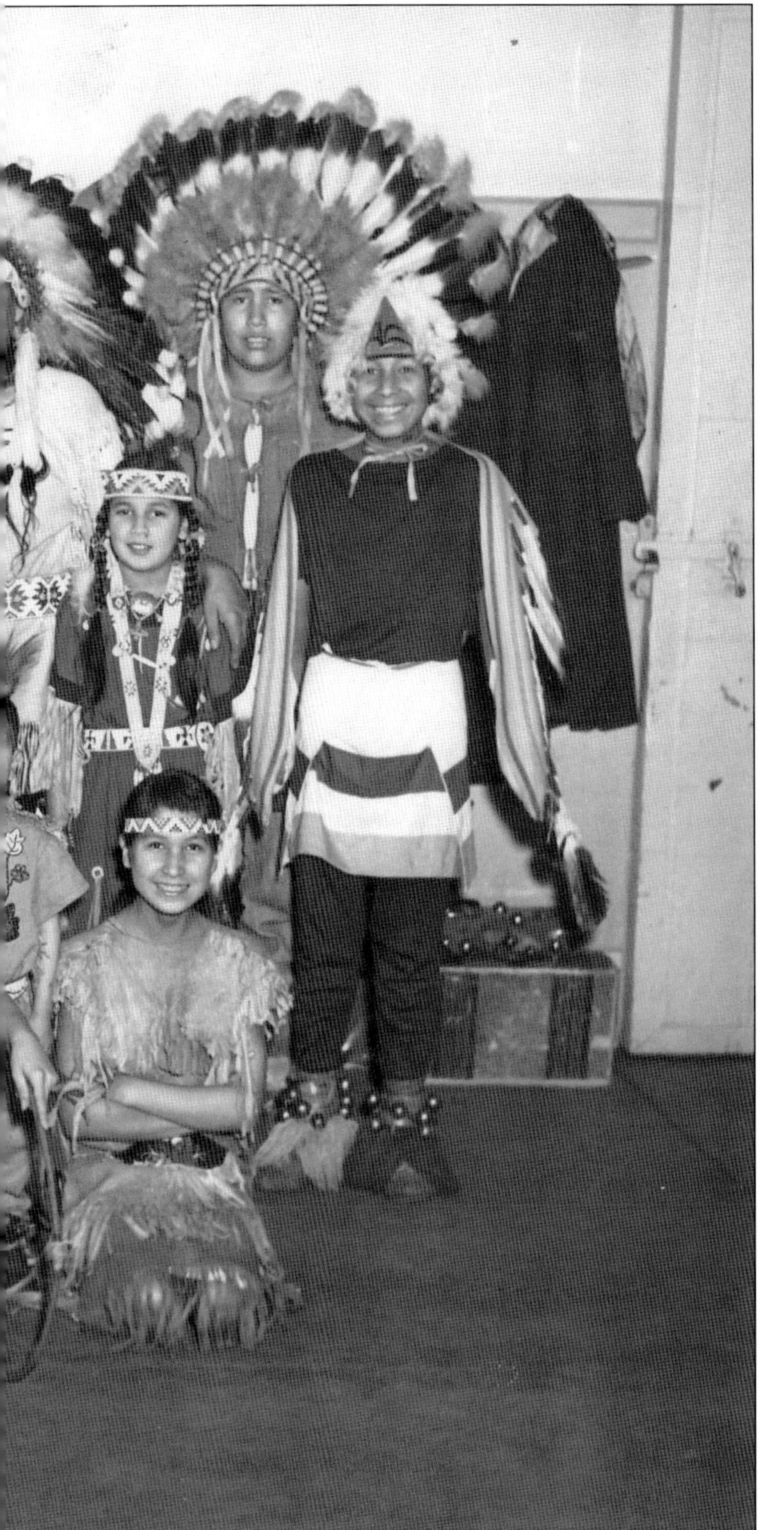

The Consolidated Tribes of American Indians dance group performed at hundreds of public and private events throughout their history. In this 1954 photograph are, from left to right, (first row) ? Webster, Doris Steffes, Opal Skenandore, and Celies Webster; (second row) Ronnie Baird and Julius Webster; (third row; standing) Estelle Webster, Alpheus Smith, Dewey Silas Jr., LaBoy Baird, Frank Smart, Rosa Smart, unidentified, and Joseph Webster. (Courtesy of Opal Skenandore.)

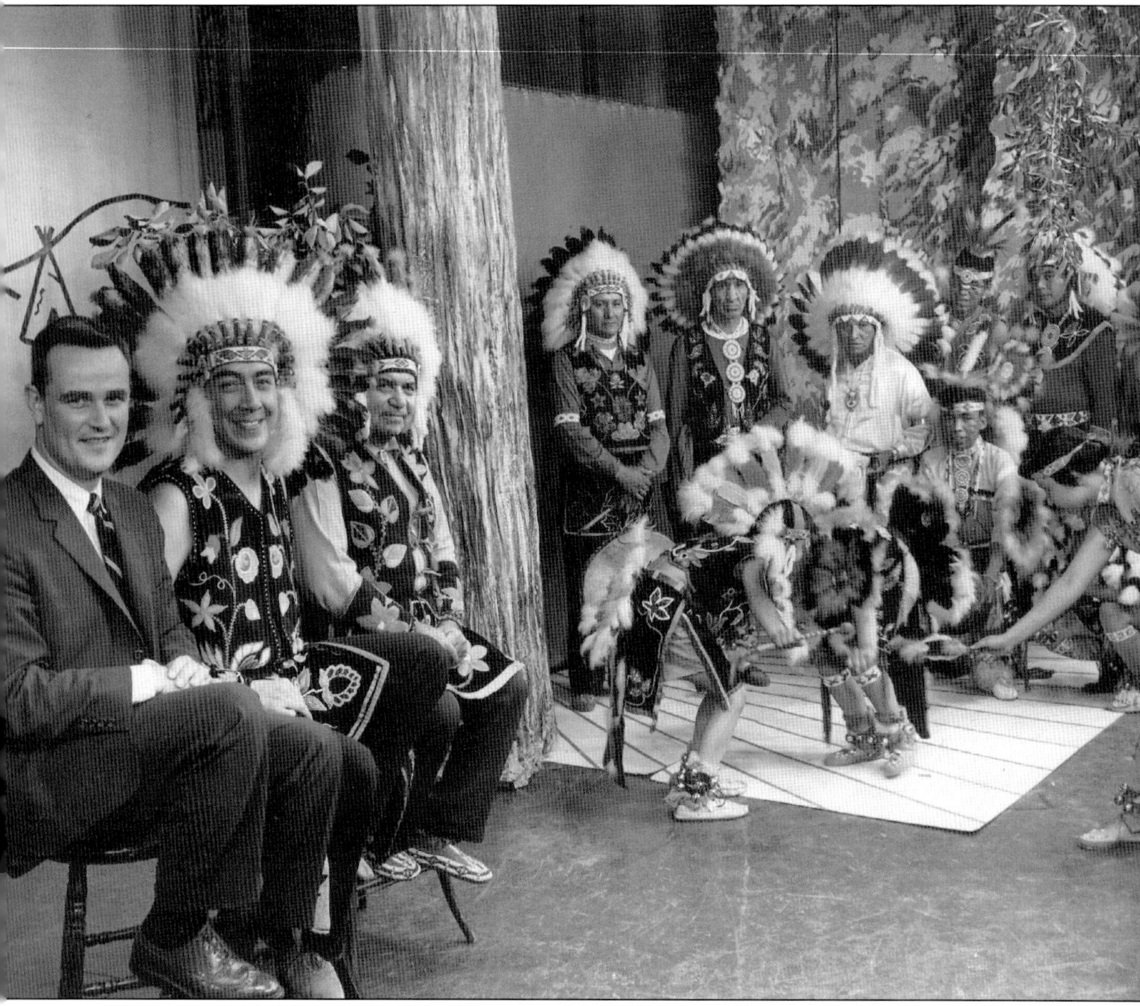

Members of the Consolidated Tribes of American Indians appear on television station WTMJ in 1957 as a promotion for their Heidelberg powwow. From left to right are an unidentified newsman, William Wheelock, Alpheus Smith, Victor Bender, four unidentified men, James Danforth, Gordon Thunder, Opal Skenandore, and two unidentified. (Courtesy of Opal Skenandore.)

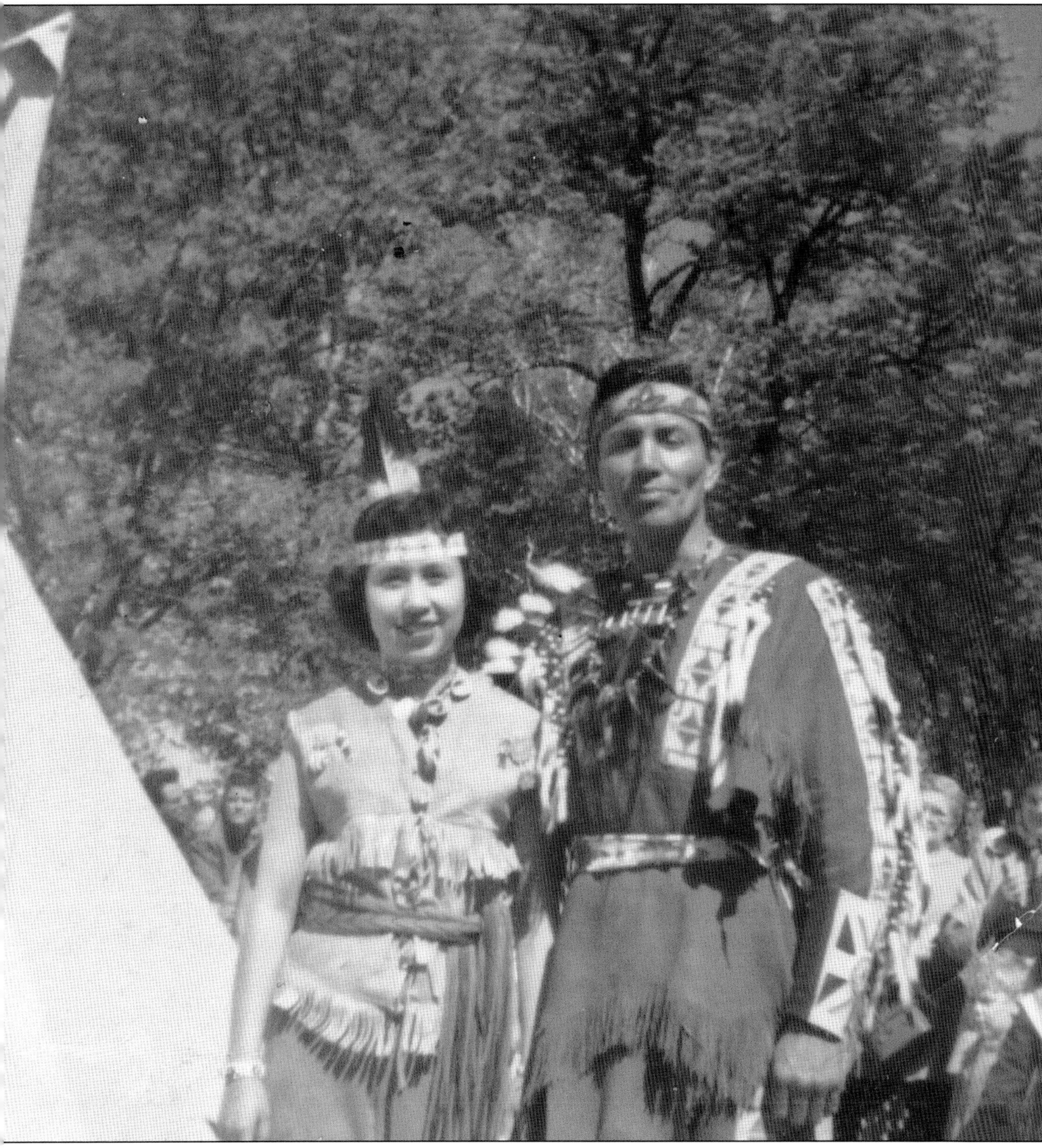

In this photograph are dancer Opal Skenandore and Jay Silverheels, better known as Tonto, the American Indian sidekick in the television series *The Lone Ranger*. He served as master of ceremonies for the Consolidated Tribes' two-day ceremony at Old Heidelberg Park in June 1957. The park was located at 5423 North Port Washington Road in Glendale, Wisconsin. Proceeds from the event were being used to create an Indian center in Milwaukee. More than 1,000 people attended the two-day event, and members of 12 different tribes danced. (Courtesy of Opal Skenandore.)

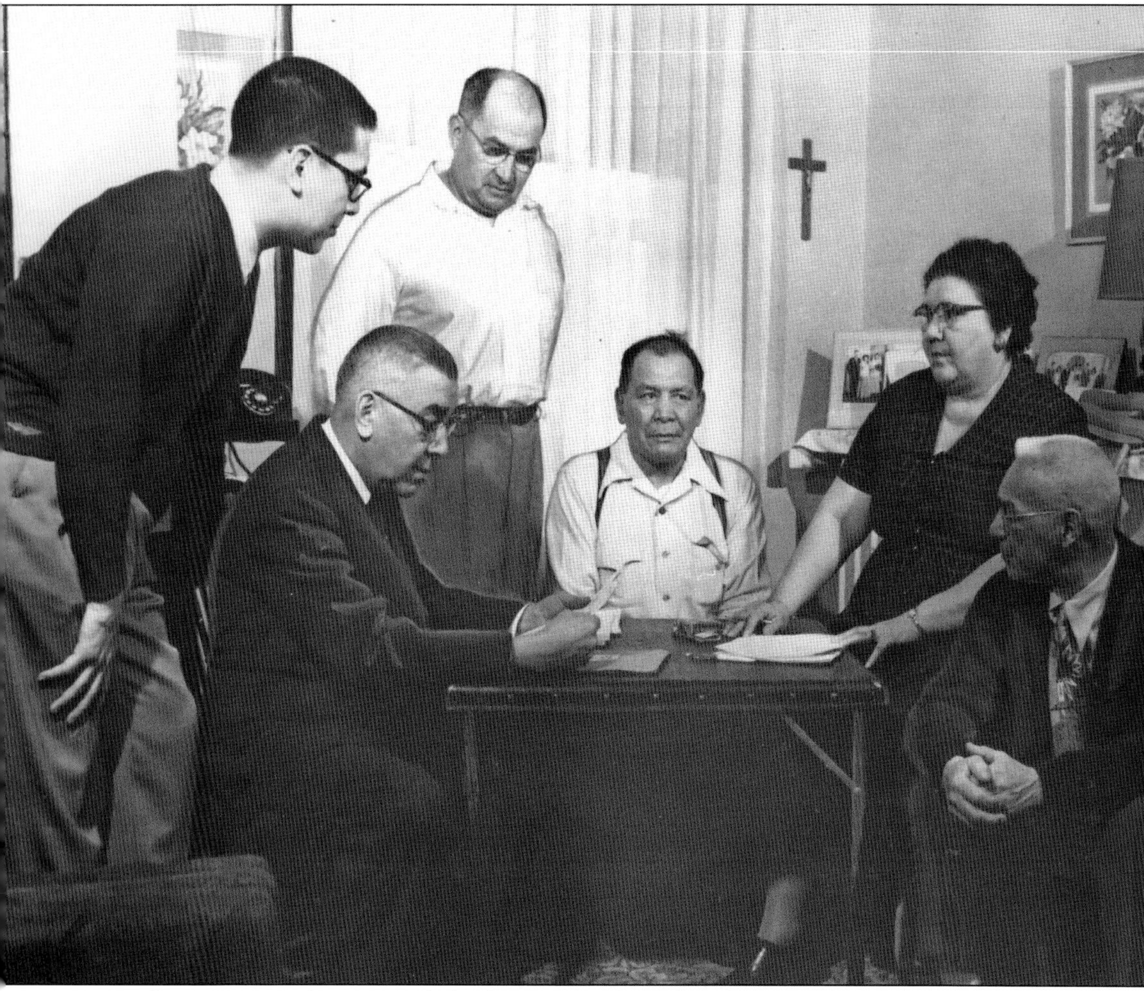

In the 1957 image above, Oneida leaders meet in the Milwaukee home of Cornelius Baird. Oneida tribal members residing in Milwaukee stayed connected to their reservation and took part in local politics at every stage of their tribal history. From left to right are William Wheelock, Morris Wheelock, Cornelius Baird, Oscar Archiquette, Ruth Baird, and John Danforth. Archiquette was the first elected tribal chairman of the Oneida Nation in 1934; he also later served four terms as vice chairman of the Oneidas. Morris was the first elected tribal chairman of the Oneida Nation in 1937 after the Indian Reorganization Act, which changed how tribes govern themselves. Wheelock also served as chairman of the Consolidated Tribes of American Indians in the 1950s. (Courtesy of the Milwaukee Public Museum.)

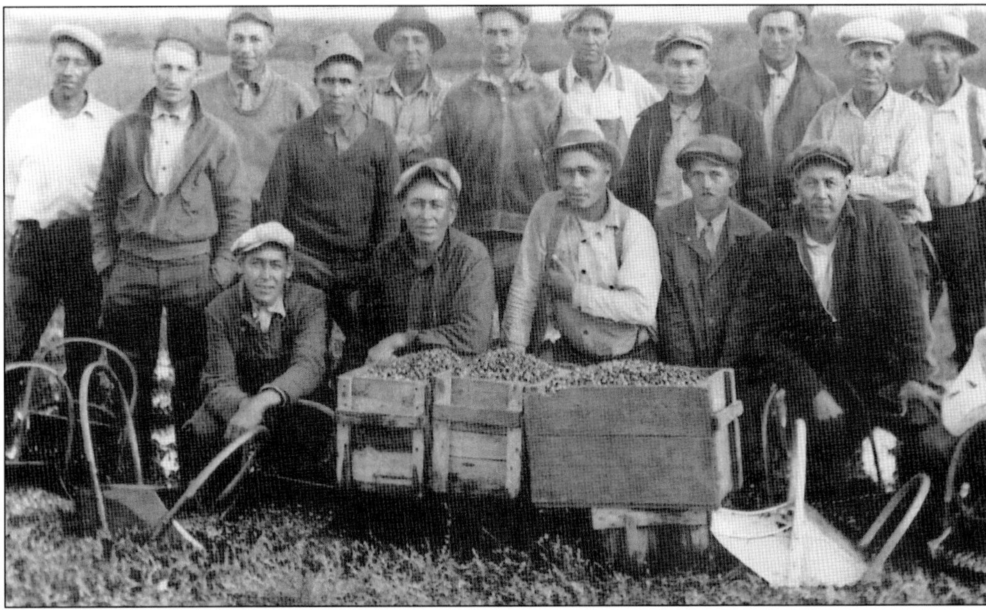

Isadore Doxtator, Oneida, is kneeling in the front left at a cranberry orchard in Wisconsin Rapids in the 1940s. Many Oneidas traveled to the cranberry marshes at harvest time to earn money to feed their families. They often lived on the marsh in bunkhouses. There was a strong sense of friendship and camaraderie because families, including parents and their children, worked together. It was an important time since not many jobs were available for Oneidas. (Courtesy of the Doxtator family.)

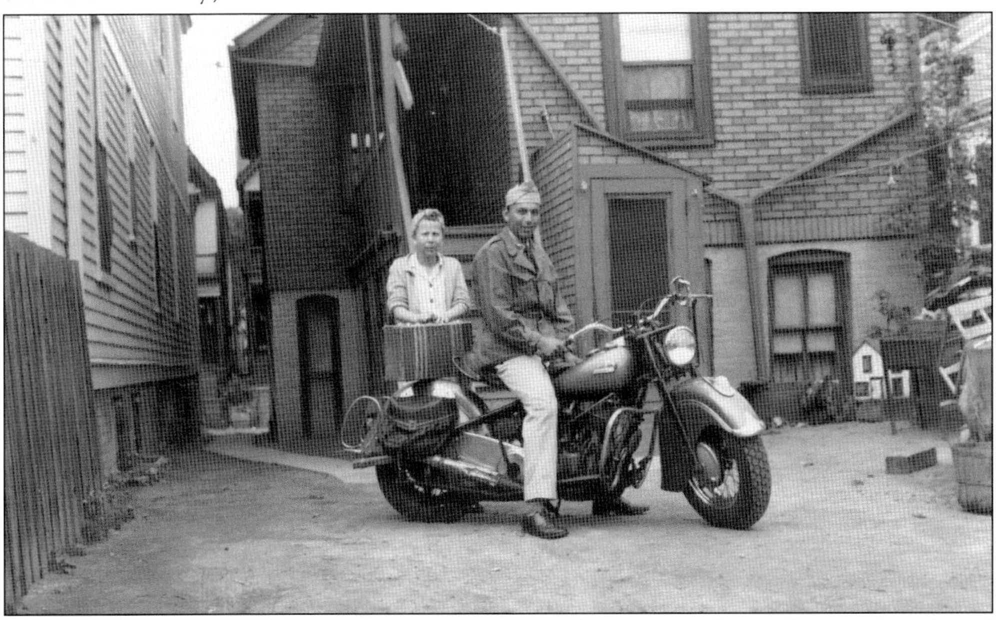

Glenn Curtis Skenadore (1929–2010), sitting on his Indian motorcycle, was born in Oneida and lived in Milwaukee for more than 50 years on Thirty-seventh Street. His mother, Miriam Hill (1900–1994), was the youngest daughter of Chief Rev. Cornelius Hill, a traditional chief of the Wisconsin Oneida. Skenadore was a veteran and member of American Legion Post No. 1 for 45 years. (Courtesy of Donna Skenadore.)

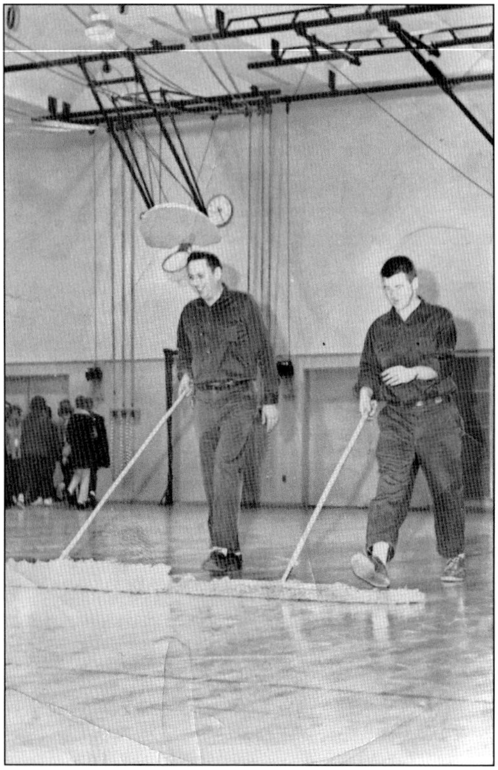

Glenn Skenadore (left) retired from working as an engineer for Milwaukee Public Schools (MPS) after 27 years. In the late 1960s, Skenadore won his lawsuit to broaden the racial application categories that the city of Milwaukee offered to include American Indians, since he was forced to choose "white." Glenn served on the Committee of 100, which formed to desegregate MPS in 1976. (Courtesy of Donna Skenandore.)

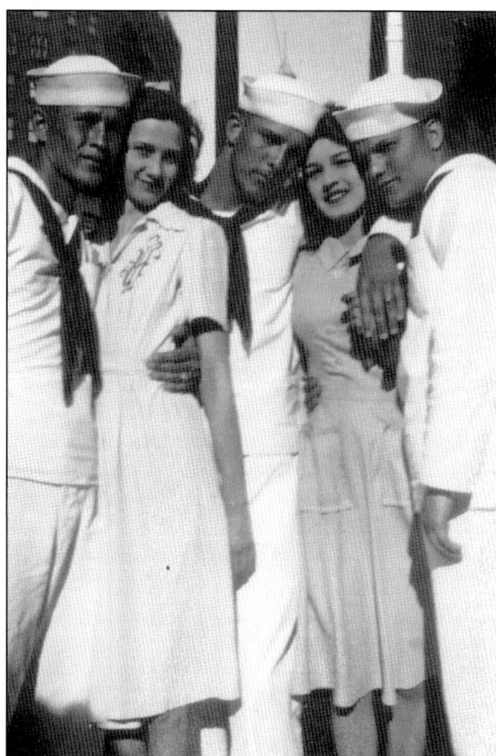

Oneida sisters Dorothy (left) and Elaine Klatt (right) were instructed by their mother, Inez Hill, to invite enlisted men who were on leave in Milwaukee during World War II to visit their home so the servicemen could enjoy a good, home-cooked meal from her kitchen. (Courtesy of Kitty Hill.)

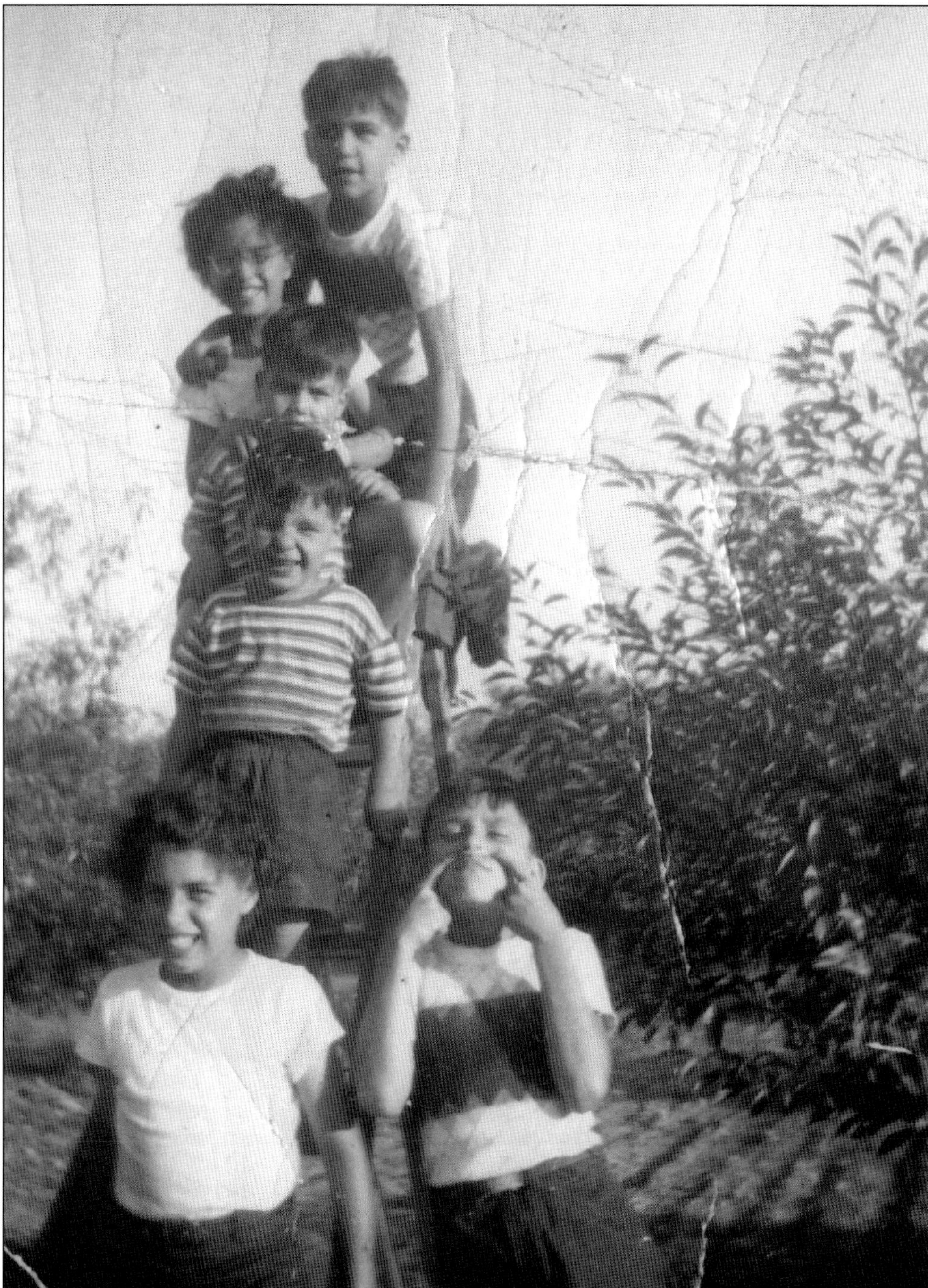

Cherry-picking was another form of migratory work that Indians in Milwaukee did during the 1940s and 1950s. The children in this photograph are, from bottom to top, Priscilla Zakhar, Paul Zakhar, Ronald Metoxen, Donald Metoxen, Patricia Zakhar, and James Zakhar. Paul remembers his family traveled by car and lived with other families in houses near the orchards. One family typically did all the cooking, and their quarters were separated by blankets. (Courtesy of the Zakhar family.)

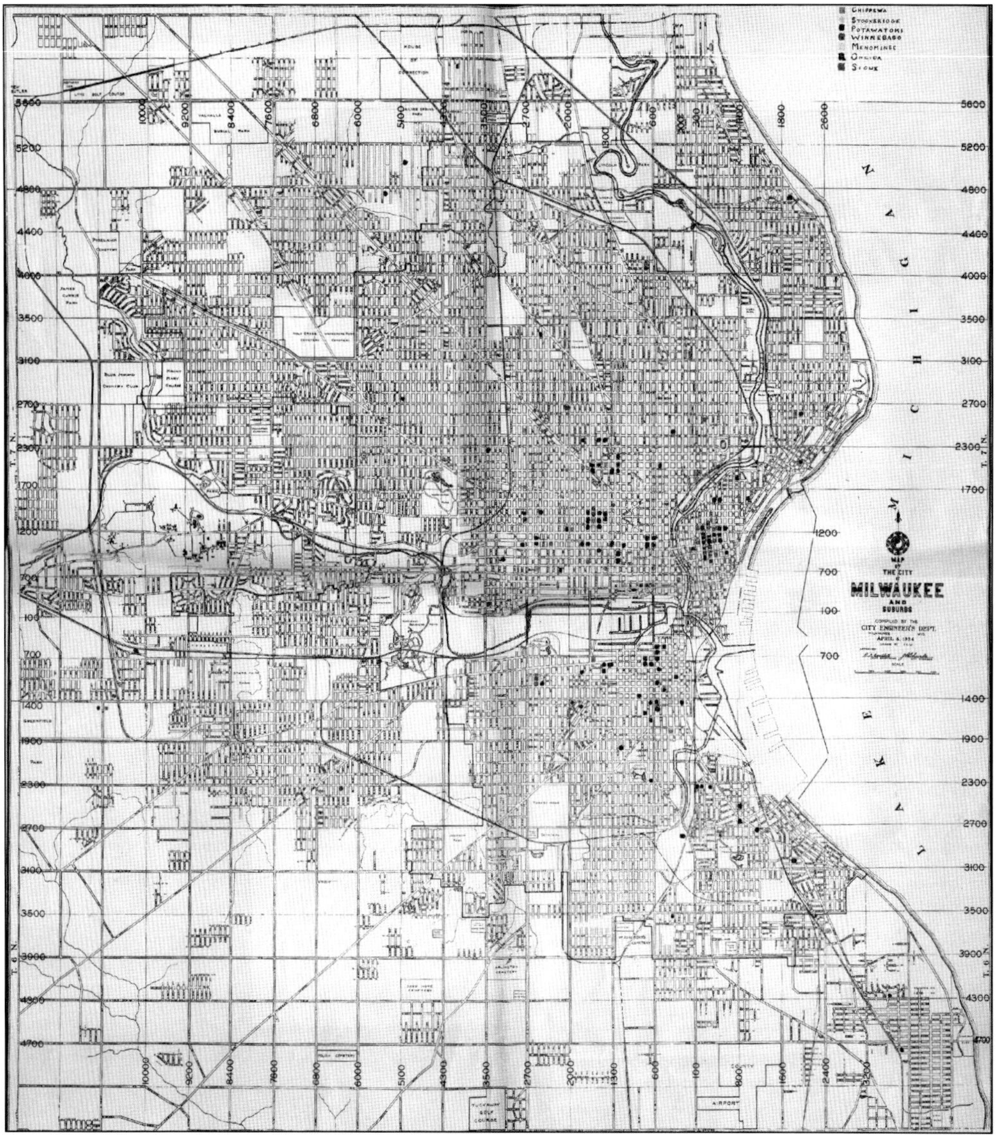

In 1955, Robert Ritzenthaler conducted a survey of American Indians in Milwaukee and created this map of Indian settlement. He worked with Oscar Archiquette, a member of the Oneida tribe who was living in Milwaukee. Ritzenthaler collaborated with Archiquette and used the Consolidated Tribes of American Indians membership list to help identify American Indians living in Milwaukee. Ritzenthaler had some difficulty gaining interviews, but he did manage to finish 75. His result was an article written with Mary Sellers called the "Indians in an Urban Situation," which found that Oneidas came to Milwaukee first and worked long-term jobs when compared to other tribal members in the city. Interestingly, almost none of the Indian people, no matter what tribe they were from, said they felt any discrimination, although they mentioned being turned down for jobs, housing, and, in one case, membership to a moose lodge. Nearly all of the American Indians enjoyed Milwaukee (with its indoor plumbing) as a place to live. (Courtesy of the Milwaukee Public Museum.)

Three

Powwow Era

The powwow era marks the transition from having one exclusive American Indian organization doing all the cultural events in the city, including powwows, to having several organizations host them. Many American Indians differ on the origins of the powwow, but most agree it began in the late 1800s with the Western Plains tribes. The men's styles may come from the war dances of different Plains Indians tribes, and the drum was the same used by the big drum societies. Many of the first songs were Plains Indians war dances and ceremonial songs.

Milwaukee-area Indians began organizing powwows in their early form during the late 1950s; in this area, most of the songs sung came from the Potawatomi, Menominee, Ojibwe, and Ho-Chunk tribes. Local Indians often wore Plains Indian–style headdresses and buckskin clothing, and some incorporated elements of their own tribe, but it was clearly still a new time for Milwaukee's Indians. In the 1960s and 1970s, the powwow locally began to take on more authenticity and became more widespread as different groups and organizations began sponsoring their own powwows.

From tribally specific reservation powwows to white hobbyist groups to intertribal groups in the city, each had their own reasons and interpretation for hosting a powwow. By the end of the 1970s, the powwow was truly an intertribal event. People from all over Wisconsin and surrounding states came to Milwaukee to participate in these events. Powwows provided a chance to embrace the unity American Indians shared as an ethnic group. People came to socialize and dance, see old friends and relatives, and make new friends.

American Indians who danced began to embrace the styles and customs of their own individual tribes and others, so there were much more unique and colorful outfits on display. As powwows evolved, more dance styles were included, like the men and women's fancy dance, women's jingle dress, and men's grass dancers, along with some of the area's first competition powwows. Powwows brought in much-needed revenue for financially struggling American Indian agencies, and they appealed to non-Indians who attended them. Powwows brought people together.

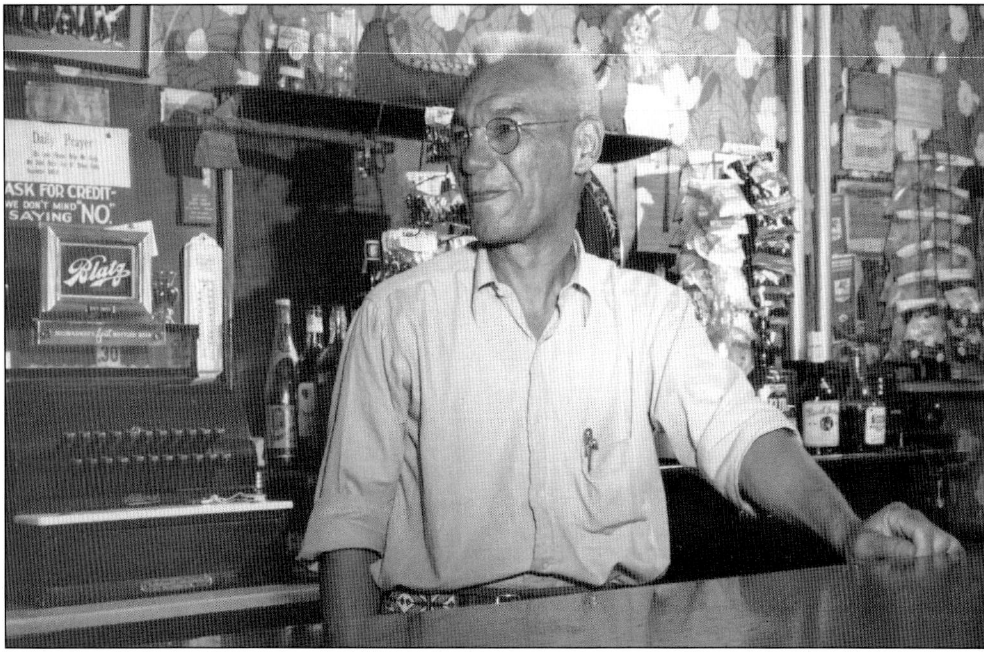

John A. Danforth, Oneida, a member of the American Indian Community in Milwaukee, became the first Indian commander of the Gen. William Mitchell American Legion Post in 1950. He ran a tavern with his wife, Nancy, called Indian John's, pictured below, by the intersection of Fifth and Bruce Streets. Taverns provided more than just socializing for American Indians in the city. For newcomers, they were places to seek out relatives, find assistance for their housing issues, find employment, and obtain general advice on surviving the challenges of the city and taking advantage of the support systems the city offered. (Courtesy of the Milwaukee Public Museum.)

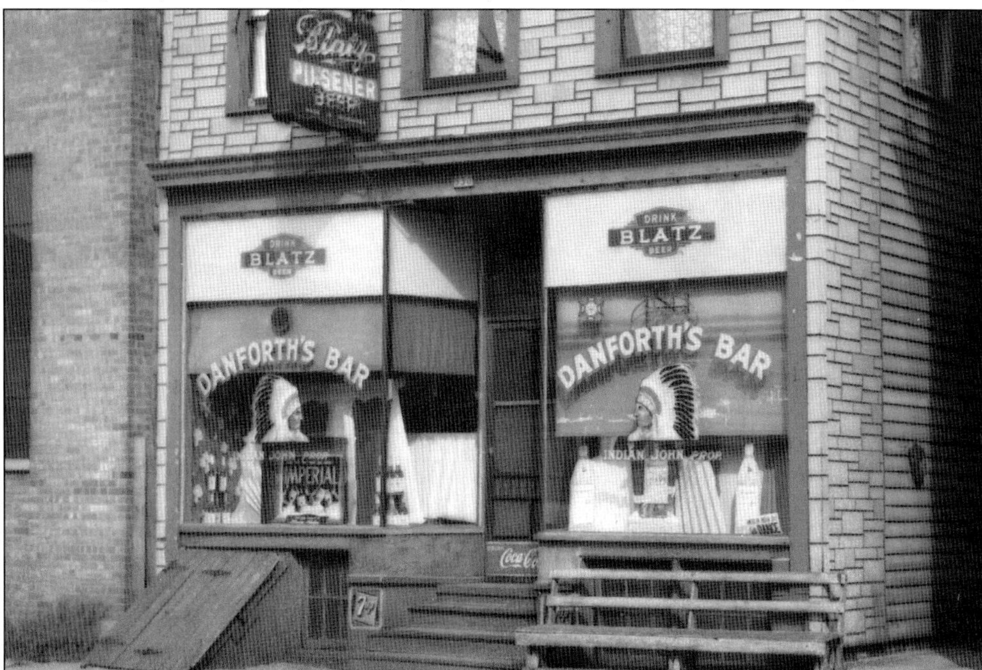

Coleman Schwamp ran the Thunderbird Tap at 1435 South Muskego Avenue. Coleman did not drink, and he made sure to refer problem drinkers to appropriate services. His bar also sponsored all-Indian athletic teams in Milwaukee. Schwamp served as chairman of the Consolidated Tribes in 1968 and 1969. His wife, Emily Schwamp, was certified as an Oneida language teacher. She taught in local schools and agencies from 1973 to 2000. (Courtesy of *Milwaukee Journal Sentinel* Archives.)

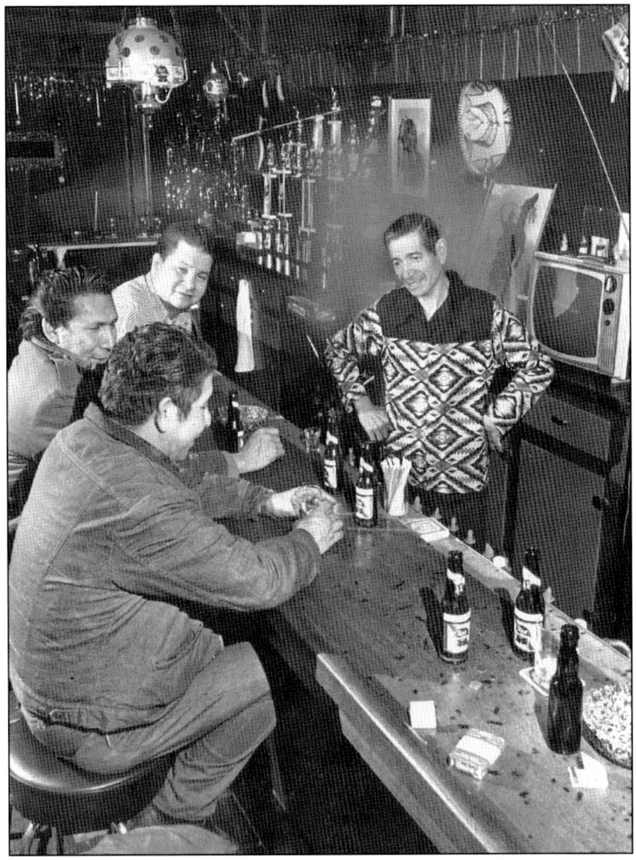

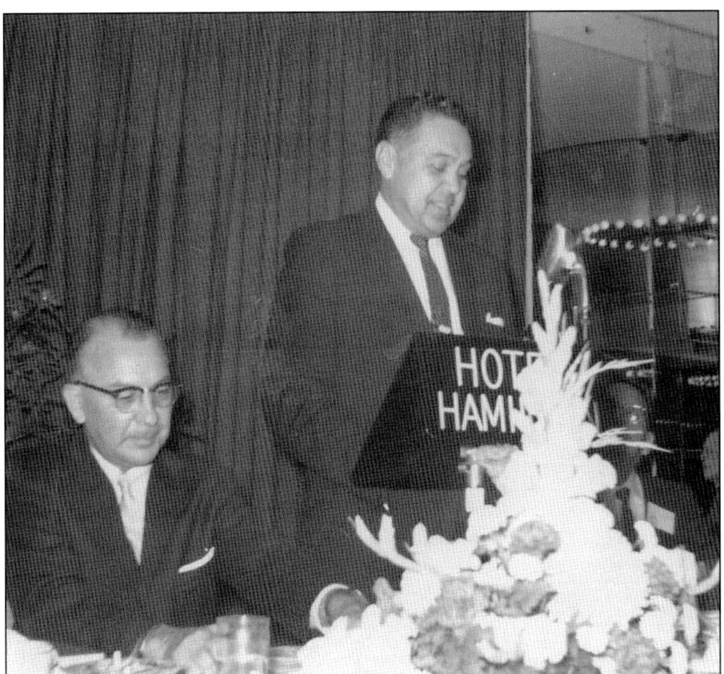

The Holiday Folk Fair celebrated its 25th anniversary November 15–17 in 1968 at the Milwaukee Arena. The honored ethnic group, American Indians, put on a folk play titled *Swift Feather Seeks a Bride*. Miss Holiday Folk Fair was Opal Skenandore, Oneida. The honored guest was Robert Bennett, Oneida, the Commissioner of Indian Affairs, pictured at left. (Courtesy of Opal Skenandore.)

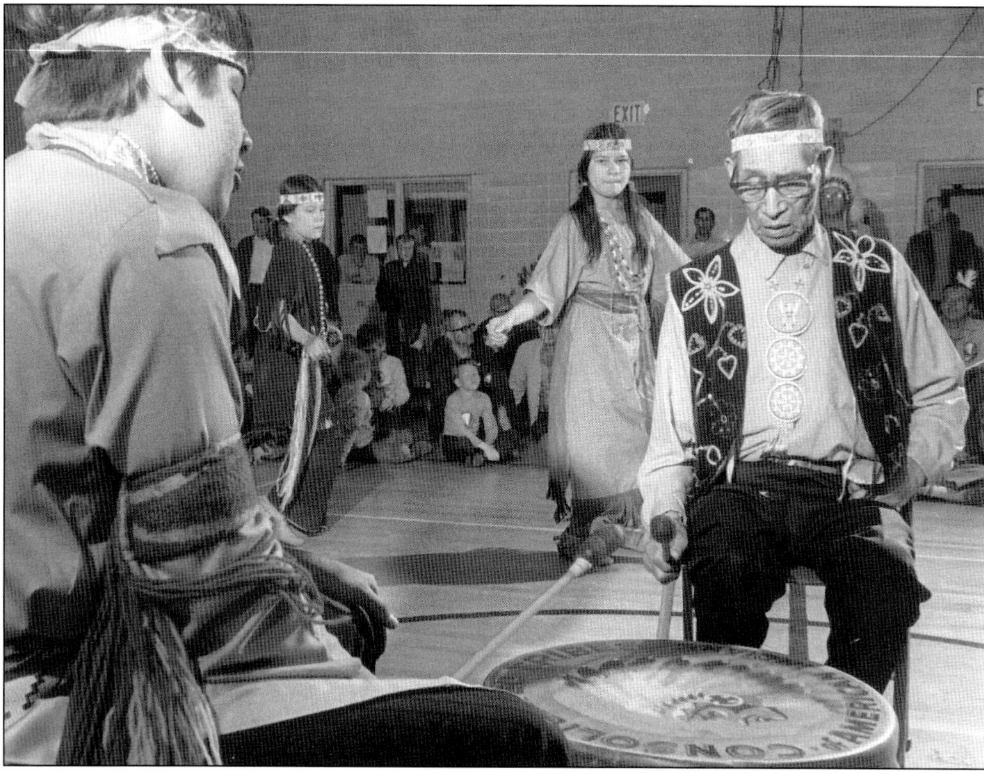

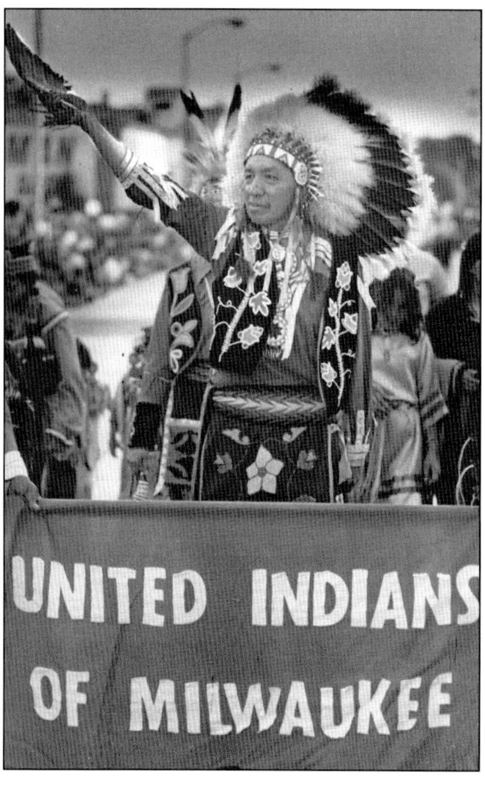

The Consolidated Tribes of American Indians began holding its powwows at Bohemian Hall in 1960. The Fifth Annual Powwow at Croatian Park in 1969 attracted more than 700 visitors, the best attendance record at the time. On March 30, 1969, Peter Waubanascum, Oneida (pictured), and members of the Consolidated Tribes performed at an event in Waukesha. Consolidated Tribes was nearing its end in 1970. It was only active for a few more years. (Courtesy of the Historic Photo Collection/Milwaukee Public Library.)

Thomas Kitchkume, Potawatomi and Ho-Chunk, is pictured in a headdress with a United Indians of Milwaukee banner for an area parade. Kitchkume is one of the founding board members of the organization, which began meeting in May 1968. They developed the organization, believing that it would be more representative of the diversity of tribes in the city than existing American Indian organizations. They also intended to have their own Indian center to offer various programs. (Courtesy of the Historic Photo Collection/Milwaukee Public Library.)

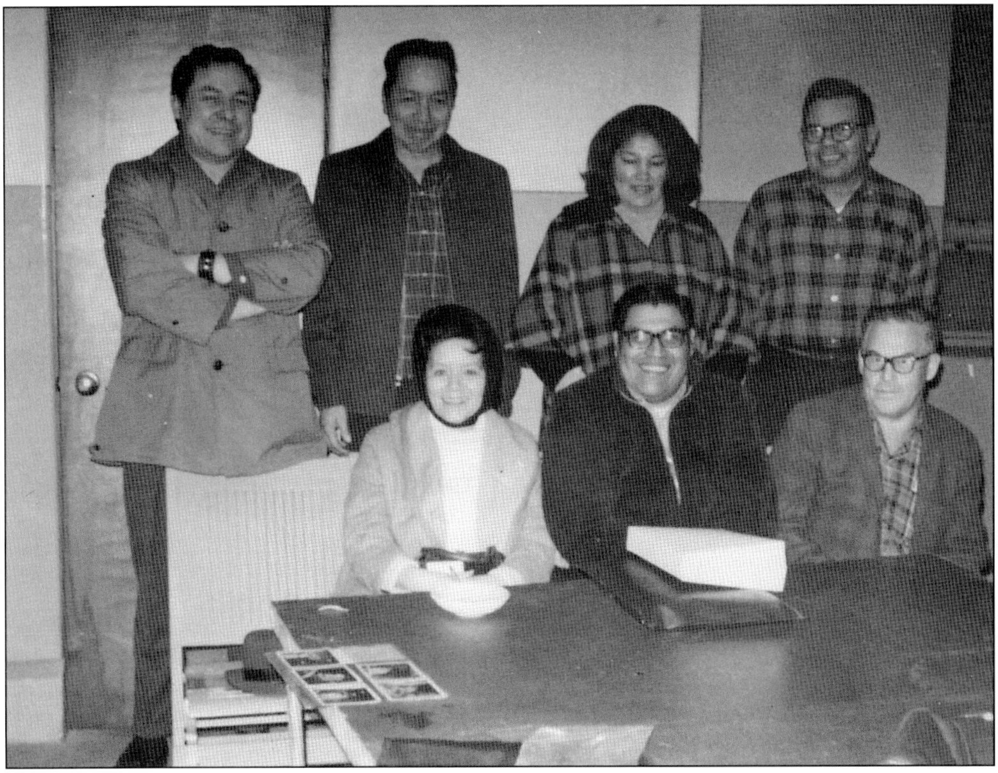

The first United Indians of Milwaukee Board of Directors, from left to right, are (first row) Petranel Martin, Ervin Funmaker, and Edward LaPlante; (second row) Wayne Martin, Thomas Kitchkume, Janette Smoke Czarnecki, and president Lawrence Jacobs. The organization filed articles of incorporation with the State of Wisconsin on March 13, 1969. In September 1969, the group was able to secure the lease to a vacant firehouse at 1554 West Bruce Street. (Courtesy of the Milwaukee Public Museum.)

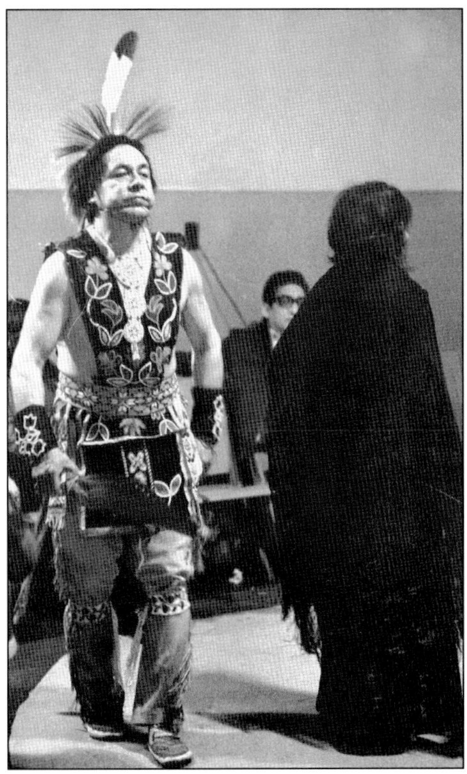

In this photograph, Wayne Martin, Menominee, wears traditional dress and dances at a local event. Besides being a founding board member of United Indians of Milwaukee, Martin also served as chairman from 1973 until 1981, then he returned to the Menominee reservation. He came to Milwaukee in 1960, and he later worked as a machine operator for 14 years. He also founded an Alcoholics Anonymous chapter in the United Indians Center. (Courtesy of the *Milwaukee Journal Sentinel* Archives.)

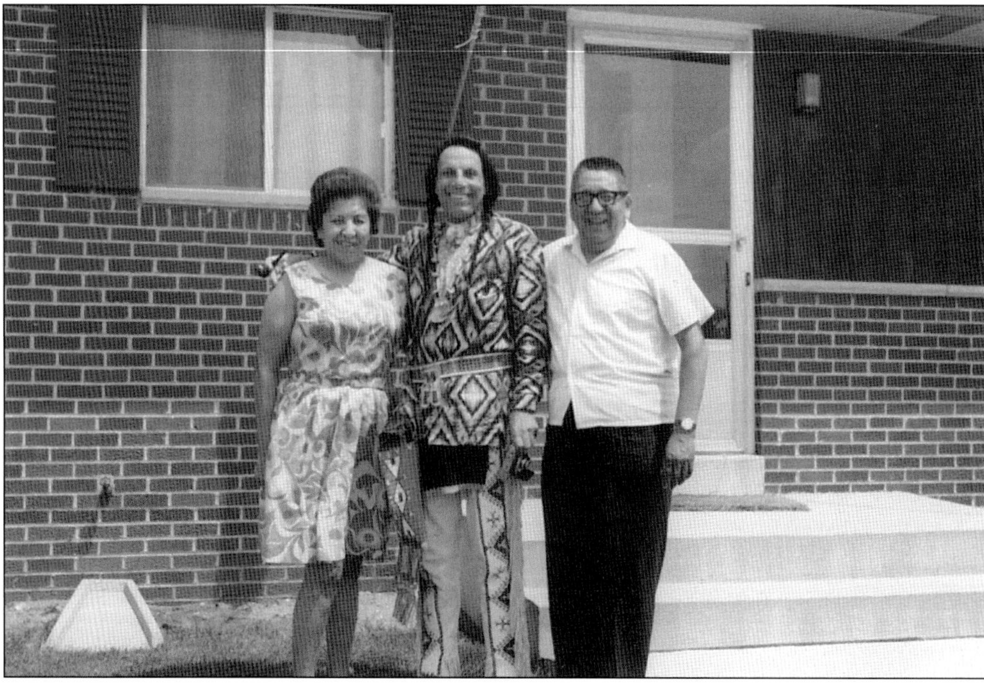

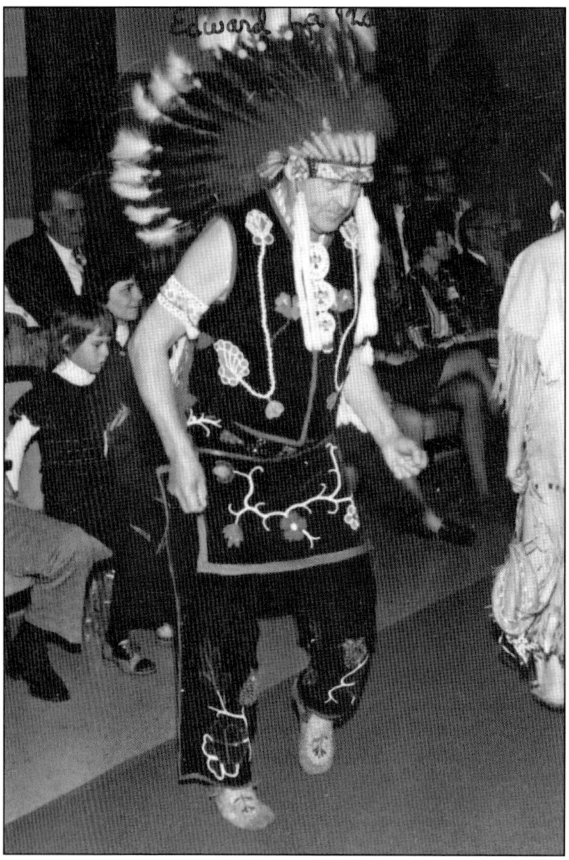

From left to right, Grace Bear, Iron Eyes Cody, and Frank Bear are pictured above in front of their home in July 1968. Cody, an actor, served as the master of ceremonies for the Consolidated Tribes Croatian Park Powwow. He played an American Indian in many movies and commercials but was actually of Italian ancestry. Frank, Oneida, a veteran of World War II and Korea, was a founding member of United Indians of Milwaukee. (Courtesy of Opal Skenandore.)

Edward LaPlante, Chippewa, is pictured here in a headdress. As a founding member of United Indians of Milwaukee, he added to his career of public service. In the 1950s, he acted as the American Indians spokesman on many local and national issues. This included serving as a delegate to the National Congress of American Indians and as commissioner of the Milwaukee Commission on Community Relations. (Courtesy of the Milwaukee Public Museum.)

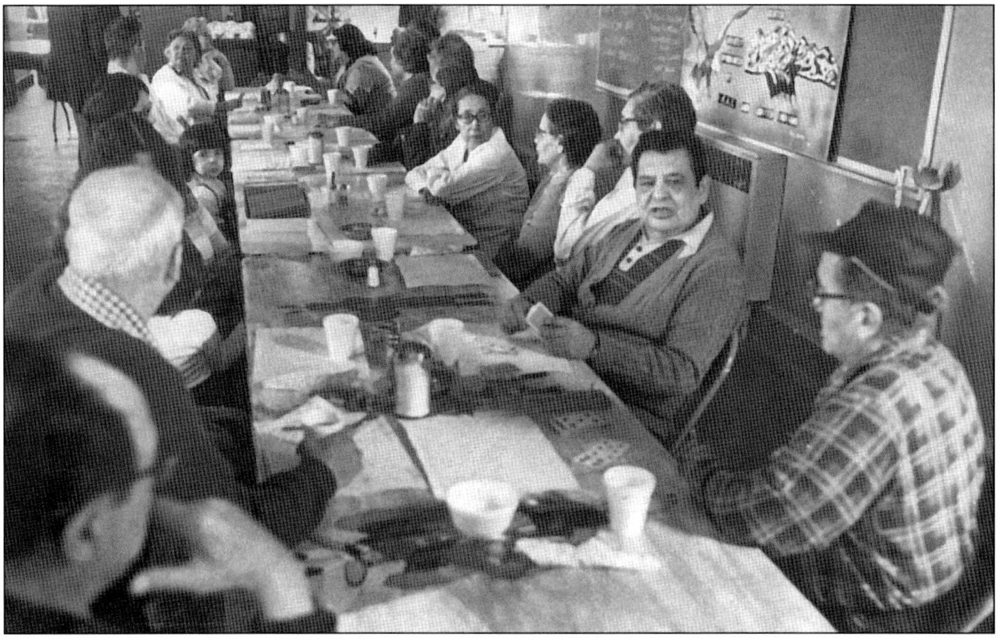

Pictured is the inside of United Indians of Milwaukee Center, located at 1554 West Bruce Street, on March 21, 1979, during the Indian elderly lunch program. The center sponsored many elderly meals and activities for the community, such as bingo and cards, youth recreation activities, basketball, pool tables, Indian dance and craft classes for the family, and Alcoholics Anonymous meetings. (Courtesy of the Historic Photo Collection/Milwaukee Public Library.)

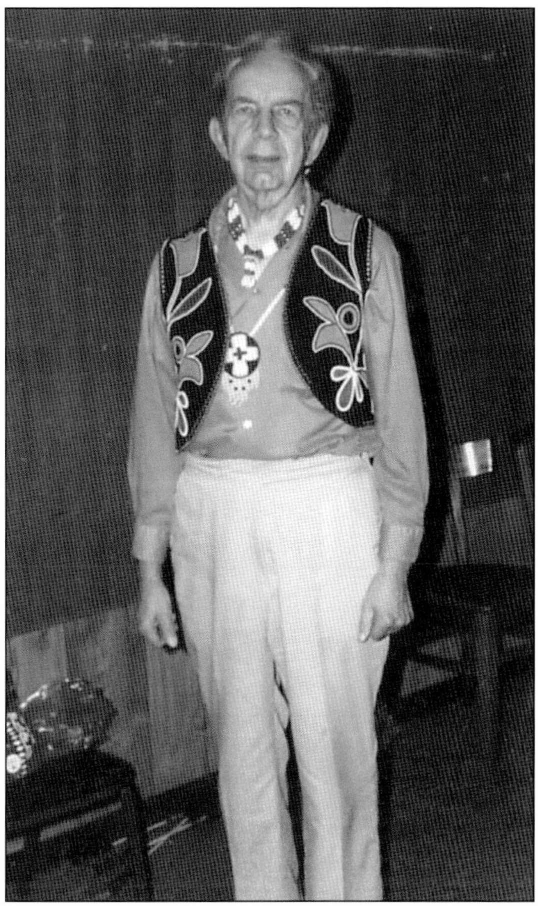

Pictured is Robert Peterman, a Milwaukee-born non-Indian. He was originally a member of a group called the Haylushka Society, which was a group of non-Indian men that were interested in American Indian culture—specifically powwow dancing and regalia. The group sponsored the first Milwaukee-area powwow in February 1967. The group disbanded in 1967, but Robert Peterman continued as a member of the United Indians. (Courtesy of the Doxtator family.)

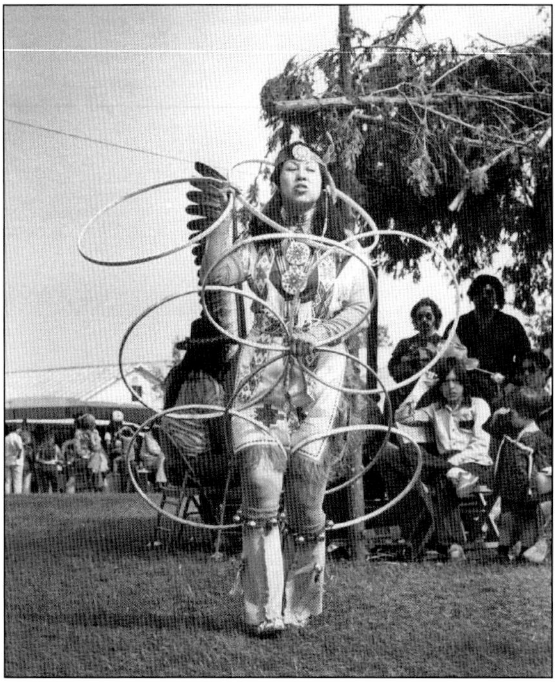

Opal Skenandore, Oneida, performed hoop dances at many local and national events and powwows. She originally learned the dance from Kenneth Powless at the Consolidated Tribes of American Indians. Here she is in July 1970, dancing with eight hoops and moving them into various shapes while keeping step with the beat of the song. She was the first female hoop dancer in this area. (Courtesy of Opal Skenandore.)

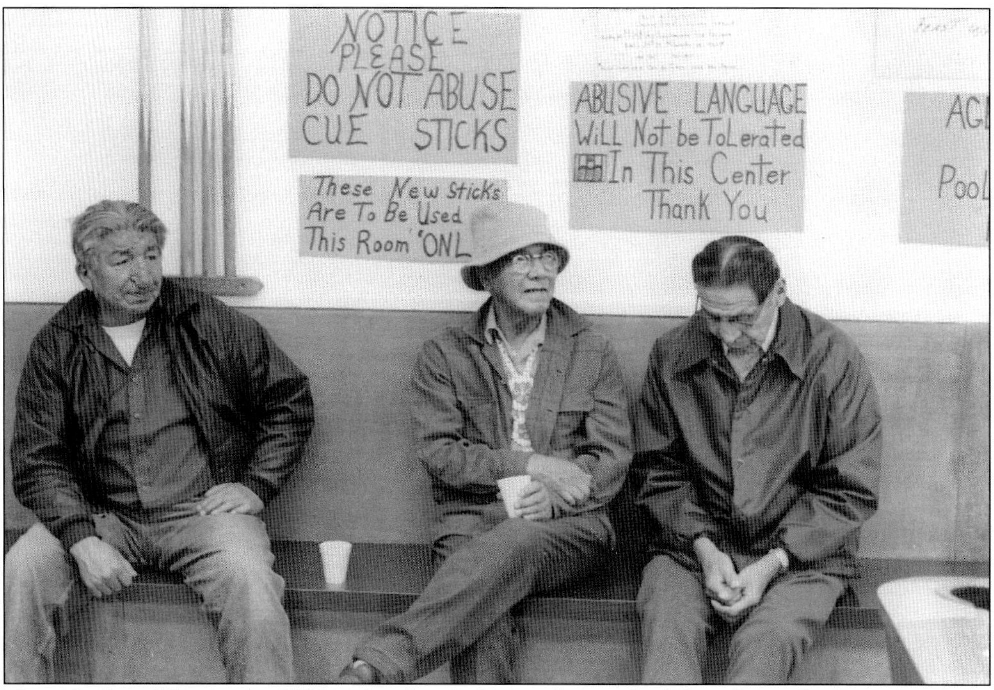

Three Indian elders in the 1970s take a break during the regular Thursday night dance practices at United Indians of Milwaukee. Barney Doud, a drum leader and respected Menominee elder, is seated far right. The dance practices were opportunities for the older men to drum and sing together and share songs, history, and protocol associated with the drum. Families also attended, and the women danced or sat and socialized while the young men danced or drummed. (Courtesy of the Historic Photo Collection/Milwaukee Public Library.)

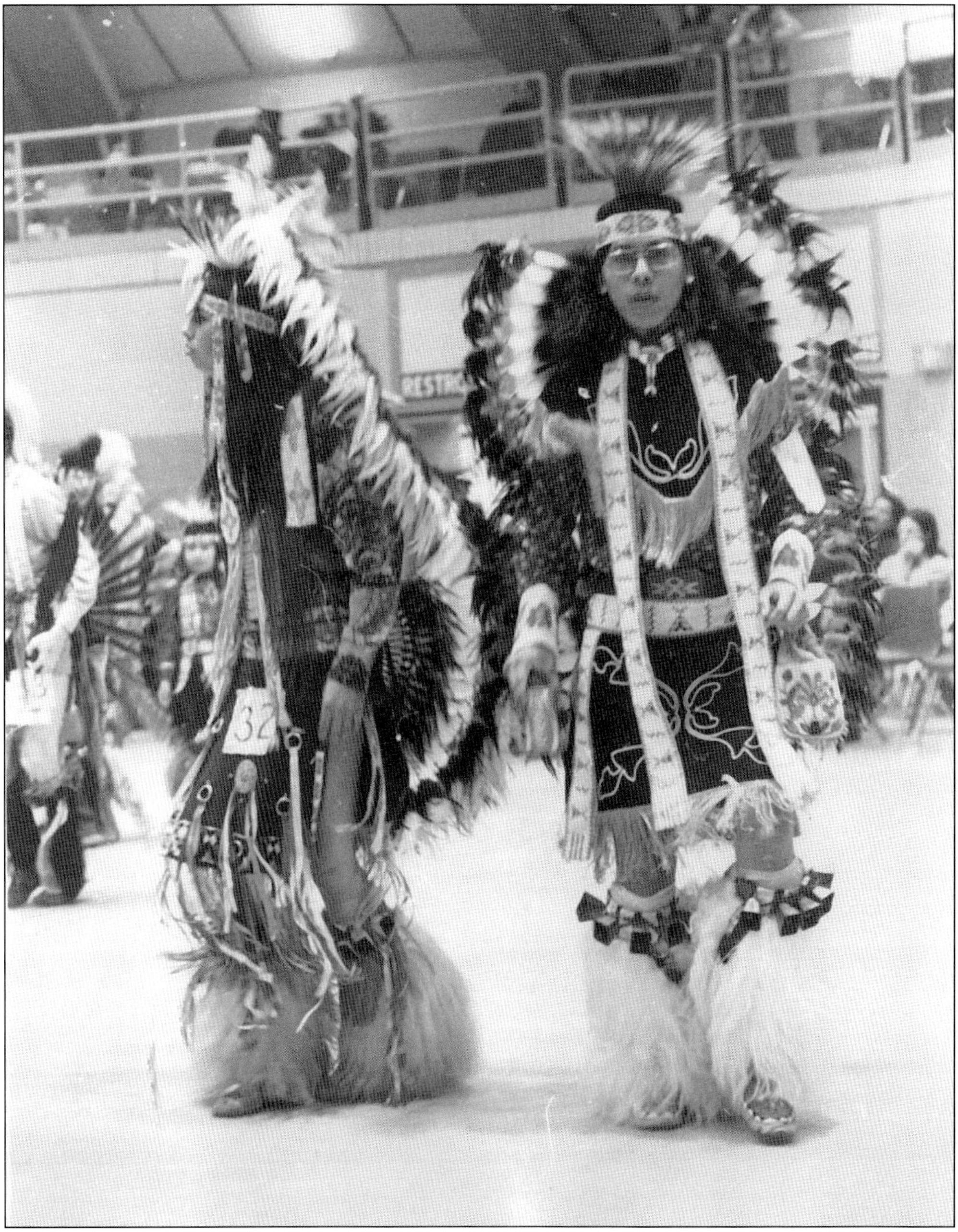

Pictured above are the Beauprey twin girls, who are Menominee. They were the daughters of Cornelia and Peter Beauprey. The girls danced in the men's fancy-dance style at the 11th Annual Greater Milwaukee Area Powwow during the weekend of February 19, 1977. A few younger females began dancing some of the men's styles in the late 1970s, specifically fancy and hoop dancing; they felt constrained by the slower women's traditional dance steps of the time. (Photograph by Joe Kazamura; courtesy of the Department of Special Collections and University Archives, Marquette University Libraries.)

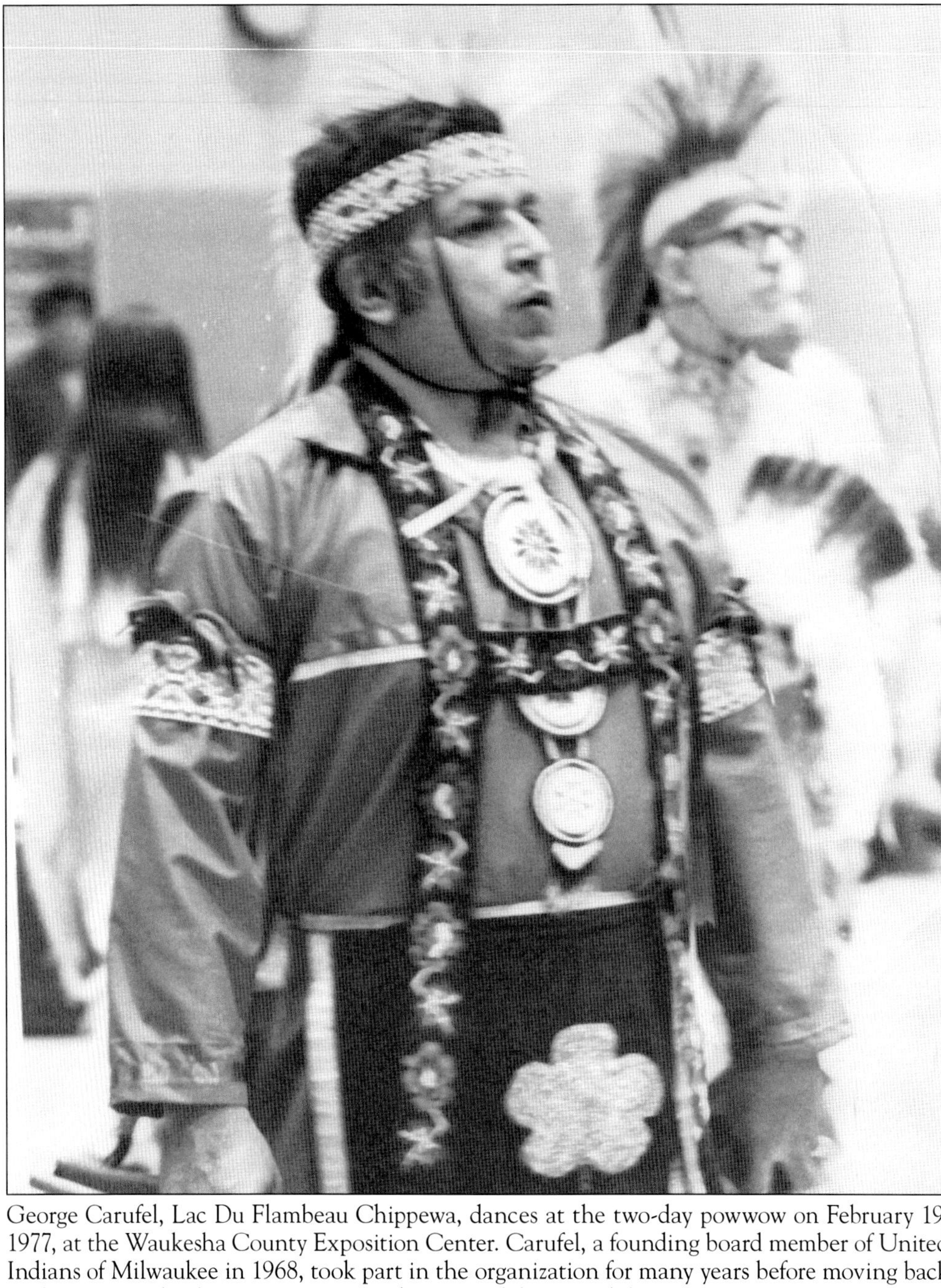

George Carufel, Lac Du Flambeau Chippewa, dances at the two-day powwow on February 19, 1977, at the Waukesha County Exposition Center. Carufel, a founding board member of United Indians of Milwaukee in 1968, took part in the organization for many years before moving back to the Lac Du Flambeau reservation in the 1980s. (Photograph by Joe Kazamura; courtesy of the Department of Special Collections and University Archives, Marquette University Libraries.)

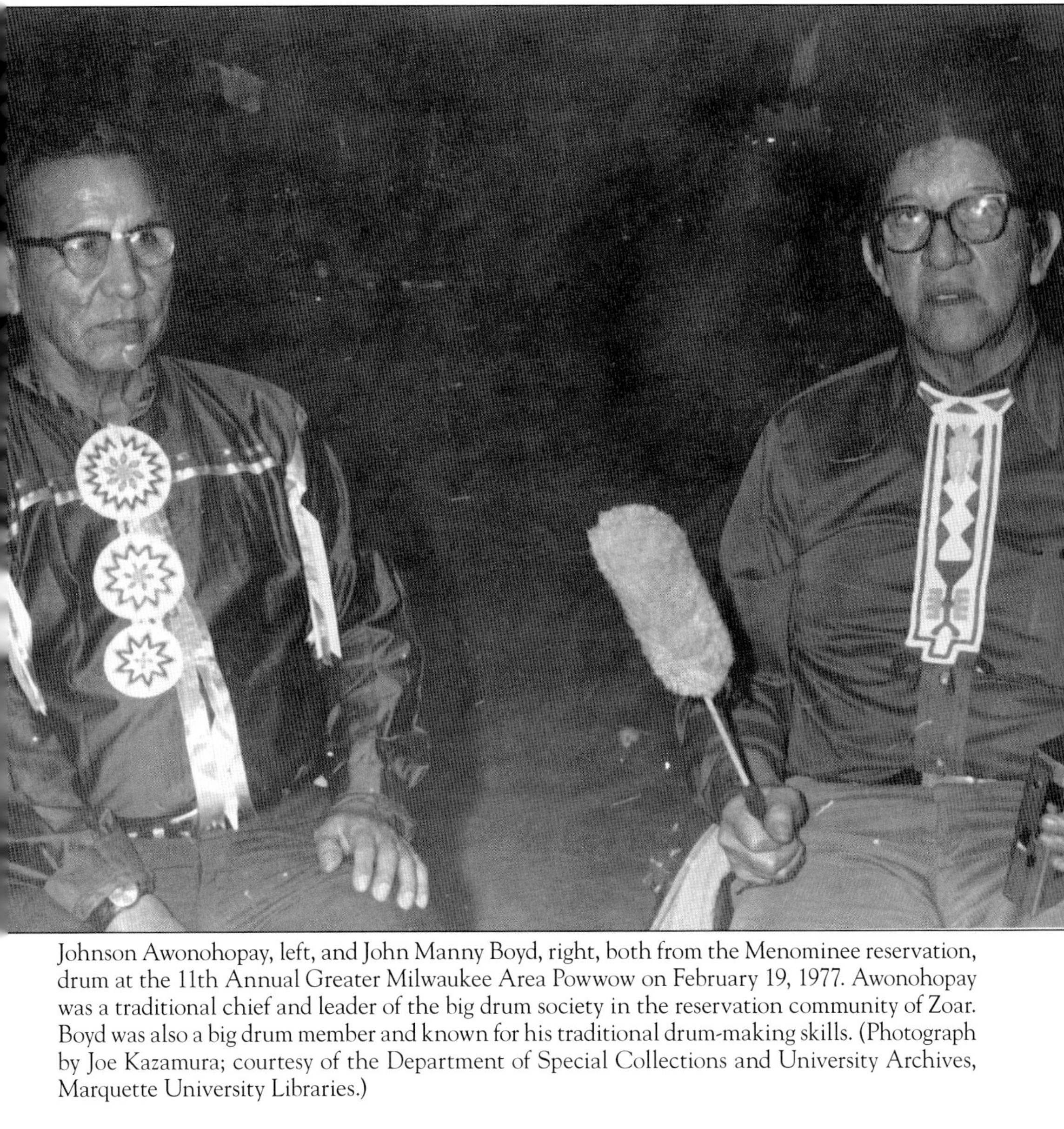

Johnson Awonohopay, left, and John Manny Boyd, right, both from the Menominee reservation, drum at the 11th Annual Greater Milwaukee Area Powwow on February 19, 1977. Awonohopay was a traditional chief and leader of the big drum society in the reservation community of Zoar. Boyd was also a big drum member and known for his traditional drum-making skills. (Photograph by Joe Kazamura; courtesy of the Department of Special Collections and University Archives, Marquette University Libraries.)

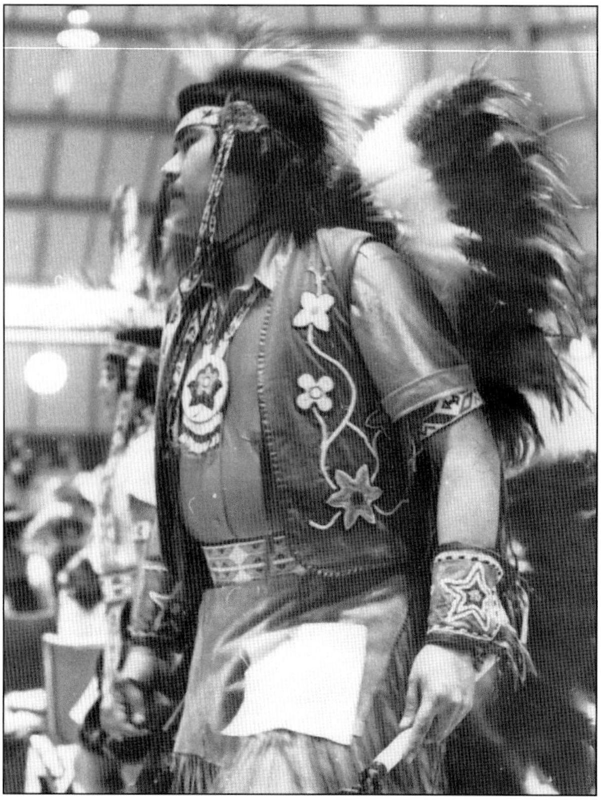

Seen at left is Alton "Sonny" Smart, Bad River Ojibwa, dressed in fancy-dance style at the Waukesha County Exposition Center in February 1977. Smart lived in Milwaukee during some of his early years because his family had relocated from the reservation. He joined the military service as a field medic and was sent to Vietnam. After military service, he later attended college and now holds a bachelor's degree and master's degree in social work, and a doctorate in sociology. He currently works as a tribal judge at the Bad River reservation and as a professor of social work at the University of Wisconsin–Stevens Point. (Photograph by Joe Kazamura; courtesy of the Department of Special Collections and University Archives, Marquette University Libraries.)

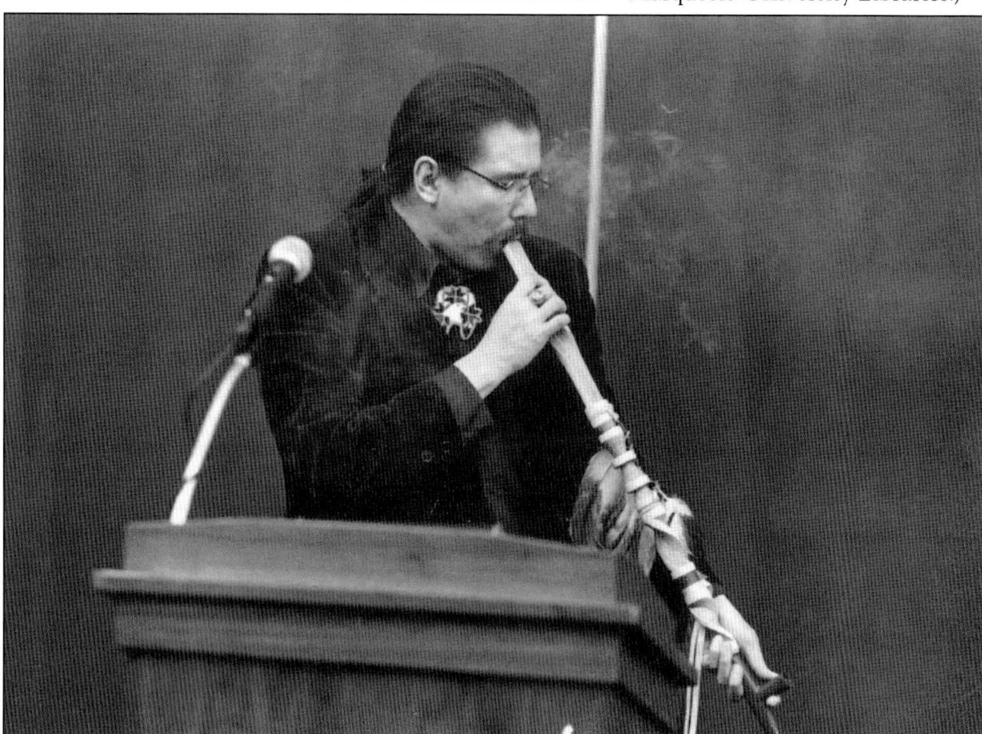

Four

Friends, Mascots, and Sports

The Milwaukee Indian community has always had relationships and interactions with others in the city that have had an impact on Milwaukee as a whole. In this section, some of those people, both Indian and non-Indian, are presented.

Anthropologists have held a long, often tension-filled, relationship with American Indians, but when one looks at the historical record of their efforts in the Milwaukee Indian community, there is little doubt that they have worked to assist and improve the lives of Indian people in the city. For instance, a good deal of the information for this book was found in the archived files of the former curator for the Milwaukee Public Museum, curator emeritus and anthropologist Nancy O. Lurie. As American Indians moved to cities in large numbers in the late 1960s and early 1970s, research on urban Indians increased, and some of the most interesting work was in this region.

The issue of mascots is contentious around the country, as well as in Milwaukee. Currently, playing an Indian mascot or character seems inappropriate. However, early on, Indian characters were played by non-Indians, and many Native Americans believed that playing the part themselves was a step forward.

Basketball, baseball, lacrosse, bowling, and boxing are a few of the team sports American Indians in Milwaukee organized and participated in over the years. These teams were usually initiated, supported, and coached by Indian people in the city. In Milwaukee, Del Porter fought for more than 40 years to keep the doors open to the club he founded, and now the club has a permanent location: Del Porter Pavilion in Kosciuszko Park.

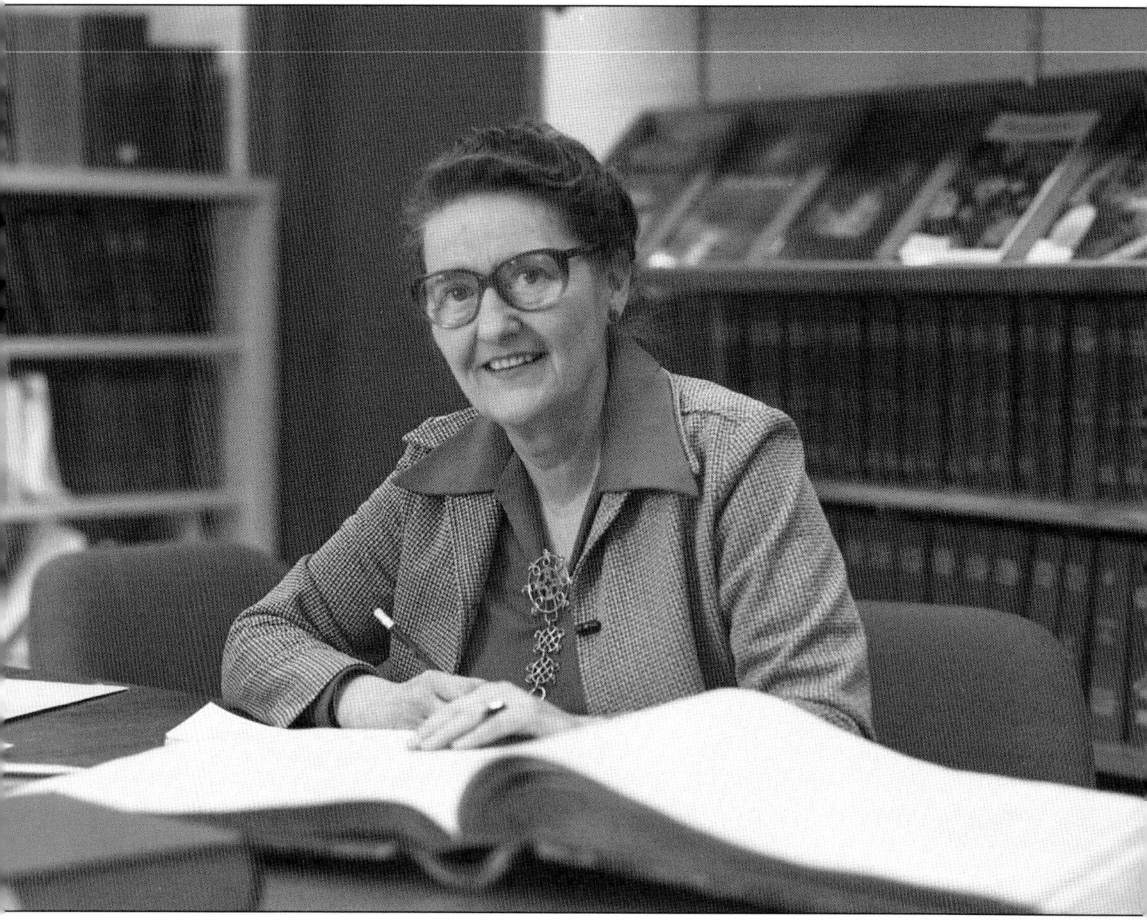

Anthropologist Nancy O. Lurie has played a major role in the Milwaukee Indian community. Lurie's 60-year career includes the writing of several books, acting as the chair of the anthropology department at UW-Milwaukee, and head curator of the anthropology department at the Milwaukee Public Museum. Along with Robert Ritzenthaler, a fellow former curator of the Milwaukee Public Museum, Lurie was one of the few who chronicled the life of urban Indians. One of her major contributions is the unique Tribute to Survival carousel at the museum. (Courtesy of the Milwaukee Public Museum.)

Sol Tax (1907–1995), along with Nancy O. Lurie, was one of the few American anthropologists who paid attention to the life of Indians in a city. Tax grew up in Milwaukee, but a large portion of his career was at the University of Chicago. Tax established a form of anthropology often referred to as "action anthropology," in which researchers use their work to help solve social problems. (Courtesy of the Milwaukee Public Museum.)

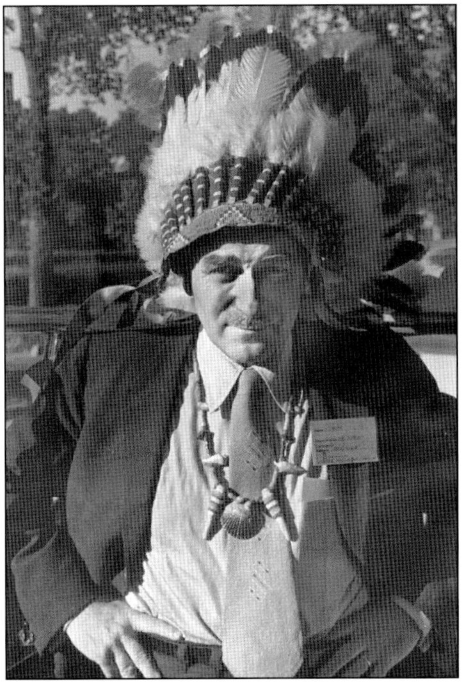

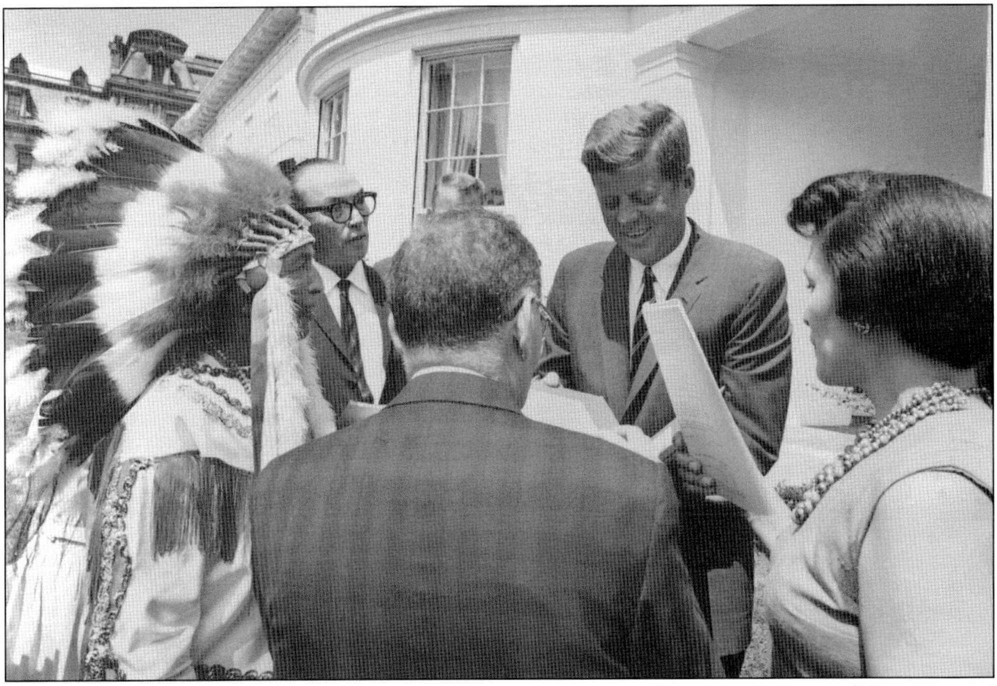

In 1961, anthropologists Sol Tax (University of Chicago) and Nancy O. Lurie (University of Wisconsin–Milwaukee) organized the American Indian Chicago Conference. At the conference, 700 American Indians from more than 80 tribal groups came to the University of Chicago to prepare the Declaration of Indian Purpose. The declaration, an attempt to present a unified Indian position to the federal government, was presented to Pres. John F. Kennedy. (Courtesy of the Milwaukee Public Museum.)

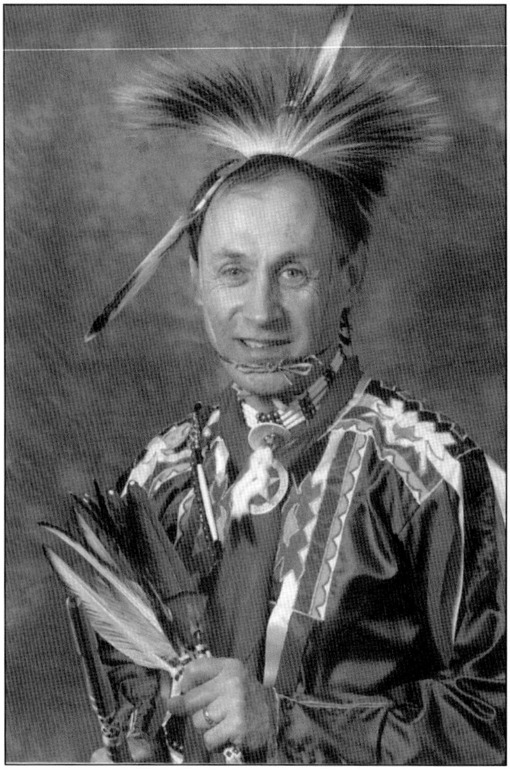

Mark Thiel is a certified archivist with the Marquette University Raynor Memorial Library. His primary responsibilities have been to gather, preserve, and service the special collections relating to the Catholic Church and Native Americans. Thiel has worked within the Milwaukee American Indian community for more than 30 years. He served with the Indian Summer Festival board and has been a longtime volunteer. Thiel has written several articles about American Indians and Indian enthusiasts that bring to light little-known people within the Milwaukee Indian community. (Courtesy of Mark G. Thiel.)

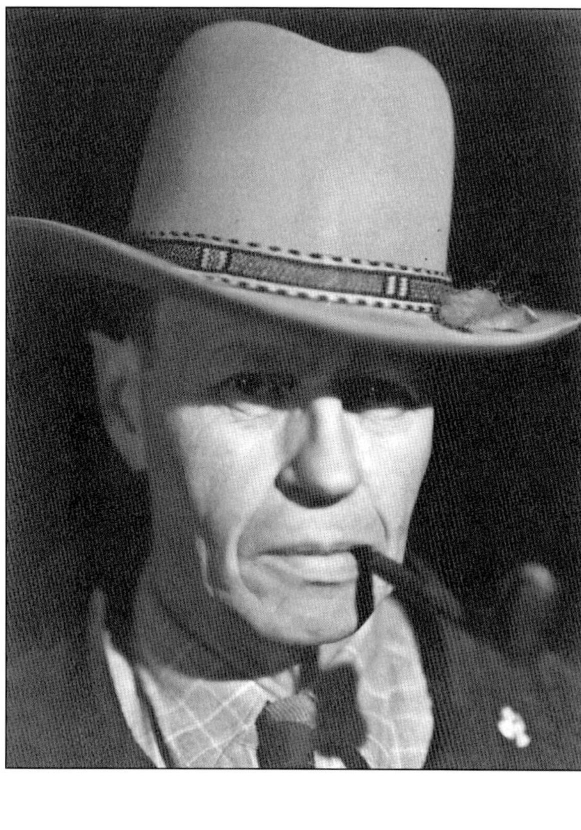

W. Ben Hunt (1888–1970) was born in Greenfield, Wisconsin, and lived in Hales Corners. Hunt's longtime interest in American Indians inspired him to tour the state and nation on a mission to experience and absorb native culture. Hunt taught Indian lore to Boy Scout leaders and wrote articles and books about making native outfits. Patrick Buckett, a protégé of Hunt's, became the Marquette University First Warrior mascot in 1953. (Courtesy of the Department of Special Collections and University Archives, Marquette University Libraries.)

Chief White Buck was Patrick Buckett, an American Indian enthusiast who hosted a television show for children on WTMJ in the 1950s. Buckett opened the debut of the Milwaukee Braves in 1953 while donning an Indian costume. As a student at Marquette, he became the First Warrior mascot. (Courtesy of the Department of Special Collections and University Archives, Marquette University Libraries.)

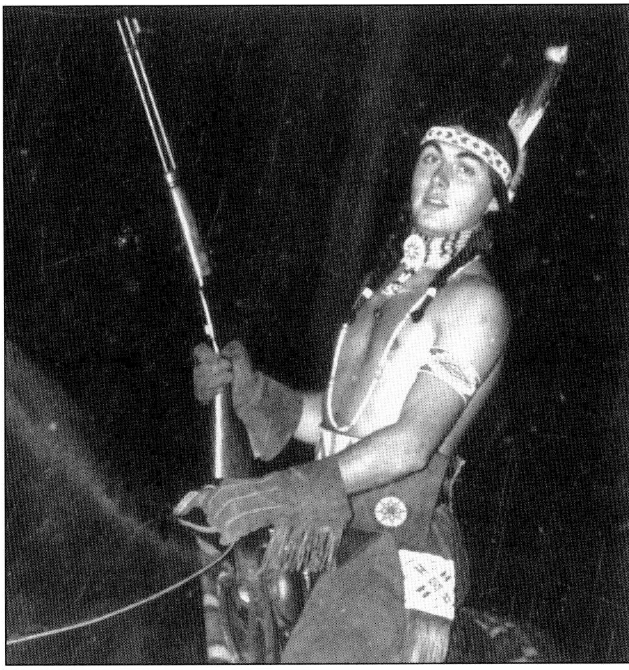

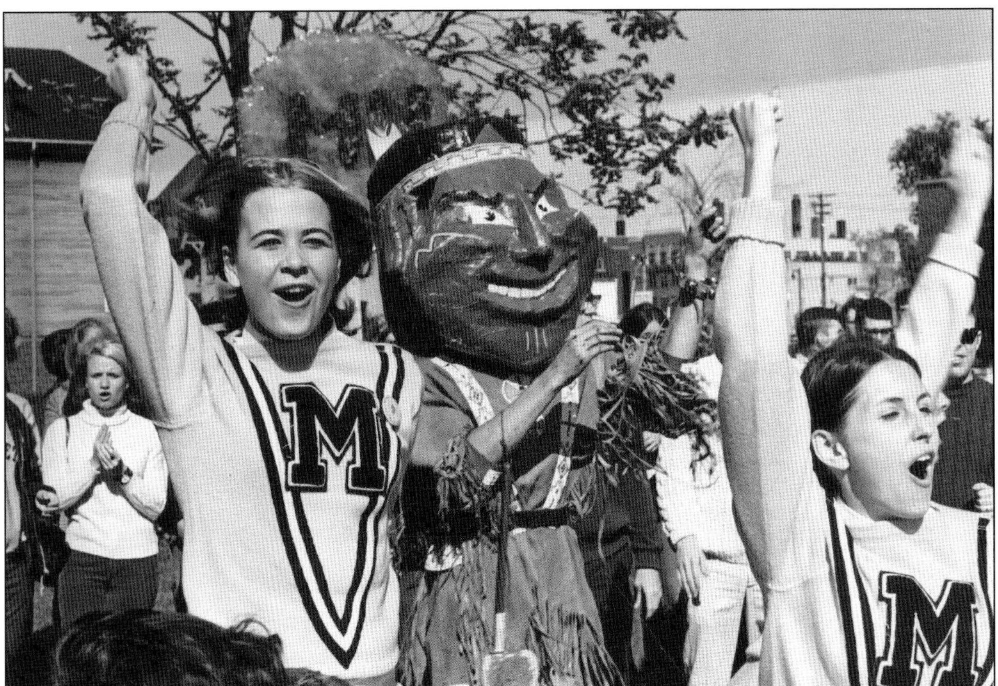

Bill Schatz was the first to play the character of Willie Wampum (1961–1971) at Marquette University. Schatz's sister Mary Ann won the bid to make the costume, which she created out of papier-mâché covered with fiberglass. The name Willie Wampum came from a student who won $5 in a "Name the Warrior" contest. In 1971, the Marquette University Student Senate requested that the administration retire the character. (Courtesy of the Department of Special Collections and University Archives, Marquette University Libraries.)

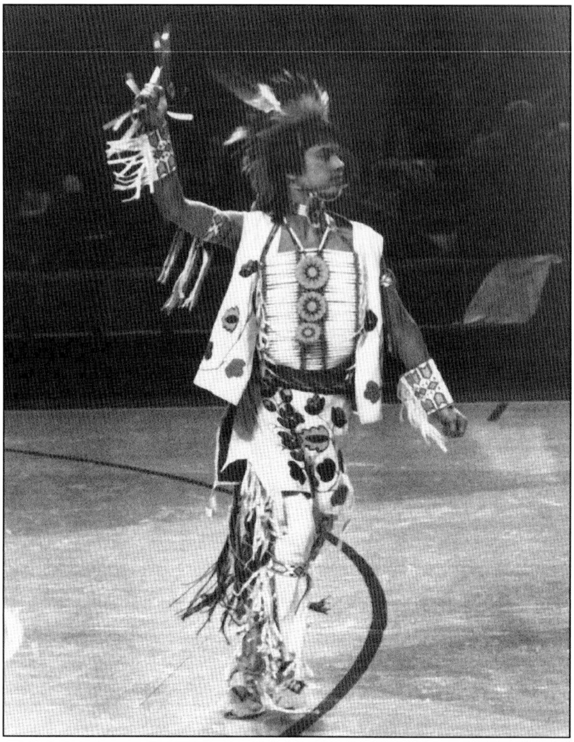

In 1979, Lila Blackdeer, whose work also appears at the Milwaukee Public Museum, was asked by American Indian students at Marquette University to make a Hocak warrior's outfit for the First Warrior mascot, which replaced the Willie Wampum mascot. After a year of work and 1,067 hours, the suit—valued at an estimated $1,500—was completed. Clifford LaFramboise, Ojibwa, was the first to wear the new First Warrior mascot outfit from 1979 to 1980. (Courtesy of the Department of Special Collections and University Archives, Marquette University Libraries.)

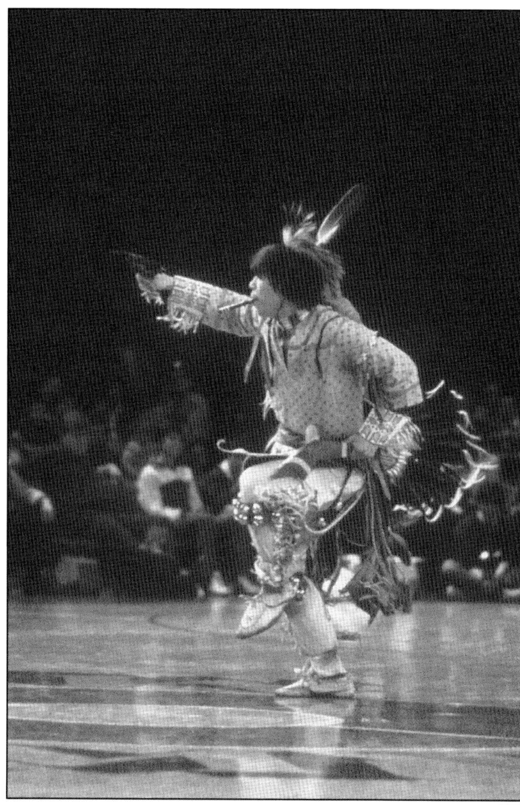

Mark Denning was a student at Marquette when he was the First Warrior mascot from 1980 to 1983. Denning's experiences led him to rethink the wisdom of Indian mascots, and he is frequently asked to speak on the issue. Denning was the Southeastern Oneida Tribal Services director for 13 years and chair of the Indian Community School in 1994. (Courtesy of the Department of Special Collections and University Archives, Marquette University Libraries.)

Richard Tourtillott, Menominee, was the final First Warrior at Marquette University from 1983 to 1986. Tourtillott, a university student who was enrolled in the Reserve Officers' Training Corps, defended the right of native people to represent themselves. Following Tourtillott's tenure, Marquette was unable to find any Indian students to take over the role. (Courtesy of Marquette University.)

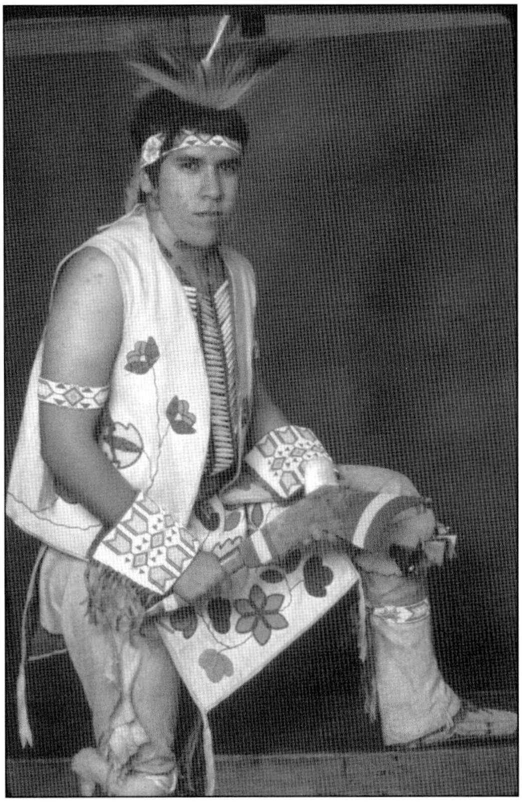

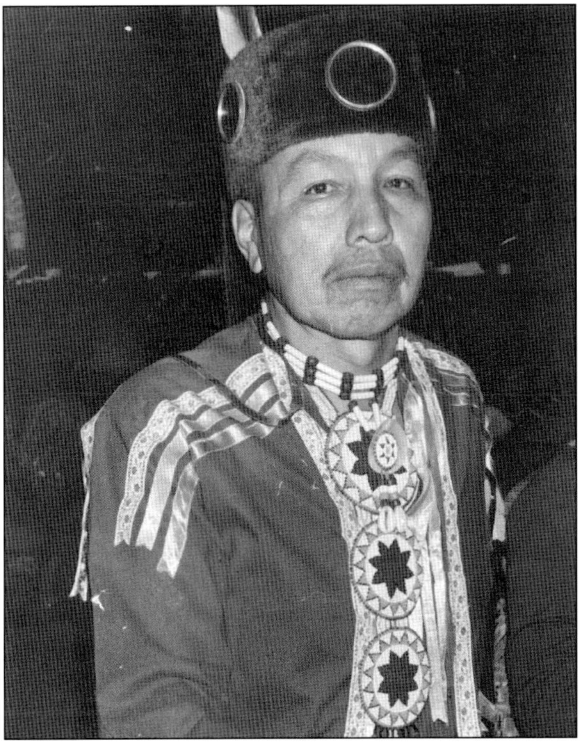

Thomas Kitchkume, Prairie Band Potawatomi and Ho-Chunk, was a traditional elder in the community and was the Milwaukee Braves mascot in the 1950s. He toured with Hank Williams Jr. and Loretta Lynn, portraying an Indian character in Williams's song "Kaw-Liga." Lynn purchased Native American arts and crafts from Kitchkume's wife, Louise, to display in her museum in Tennessee. (Photograph by Joe Kazamura; courtesy of the Department of Special Collections and University Archives, Marquette University Libraries.)

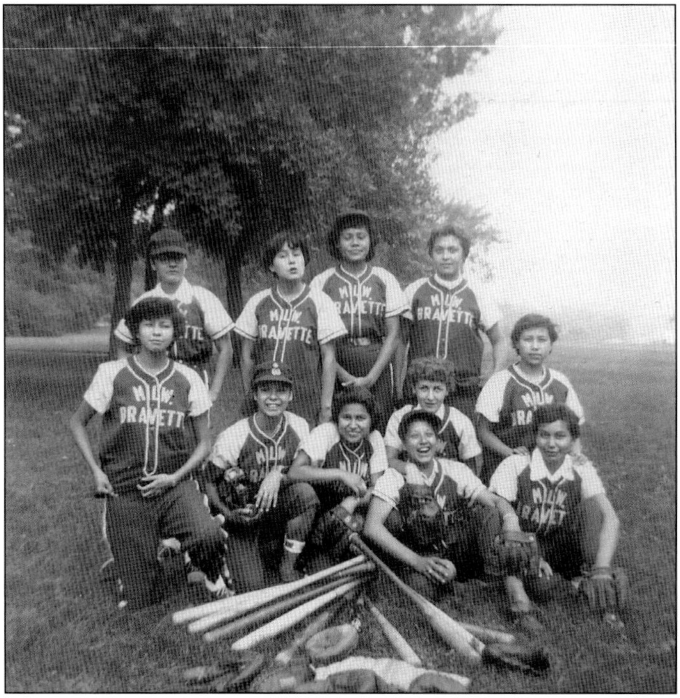

The Milwaukee Bravettes were organized and funded by the Women's Guild of Milwaukee and coached by Frank Bear, Oneida, who was a founder of the United Indians. In the photograph are, from left to right, (first row; kneeling) Marge Jackson, Ellen Danforth, Estelle Webster, Marlene Silas, and Lydia Parker; (second row; kneeling) Karen ? and Opal Skenandore; (third row) Alberta House-Metoxen, ? Elm, unidentified, and Erma Wheelock. (Courtesy of Opal Skenandore)

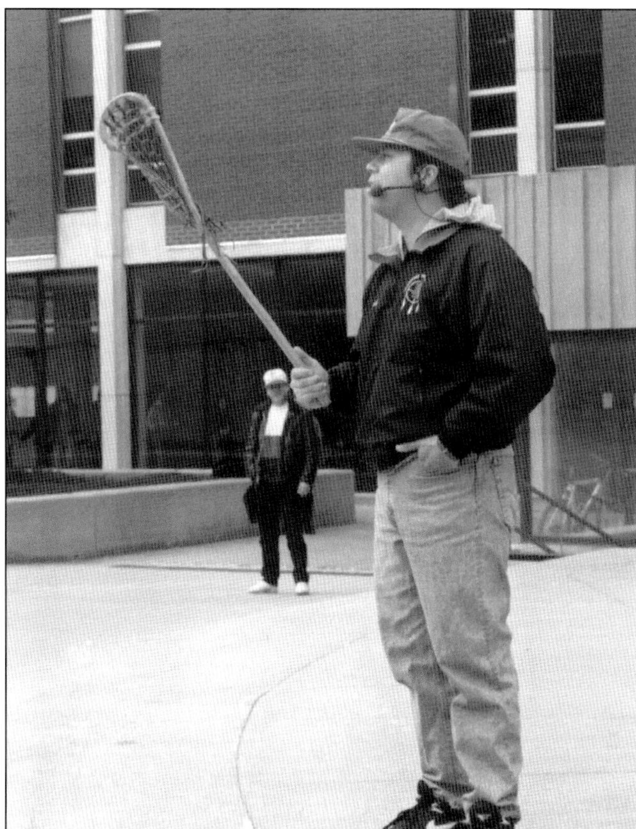

The Indian Summer Festival revived the native game of lacrosse in Milwaukee in the summer of 1987. Board member Mark Denning (pictured) assembled a team with help from Marquette University students. The club became popular with both Indian and non-Indian members who then helped initiate teams, many of which are recognized by the Wisconsin Interscholastic Athletic Association in Milwaukee-area high schools. (Courtesy of the UWM American Indian Student Services.)

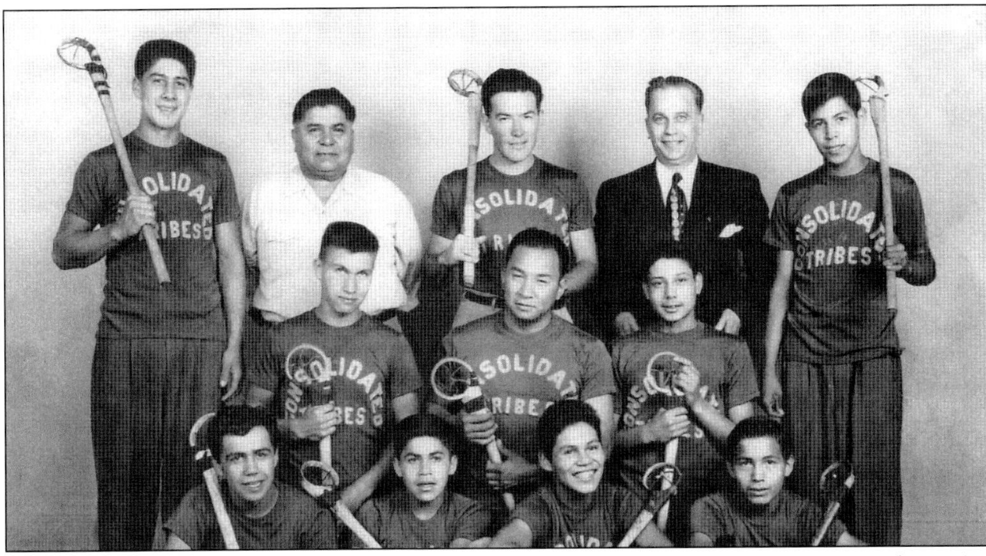

The Consolidated Tribes of American Indians supported several sports teams in the 1950s, including a lacrosse team. Pictured above, from left to right, are (first row) Robert Pero, Myron "Chubby" Skenandore, Kenneth Skenandore, and James Webster; (second row) Oscar Davids, Theodore Powless, and Eugene Silas; (third row) Lyle Ninham, Alpheus Smith, coach Kenneth Powless, Al Seager, and Francis Webster. Not pictured are Rupert Smith, William Pero, Michael Coleman, and Francis Coleman. (Courtesy of Dona Yahola.)

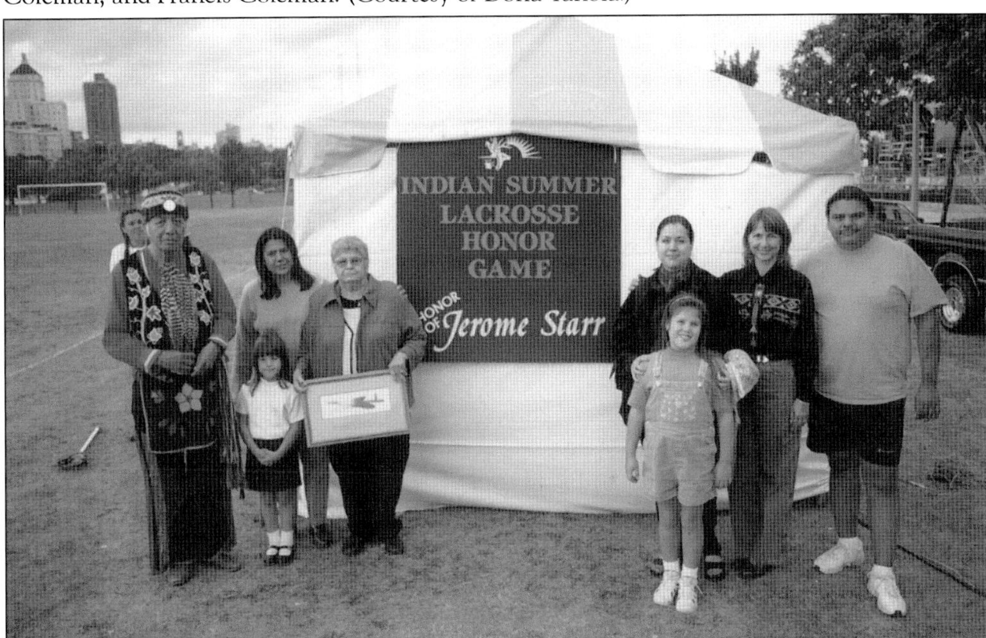

Lacrosse's primary purpose is as a medicine game. Lacrosse has been used historically to settle disputes, avoid warfare, heal the sick, and lift the spirits of individuals and families, as well as provide entertainment. A memorial lacrosse game was held at the Indian Summer Festival for the family of Jerome Starr. Starr was an ironworker who died in 1999 in the Big Blue crane accident at Milwaukee County Stadium. (Courtesy of Sharon Skenandore.)

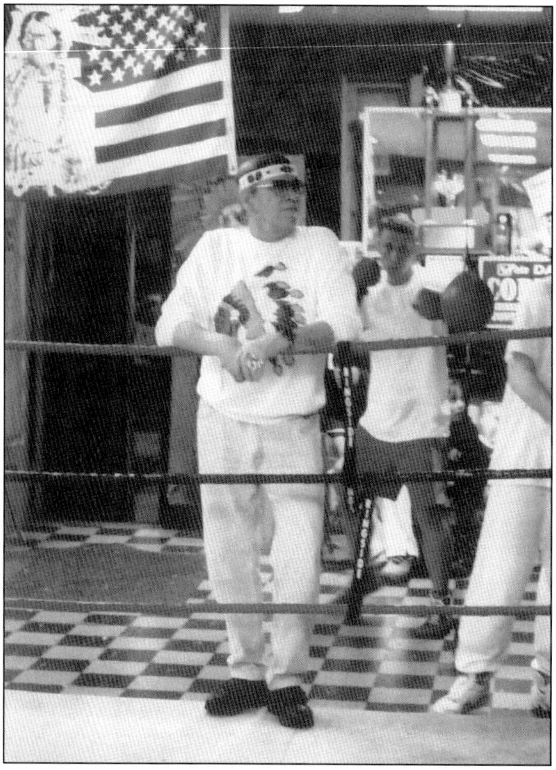

Del Porter (1933–2008), White Earth Ojibwa, founded Ace Boxing in 1960 and ran it in some form in several locations for 47 years. Porter was the son of Theodore "Cyclone" Porter, a club boxer who cofounded Ace with his son. Porter had 14 children and is survived by his wife, Diane. She and their daughter Deanna have coordinated the Indian Summer Festival Pow Wow for 23 years. (Courtesy of Diane Porter.)

Del Porter's Ace Boxing never charged or made money. He trained hundreds of young men in Milwaukee, including native youth, giving them focus and a place off the streets. In the mid-1990s, Porter trained the first woman to win a Golden Gloves title. Porter retired from the Milwaukee County Transit System and was nearly dismissed for wearing his trademark headband in honor of his father and heritage. (Courtesy of Diane Porter.)

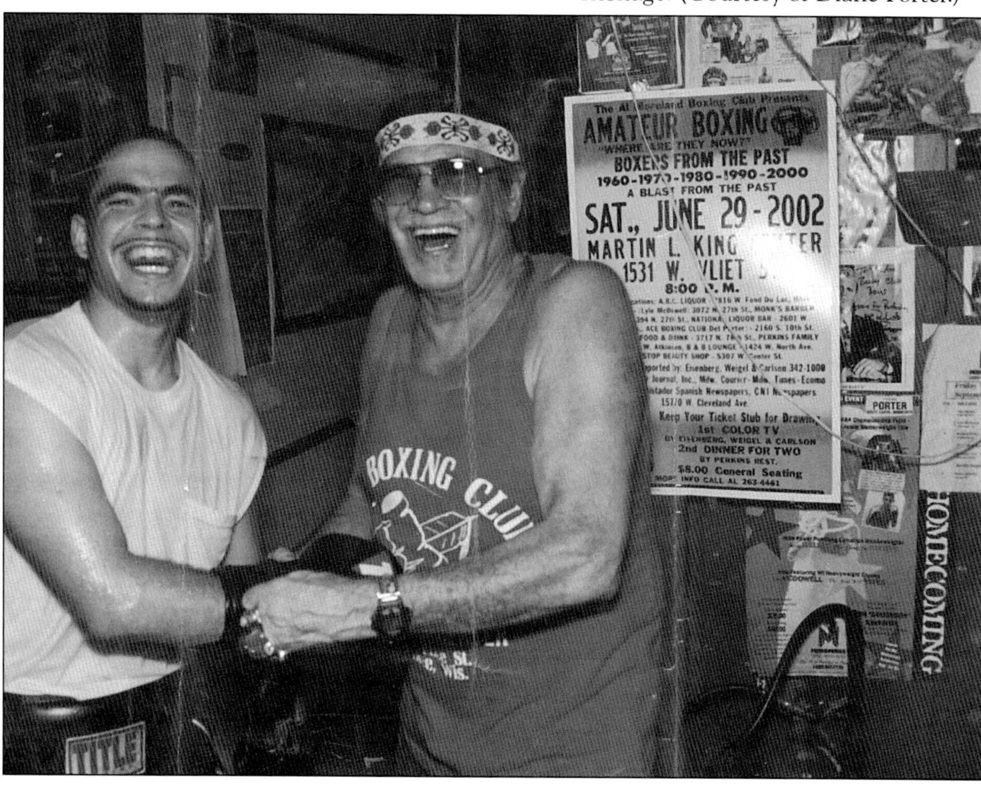

Five

Red Power Movement

In the 1970s, a new phase took hold for many American Indian communities across the county, and Milwaukee was no exception. This period is often referred to as the Red Power movement, which took prominence. For many American Indians, it was a time of empowerment and taking pride in their culture and identity. Most Americans saw this as an extension of the civil rights movement. American Indian activists were inspired by the gains of the civil rights movement, but they also saw their issues as separate. American Indians knew their issues also revolved around federal treaties and being members of sovereign nations who dealt with the federal government as equals. American Indians did not want to be absorbed into the great melting pot, but they wanted to be allowed to live as the indigenous people of this land. In urban areas, they shared common issues with other communities of color, including discrimination in housing, employment, and access to quality education.

There were more than 4,000 reported American Indians in Milwaukee in 1973, and these residents came from many different tribes statewide and nationally. Along with being consistently undercounted in the census, they also made up one of the smallest ethnic groups. They fought to show the rest of the city they existed and had issues they wanted to have resolved.

Through the 1930s to mid-1960s, only one primary American Indian organization in Milwaukee existed, but by the late 1960s and through to the early 1970s, there were more than 10. These 10 organizations served the social, spiritual, health, and educational needs of the urban Indians in Milwaukee. The methods they used to draw attention to their issues were different. From political lobbying and appealing to protest and the occupation of public and private areas, they took their future into their own hands. It was a grassroots movement that led from the bottom up and swept across the country, from distant, isolated rural reservations in the West to the crowded, bustling urban centers in the East—and Milwaukee Indians took to it with open arms.

The American Indian Information and Action Group formed in March 1969. In February 1970, it began receiving a $5,000 grant from a Methodist quadrennial emphasis committee and was able to rent an office at 1414 North Twenty-seventh Street in Milwaukee. The group operated as a social service organization and took part in activities intended to improve the housing, employment, and social welfare of urban American Indians. It published a quarterly newsletter called *Smog Signals*. (Courtesy of the Milwaukee Public Museum.)

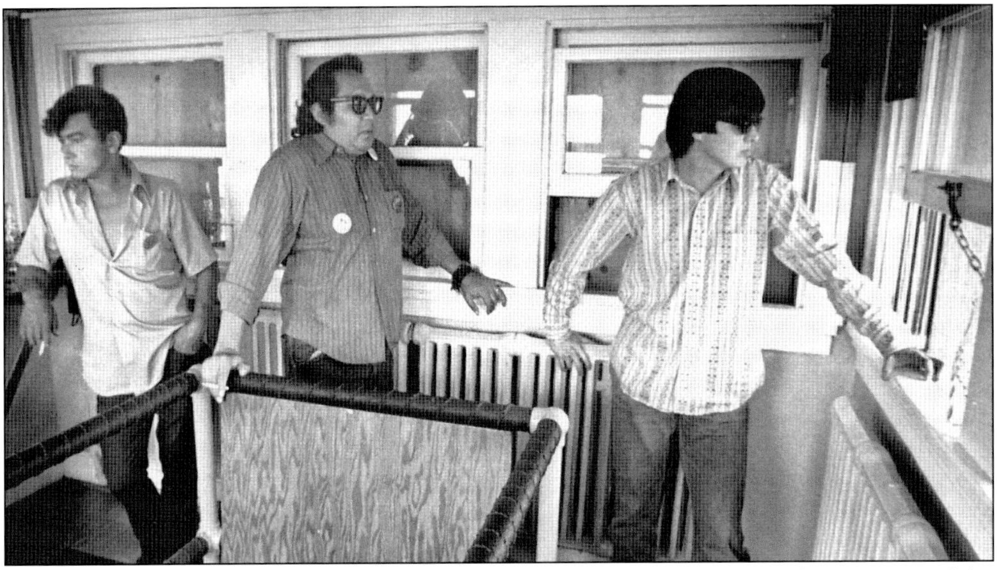

Members of the Milwaukee chapter of the American Indian Movement took possession of the Coast Guard station at Milwaukee's lakefront on August 14, 1971. Standing in the Coast Guard's tower from left to right are George Gardner, Herbert Powless, and Jerome Starr. Powless was chairman and Starr was cochairman of the Milwaukee chapter of the American Indian Movement. Starr was later killed at the Miller Park Big Blue crane collapse on July 14, 1999. (Courtesy of the *Milwaukee Journal Sentinel* Archives.)

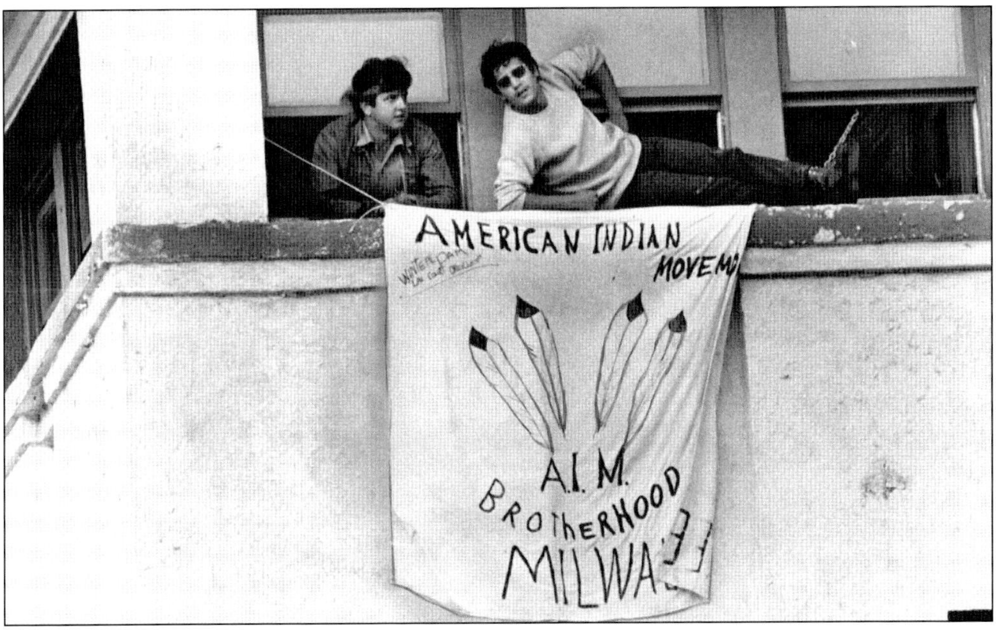

On August 15, 1971, two days into their occupation of the abandoned Coast Guard station, two members of the American Indian Movement are shown flying their flag from the windows. The Milwaukee American Indian Movement occupied the building under the authority of an 1868 treaty between the Lakota Sioux and the federal government that allows non-reservation Indians to file claims on government land "not used for a specific purpose." (Courtesy of the *Milwaukee Journal Sentinel* Archives.)

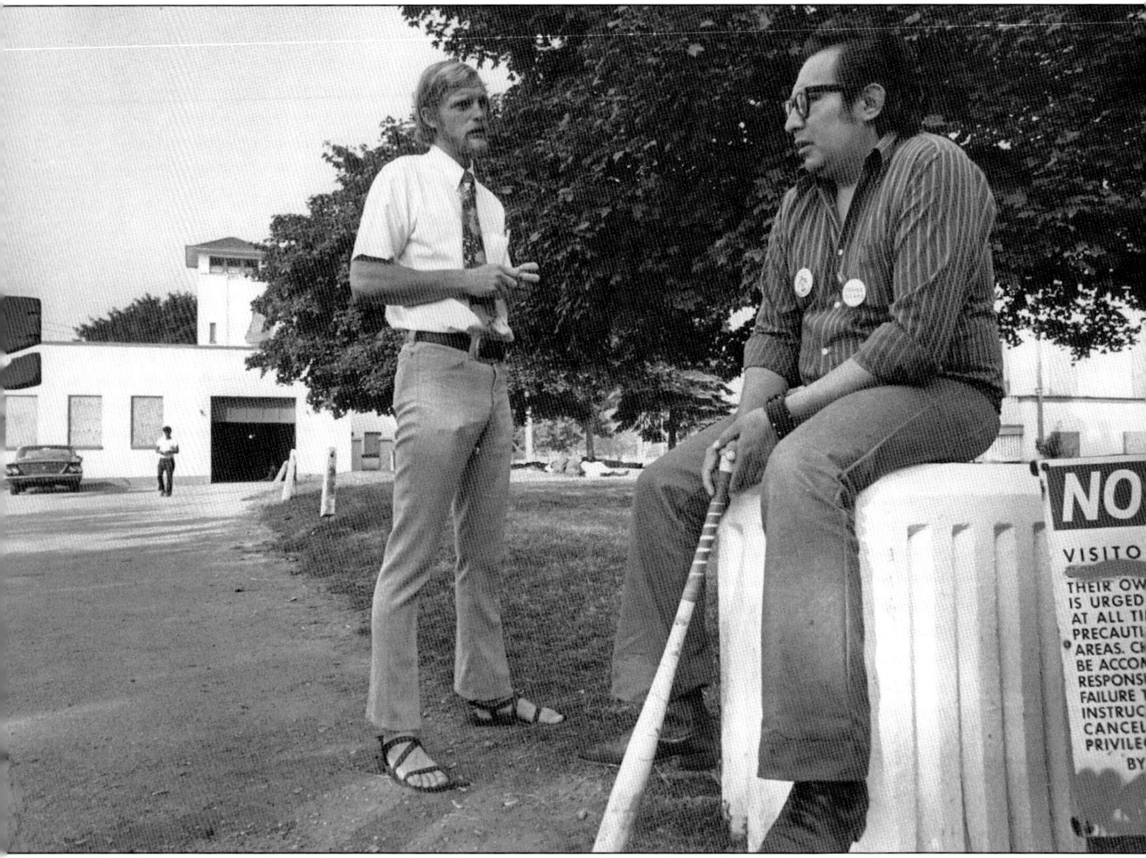

Thomas E. Dixon (left), an attorney on Indian affairs from the Milwaukee Legal Service, and Herbert Powless (right), chairman of the Milwaukee chapter of the American Indian Movement, discuss issues near the entry to the Coast Guard station. Powless, Oneida, grew up on the Oneida reservation near Green Bay. Powless later enlisted and became a US Marine. After his discharge, he came to Milwaukee. He worked as an ironworker and also for American Motors Corporation for nine years. He founded the Milwaukee chapter of the American Indian Movement in 1968. He also served as a national field representative for the movement. After previous personal incidents with alcohol, Powless later founded the American Indian Council on Alcoholism in 1973. He later served four years in prison for charges related to the 1973 Wounded Knee takeover in South Dakota. (Courtesy of the Historic Photo Collection/Milwaukee Public Library.)

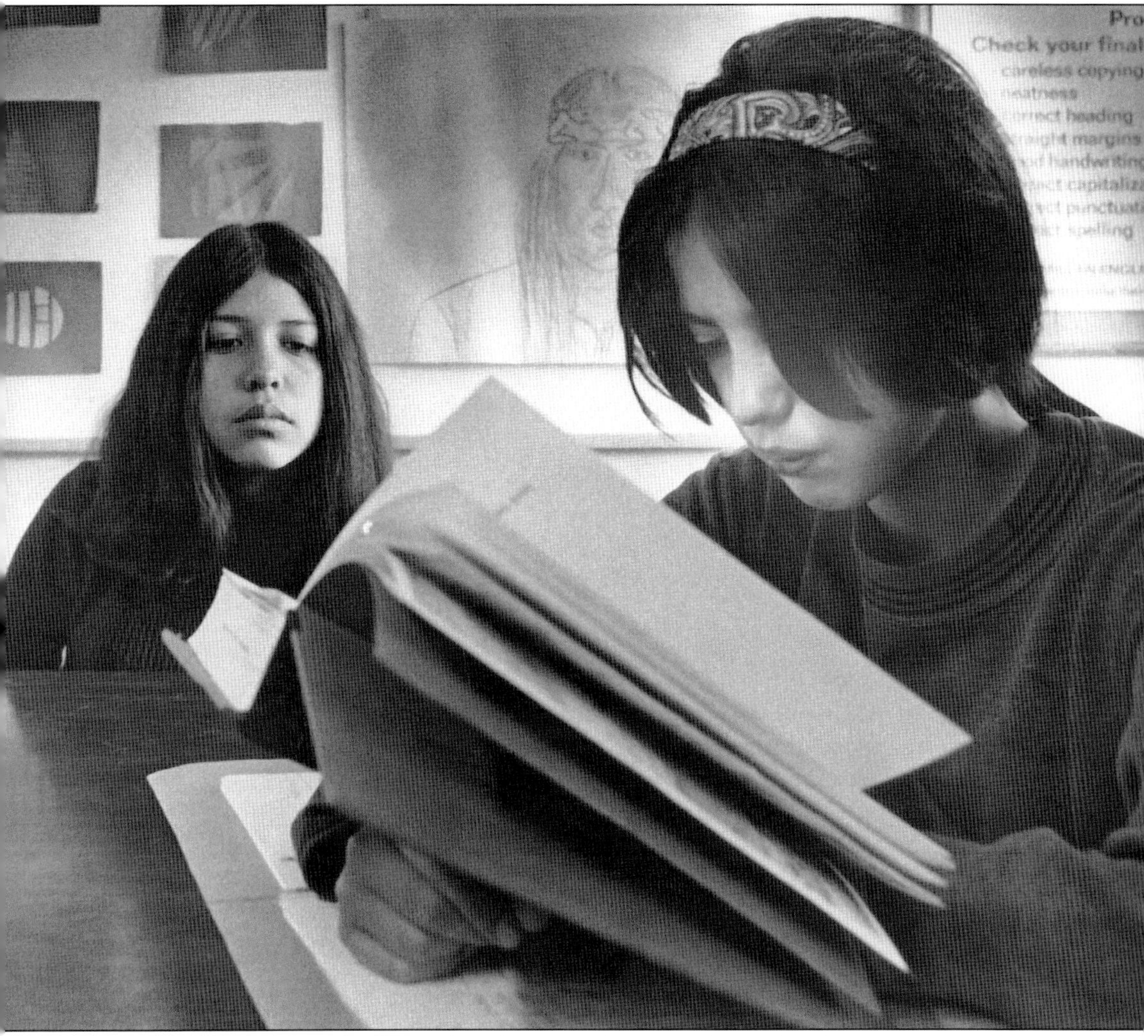

Pictured is an inside view of a Coast Guard station classroom. Days after the occupation of the station, the Indian Community School moved into one of the buildings. In the photograph are Lorene Doxtator (left), age 14, and Marie LeMieux (right), age 15, who both attended the Indian Community School. In 1975, Doxtator graduated from the high school, which was formed in 1969 by three Indian mothers: Marge Stevens, Marge Funmaker, and Darlene Neconish. Its prior location was in a church basement. Each year, the school served about 75 students in both elementary and high school. (Courtesy of the Historic Photo Collection/Milwaukee Public Library.)

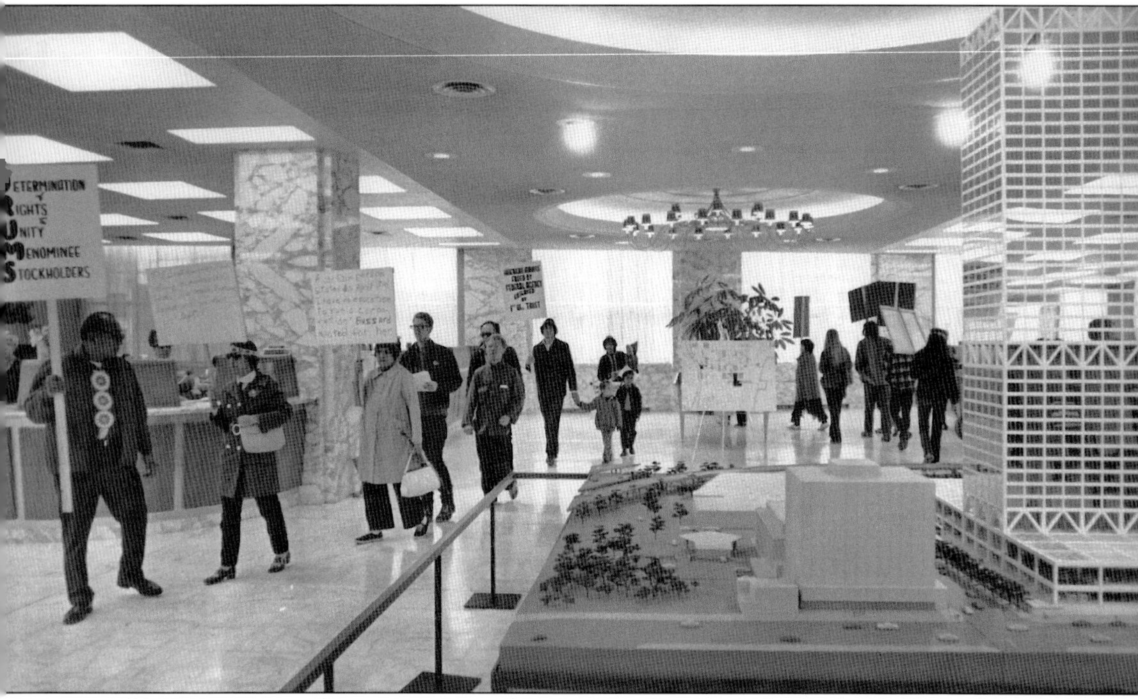

The Menominee tribe was terminated in a 1954 congressional act that did not go into effect until April 30, 1961. They lost their status as a federally recognized tribe, and their reservation became a county. The Menominee were expected to be self-sufficient and provide all their own services. All of the tribe's lands and assets went into a new entity, Menominee Enterprises, Inc. The corporation was a seven-member board of elected trustees that made all the voting decisions for the shareholders. Each Menominee Indian initially received 100 shares of stock, equaling one vote during elections. A new group that was critical of Menominee Enterprises formed, known as DRUMS (Determination of Rights and Unity for Menominee Stakeholders). They advocated for the elimination of the trustees. Pictured here is a DRUMS protest in June 1971 at the First Wisconsin Trust Building at 735 North Water Street in Milwaukee. The group also lobbied Congress for restoration of the federally recognized tribal status. Finally, on December 22, 1973, Pres. Richard M. Nixon signed the Menominee Restoration Act into law. (Courtesy of the Historic Photo Collection/Milwaukee Public Library.)

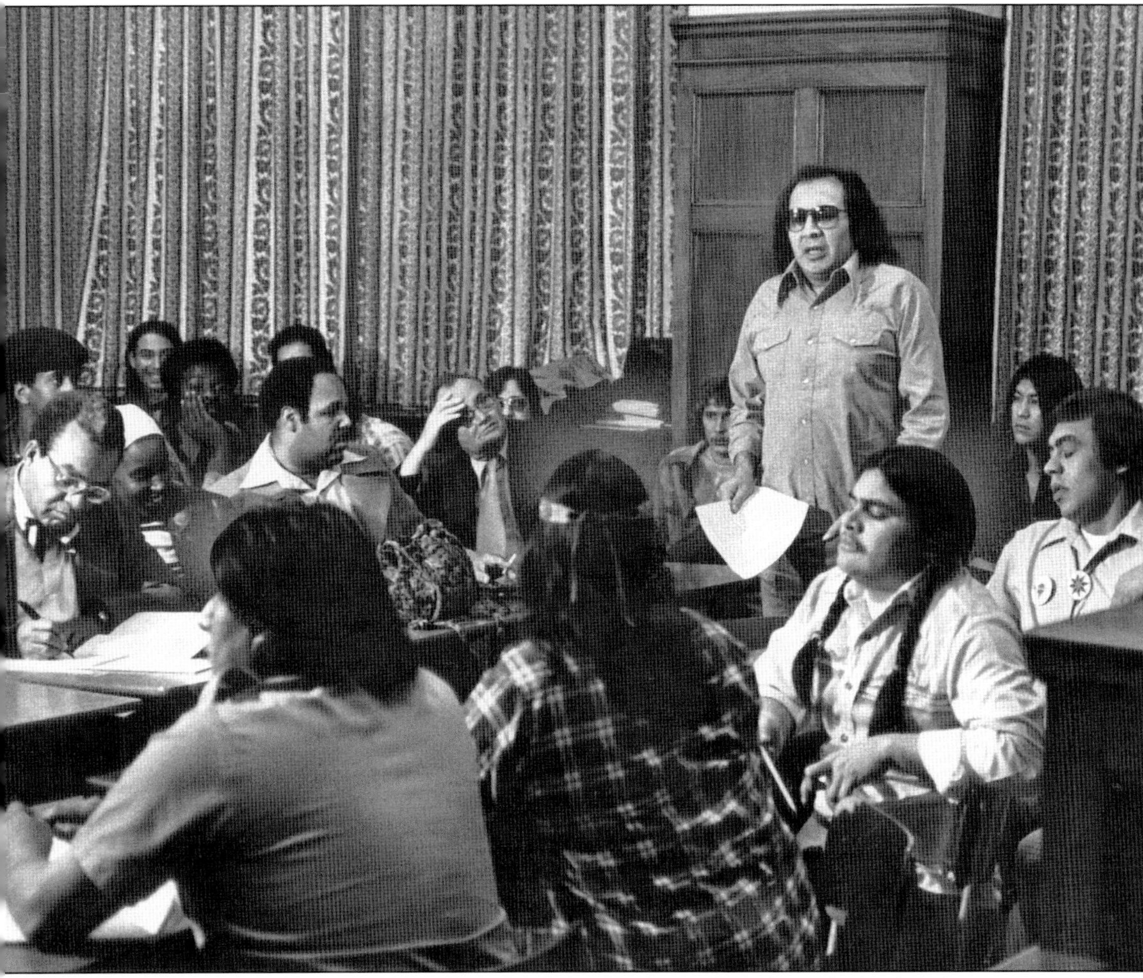

On November 13, 1975, National Indian Youth Council members from the Milwaukee Area Technical College (MATC) met with members of the Indian community, including Herbert Powless (standing) of the Milwaukee chapter of the American Indian Movement. Growing dissatisfaction and anger with the school administration under district director William L. Ramsey led to a series of complaints and protests from September through November 1975. One of the students' main complaints was that they had no office for an American Indian advisor to counsel, advise, and provide tutoring for them. In reaction to the school's lack of action, the students occupied a vacant room on November 6. Steven Perion, president of the Indian student chapter, issued a list of 16 demands to the student government including past requests for office space, emergency financial-aid funding, and the establishment of an Indian studies program with an Indian instructor to teach it. After an unsatisfactory response to the demands, the room occupation continued. (Courtesy of the *Milwaukee Journal Sentinel* Archives.)

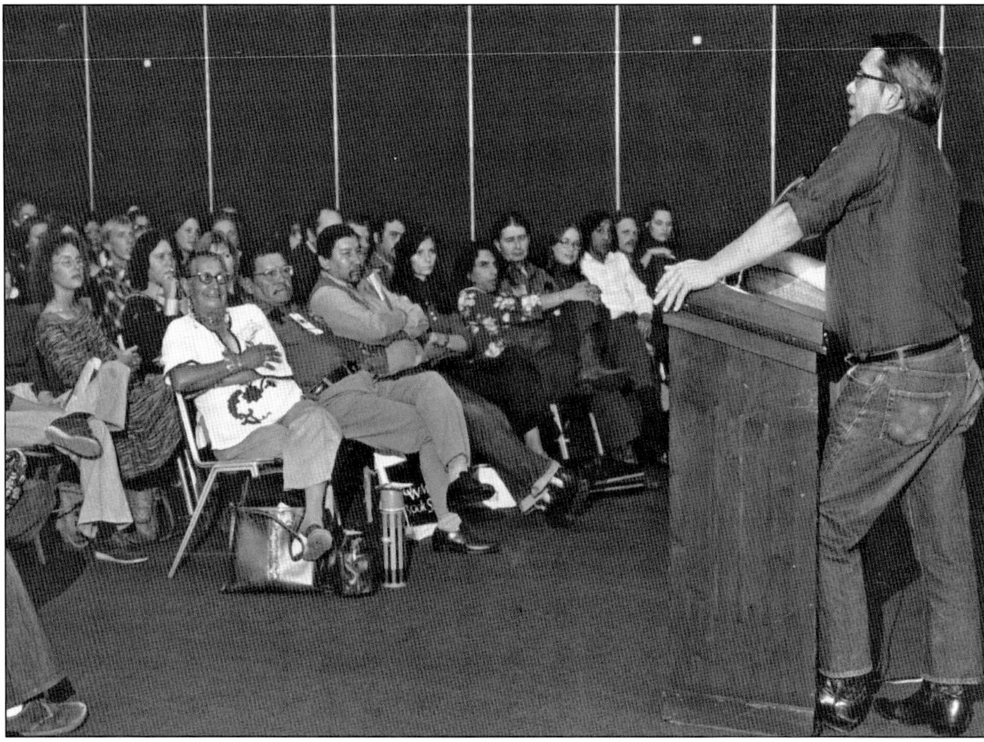

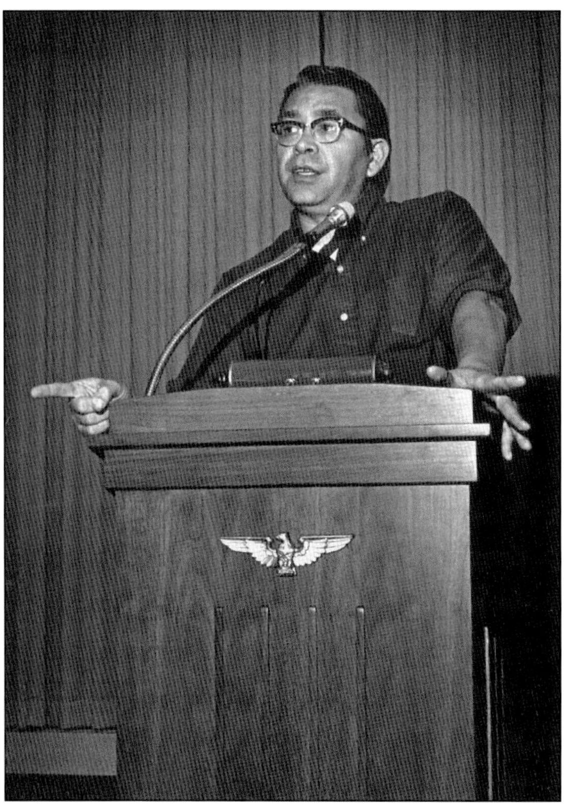

The Wisconsin Indian Education Conference took place September 9–11, 1976. The event was at the University of Wisconsin–Milwaukee. Students in the Native American Student Movement (NASM) and UWM American Indian faculty organized the event. On Friday, September 10, at 8:00 p.m., the featured speaker was a nationally known American Indian writer, Vine DeLoria Jr., pictured at left. He wrote the books *Custer Died for Your Sins* and *God Is Red*. These books were seen as the literary manifestos behind the Red Power movement. DeLoria was regarded as the academic leader of the movement towards American Indian empowerment in the 1970s. He has written and published more than 20 books. (Photograph by John W. Alley; courtesy of American Indian Student Services.)

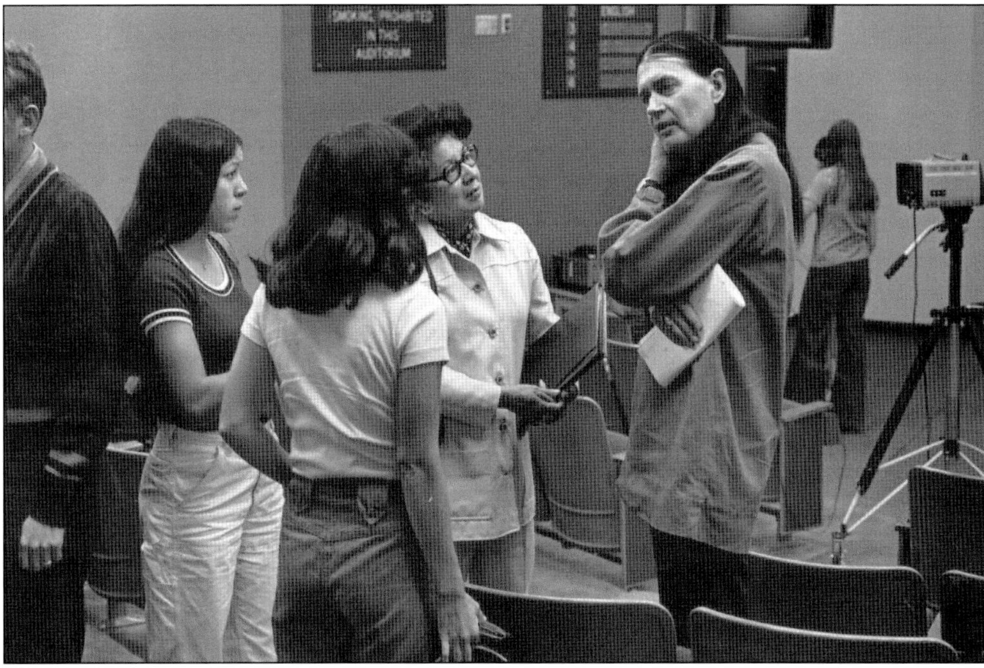

William Hawk (right), an American Indian lecturer in the anthropology department at the University of Wisconsin–Milwaukee, was told he would not be rehired by the university due to budget problems in the beginning of February 1979. That announcement kicked off protests on the university's campus. (Photograph by Alan Magayne-Roshak; courtesy of American Indian Student Services.)

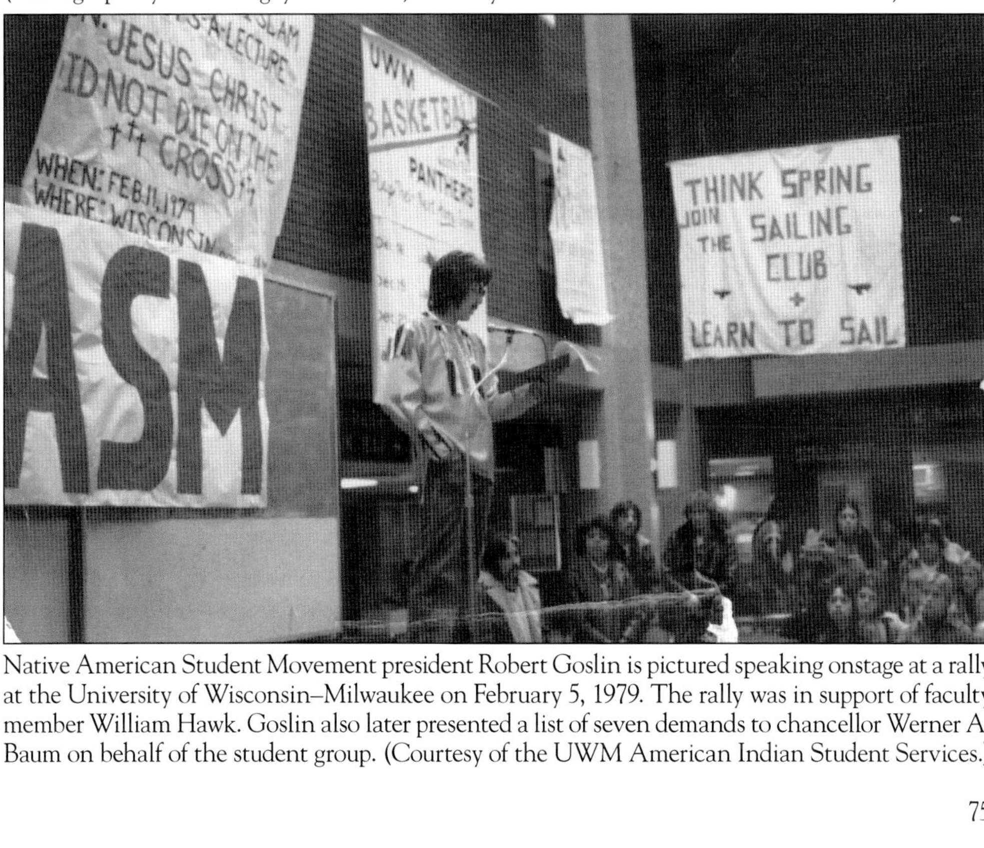

Native American Student Movement president Robert Goslin is pictured speaking onstage at a rally at the University of Wisconsin–Milwaukee on February 5, 1979. The rally was in support of faculty member William Hawk. Goslin also later presented a list of seven demands to chancellor Werner A. Baum on behalf of the student group. (Courtesy of the UWM American Indian Student Services.)

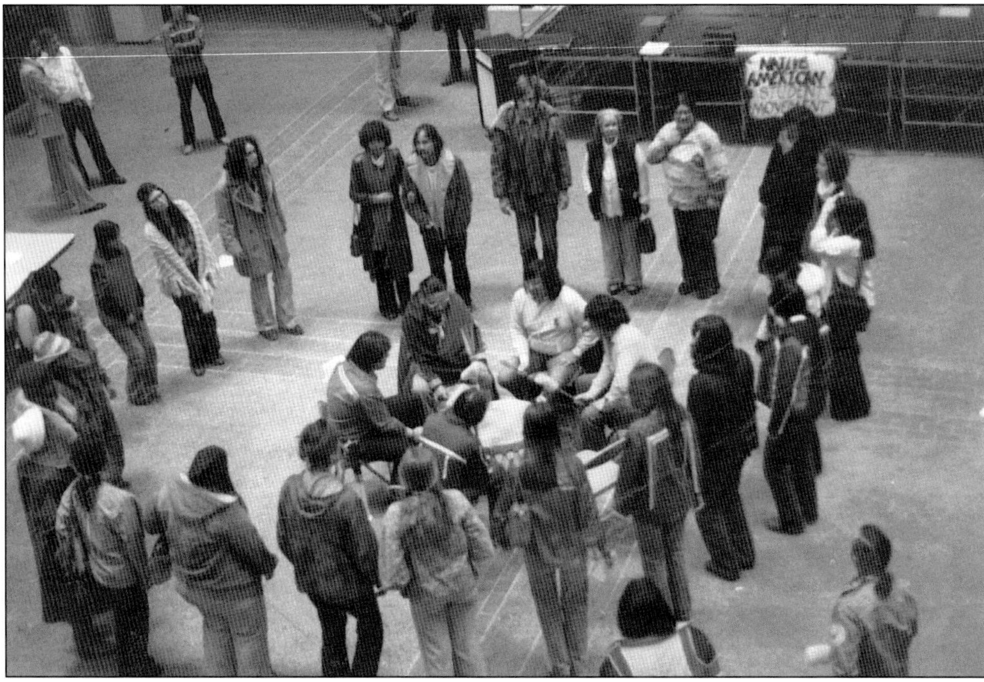

NASM members from the University of Wisconsin–Milwaukee and community members participate in a round dance around the drum in the UWM Student Union building. The rally against further budget cuts was attended by 250 to 300 people. (Courtesy of the UWM American Indian Student Services.)

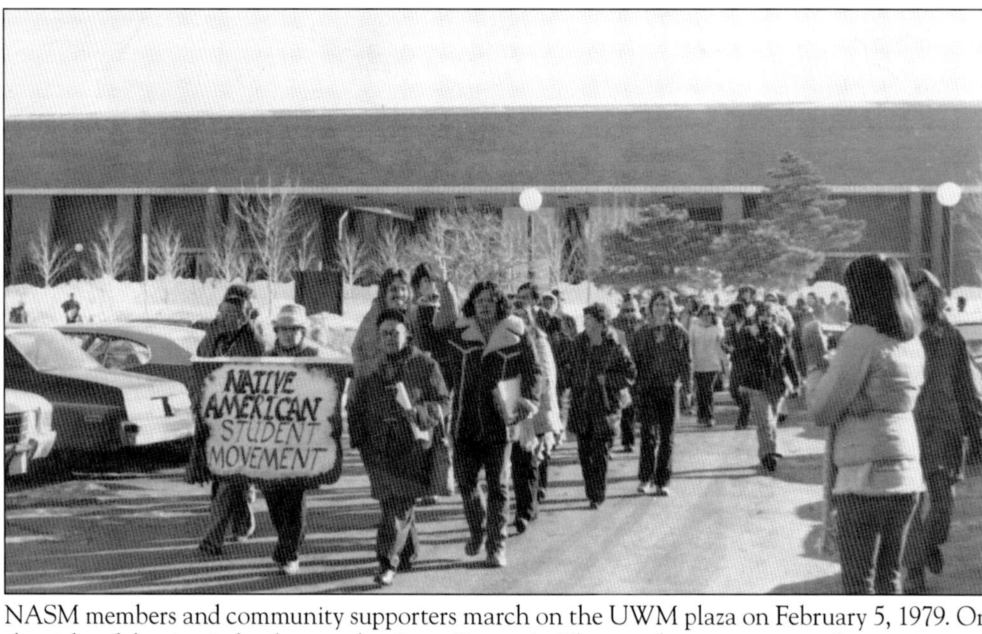

NASM members and community supporters march on the UWM plaza on February 5, 1979. On the right of the sign is faculty member Irene Pyawasit. The march was to protest the termination of William Hawk and demand more American Indian staff, including an open position for a counselor. (Courtesy of the UWM American Indian Student Services.)

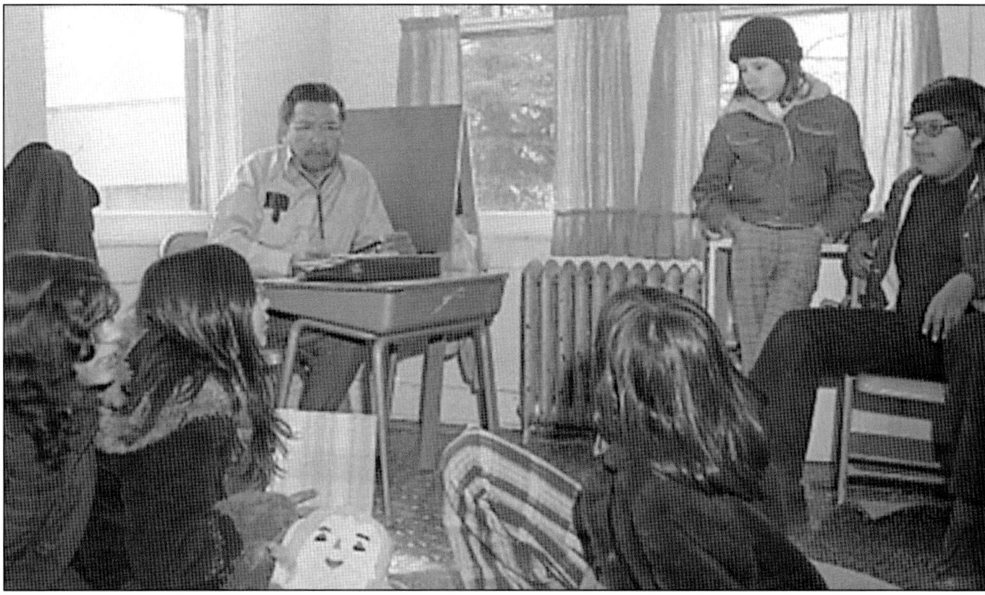

Wallace Pyawasit, Menominee of the Zoar community on the Menominee reservation, is pictured above at the Indian Community School's Coast Guard classroom in 1975. He is also pictured in the 1979 photograph below at a benefit for American Indian elders. Pyawasit served as a drum chief in the Menominee Big Drum Society. He also worked as a culture and crafts teacher at the Indian Community School. He later taught an American Indian dance class at the University of Wisconsin–Milwaukee. He was a respected elder and spiritual leader to many urban American Indians in Milwaukee. Milwaukee students and community members attended his funeral services on the Menominee reservation in 1982. In honor of him, an award is presented in his name each year at the University of Wisconsin–Milwaukee by the American Indian Student Services for outstanding community service. (Above, courtesy of the UWM Libraries Archives Department; below, courtesy of the Doxtator family.)

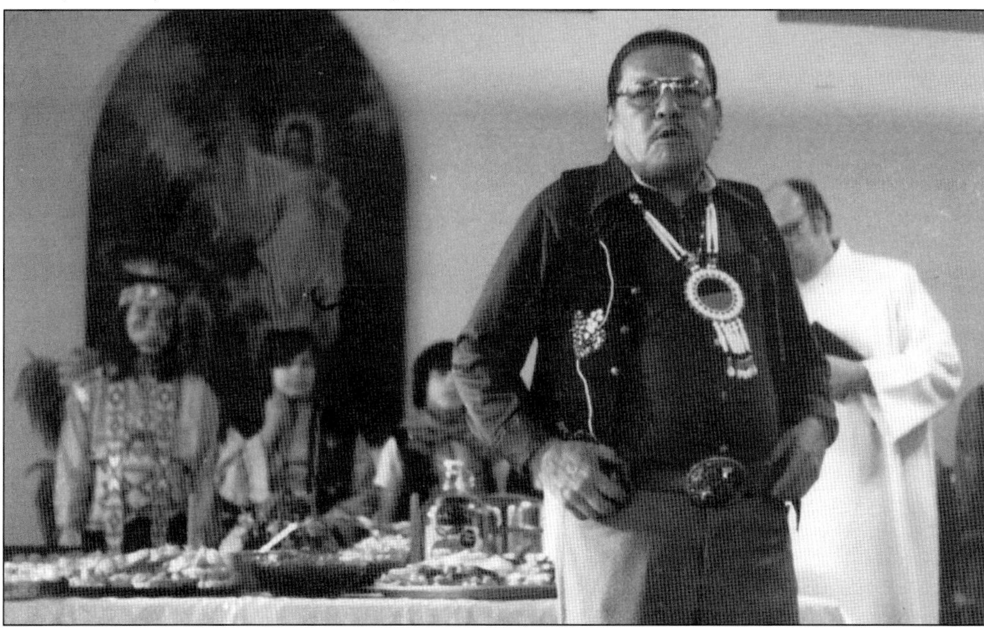

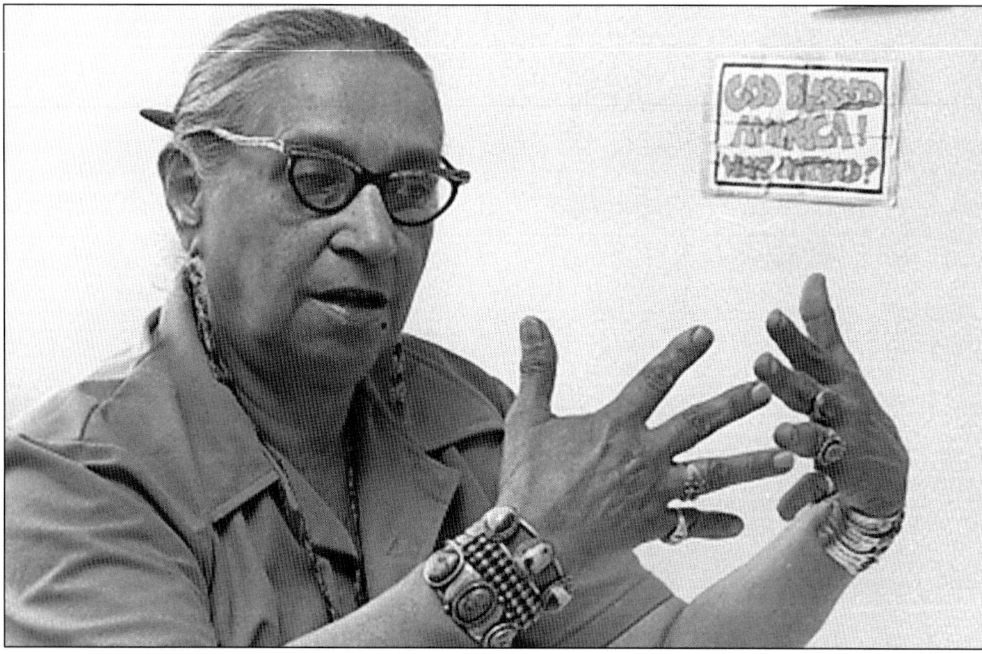

Pictured above is Irene Mack Pyawasit, Menominee, in the Native American Student Movement office at the University of Wisconsin–Milwaukee. She worked as a teacher at UWM where she taught Menominee language and culture. She also served as a recruiter for American Indian students. In 1975, she married Wallace Pyawasit in Rosebud, South Dakota. (Courtesy of the UWM Libraries Archives Department.)

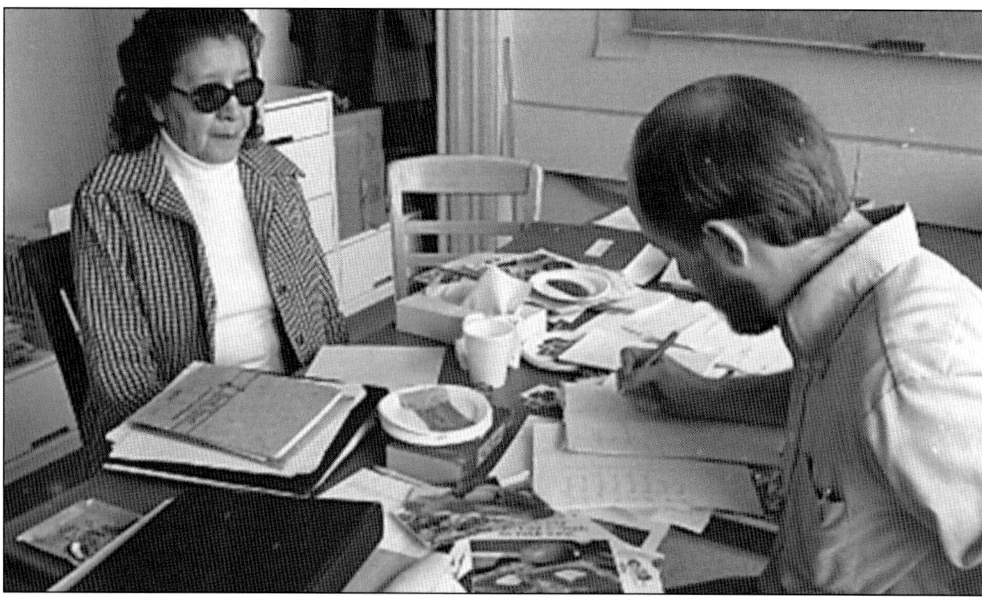

Maria Hinton, Oneida, worked with the Wisconsin Native American Languages Project at the University of Wisconsin–Milwaukee on the Oneida language consultant staff. The program, which lasted from 1973 to 1976, was a federally funded program under Title IV of the Indian Education Act. The goal of the program was to preserve and teach Wisconsin tribal languages to adults and children of those communities. (Courtesy of the UWM Libraries Archives Department.)

Members of the Milwaukee-area American Indian community marched to support the occupation of Wounded Knee on March 25, 1973. Carrying banners and drumming, the group marched from the University of Wisconsin–Milwaukee to Locust Street and Lake Drive, the site of an Indian burial ground. The occupation of Wounded Knee, South Dakota, by the American Indian Movement and Oglala Lakota community members began on February 27, 1973. (Courtesy of the *Milwaukee Journal Sentinel* Archives.)

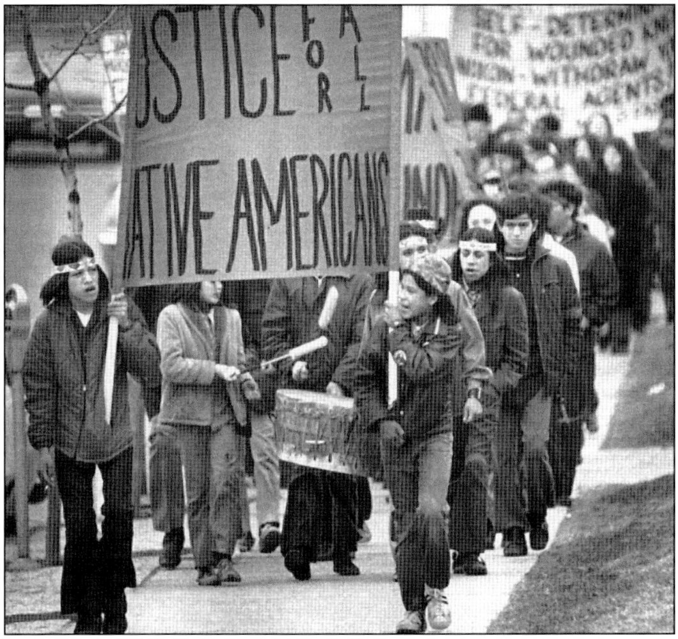

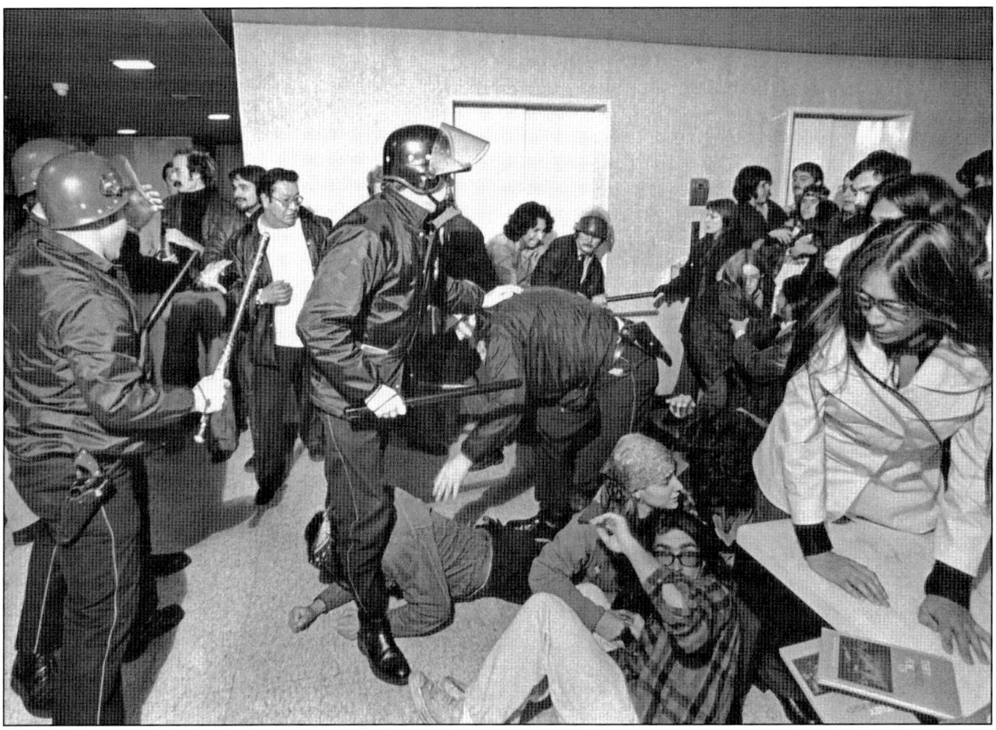

American Indians and their supporters clashed with Milwaukee police at the Memorial Center on November 19, 1975, in Milwaukee. The group of 50, which included Fr. James Groppi, protested the appearance of Douglas Durham, an undercover informant working for the Federal Bureau of Investigation who had infiltrated the American Indian Movement. Durham was invited to speak at a meeting of the John Birch Society. Thirteen protestors were arrested and five were injured. (Courtesy of the *Milwaukee Journal Sentinel* Archives.)

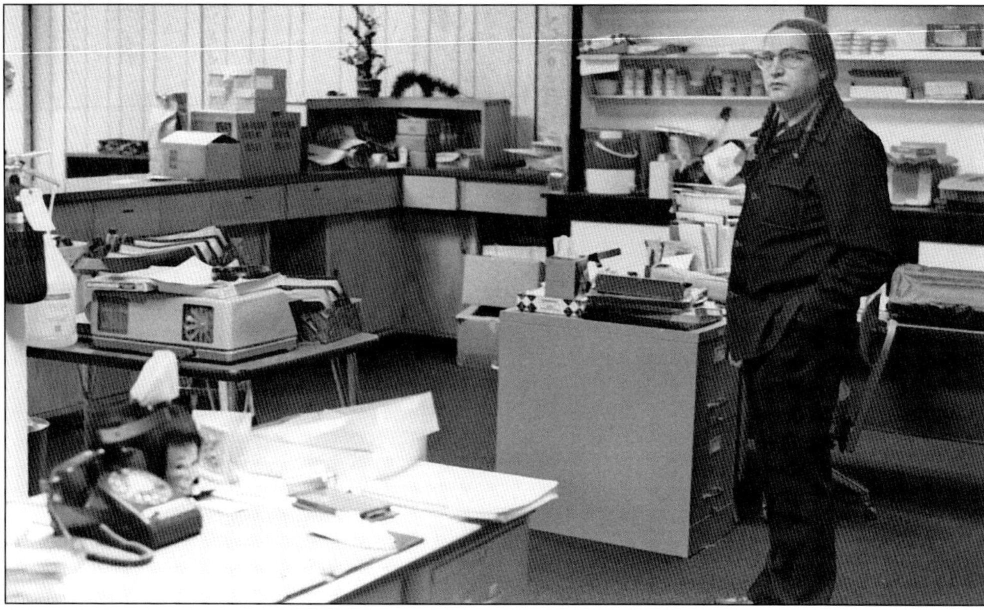

John Clifford, Lakota, originally from the Rosebud reservation in South Dakota, moved to Milwaukee in 1957. In 1973, he began his work as coordinator with the WE Indians Program. Clifford retired from this position within the Milwaukee Public School system in April 1997. The program provided teachers and tutors for extra academic help, support services for families, and instruction to students in Woodland tribal cultures. (Courtesy of the Historic Photo Collection/ Milwaukee Public Library.)

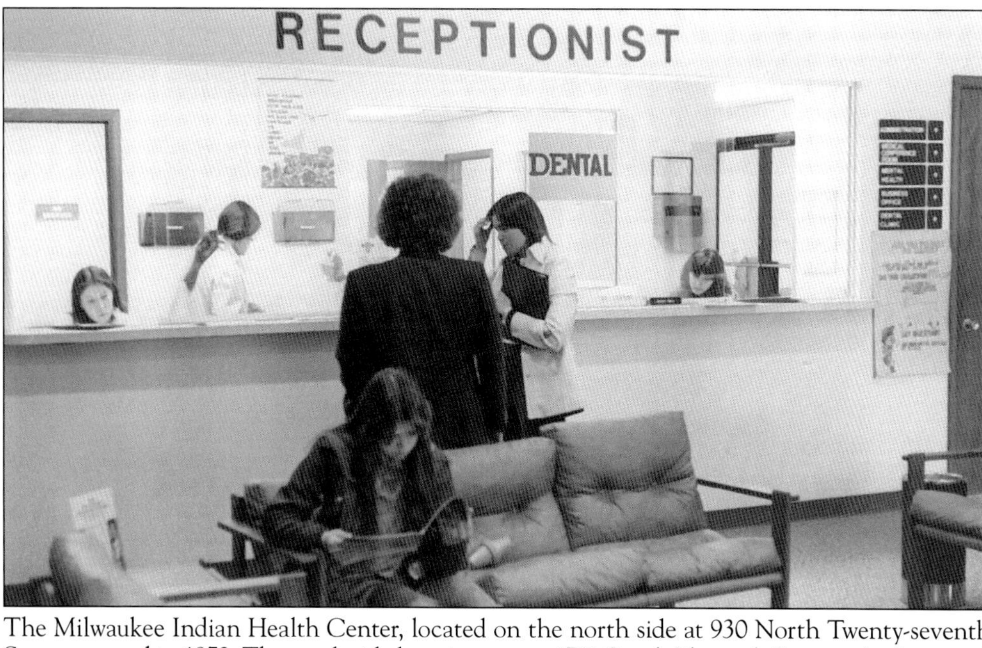

The Milwaukee Indian Health Center, located on the north side at 930 North Twenty-seventh Street, opened in 1972. The south side location was at 1711 South Eleventh Street, which opened in 1974. Both locations closed in April 1999. The clinics received federal funding from Indian Health Services. They offered medical, dental, lab, and pharmacy services with fees based on patients' ability to pay. (Courtesy of the Historic Photo Collection/Milwaukee Public Library.)

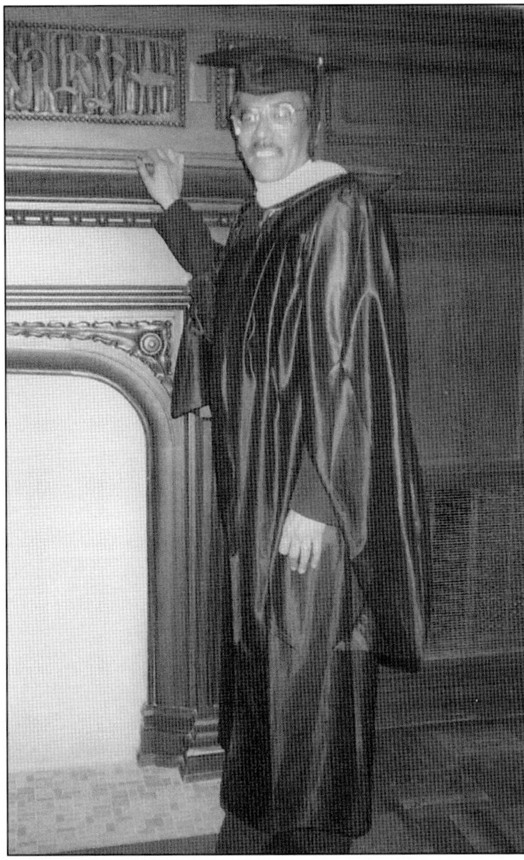

James "Jim" LaGoo, Bad River Chippewa, taught for two years as a social studies and culture teacher at the Indian Community School's Coast Guard site in the 1970s. In 1978, he started working at the Milwaukee Area Technical College as a Native American studies teacher. One of the classes he taught was "Wisconsin Indian: Past/Present/ Future." (Courtesy of Diane Amour.)

The Indian Urban Affairs Council, located at 1410 North Twenty-seventh Street, was a coalition of seven American Indian organizations that provided social services to the urban Indian community of Milwaukee. The member groups were the American Indian Information and Action Group, United Indians of Milwaukee, the Indian Community School, the American Indian Welfare Rights, the Determination Rights and Unity for Menominee Stockholders (DRUMS), the Native American Student Union of UWM, and the American Indian Student Union of Marquette University. (Courtesy of the Historic Photo Collection/Milwaukee Public Library.)

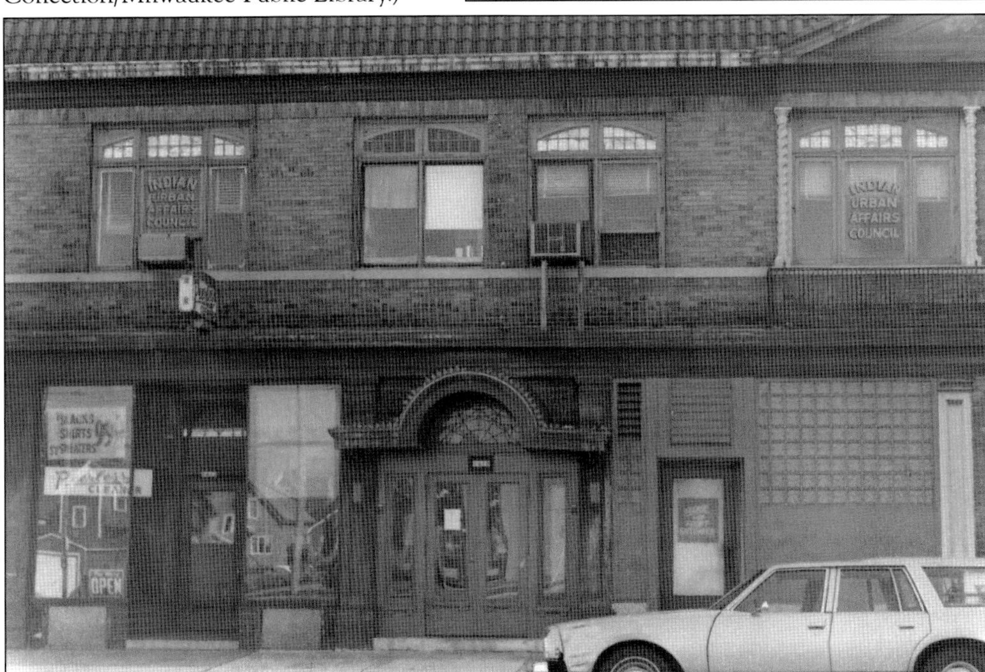

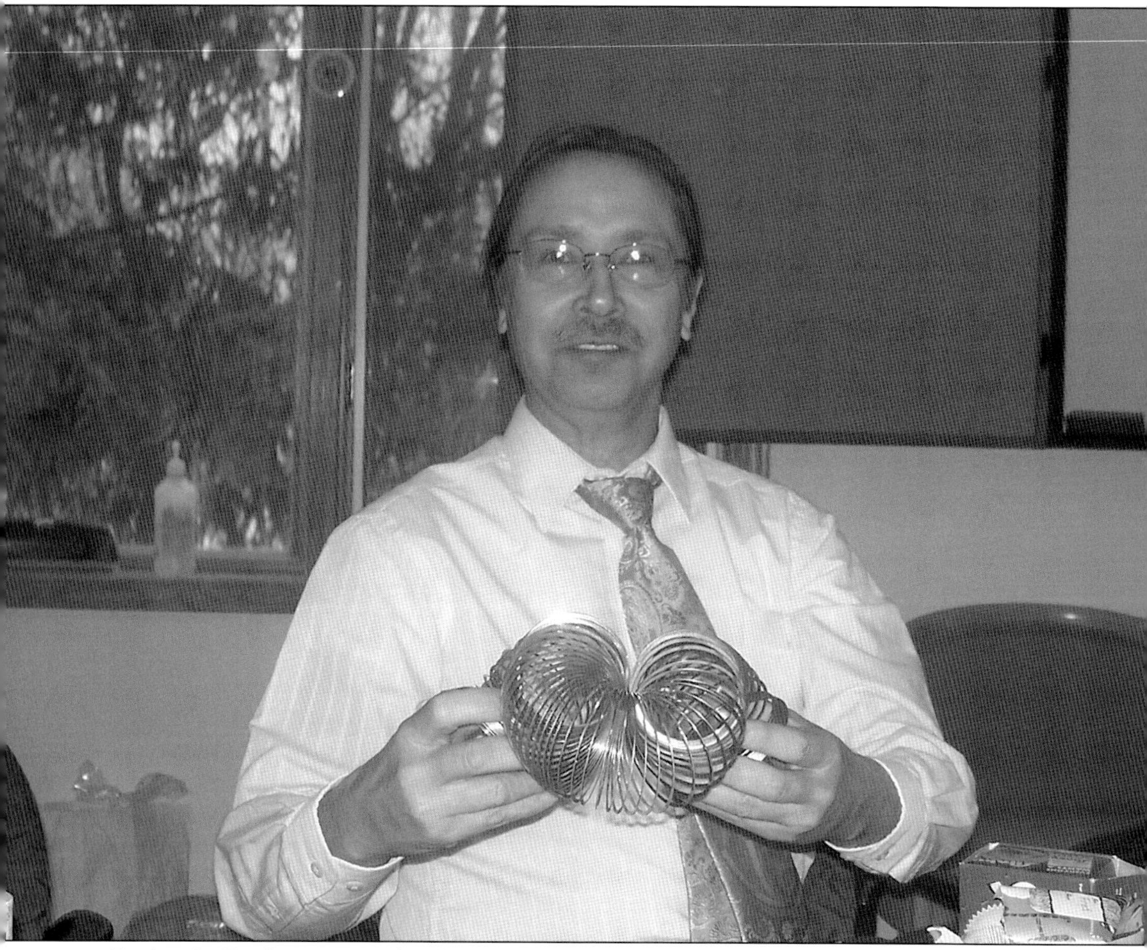

Frederick "Fred" Muscavitch, PhD, Oneida, was a longtime resident of Milwaukee. He was a former teacher at the Indian Community School's Coast Guard site. He later became executive director of the Milwaukee Area American Indian Manpower Council, Inc. Muscavitch served in this position for more than 10 years. He was also instrumental in starting the Southeastern Oneida Tribal Services program for Oneidas in Milwaukee. He moved to Oneida, Wisconsin, in 1992. (Courtesy of Fred Muscavitch.)

Six

EMERGENCE PRESENCE

By the 1980s, Indian people in Milwaukee were practicing and participating in more cultural activities. The combination of renewed cultural expression of the powwow era with a political consciousness from the Red Power era encouraged new forms of organizations and goals of Indian people in Milwaukee. The Indian Community School reorganized and partnered with the Forest County Potawatomi and established trust land for the tribe and a stable source of funds for the school. The United Indians of Milwaukee that formed in 1968 surpassed the Consolidated Tribes of American Indians in membership and became the focus of Indian social gatherings, providing much of the cultural programming for Milwaukee schools, festivals, parades, and fairs. The Catholic church recognized that the needs of its urban Indian members were not being met, so with help from Archbishop Rembert Weakland, they formed the interdenominational Siggenauk Center, which blended Christianity and native traditions. American Indians in Milwaukee still danced, set up villages, held powwows, and struggled to secure a better form of education for their children, but during this period, enduring Indian institutions emerged with more control and voice.

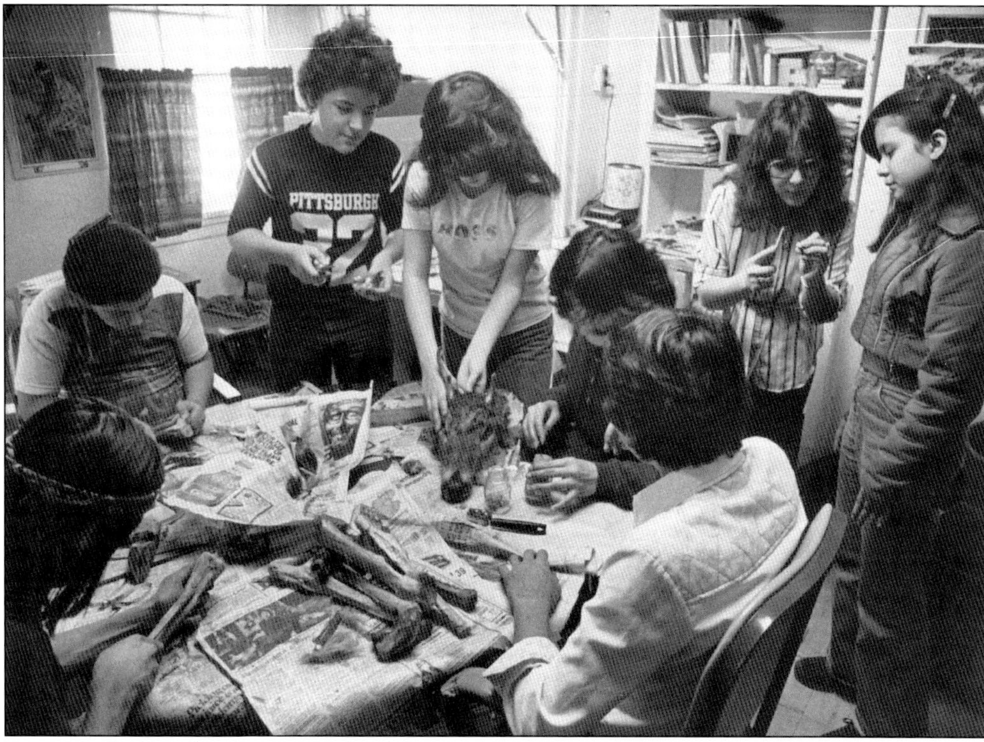

In 1980, the Bartlett Avenue School became home to the Indian Community School (ICS) following a complicated deal between the federal government, the City of Milwaukee, Milwaukee County, and Milwaukee Public Schools. The Bartlett Avenue School was well attended and expanded to about 120 students in kindergarten through 12th grade, and it was fully accredited. Like the Coast Guard station before it, the Bartlett building was not ideal—the building was run-down and the grounds lacked a play area. The school's primary funding source was cut by the Reagan administration, and the school was forced to close its doors in 1983. (Both courtesy of Drew LaBelle.)

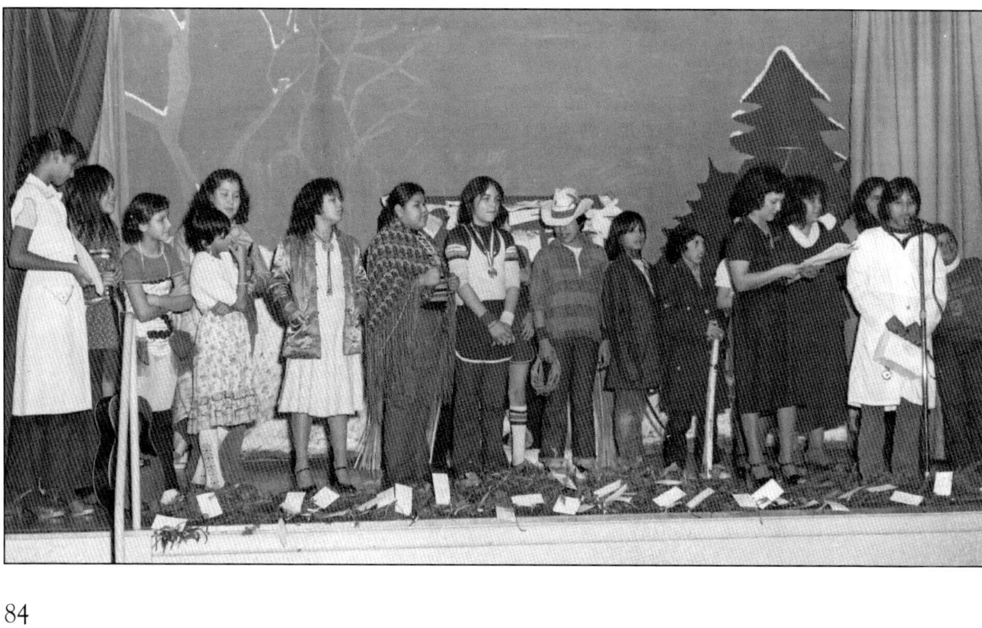

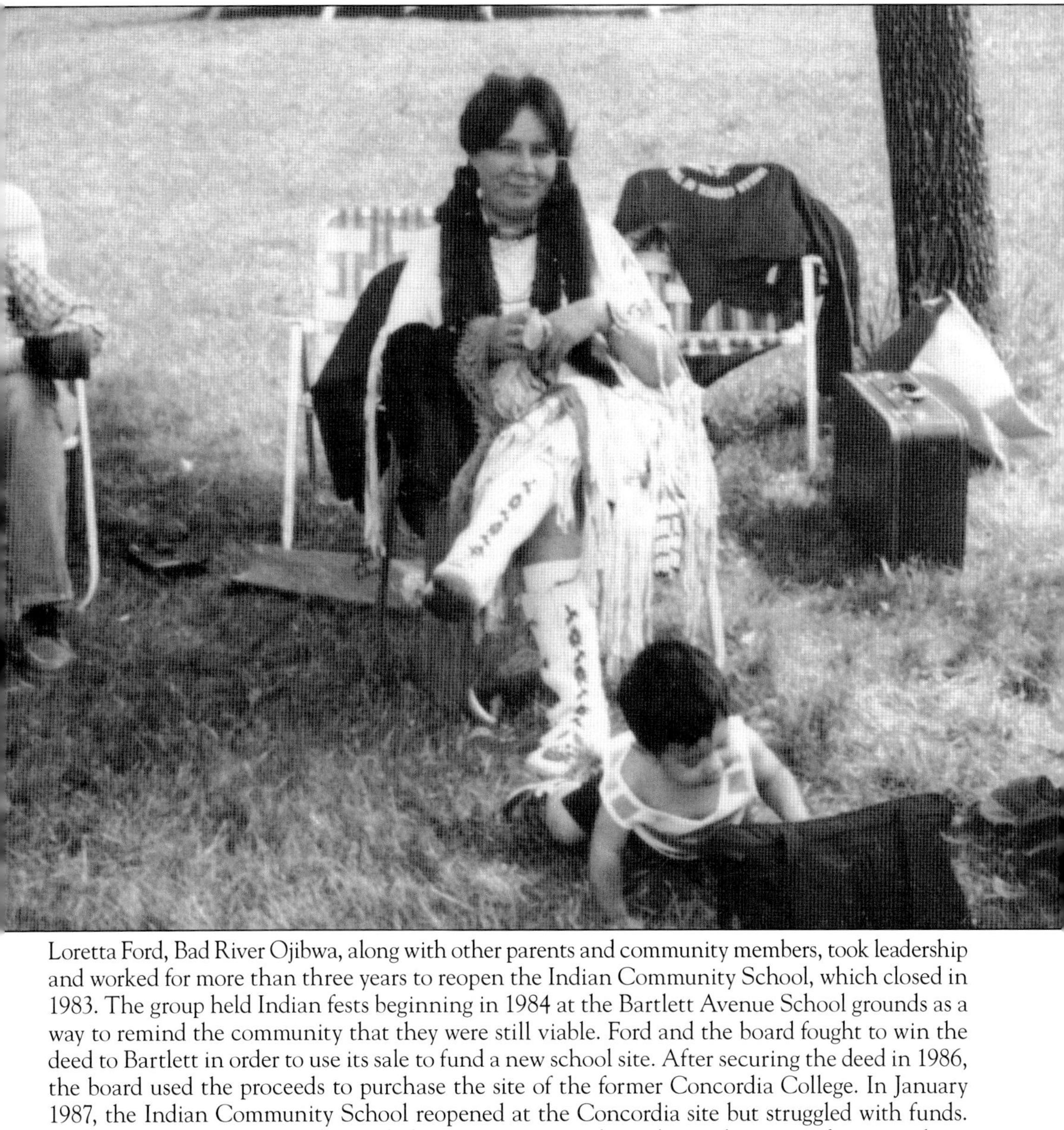

Loretta Ford, Bad River Ojibwa, along with other parents and community members, took leadership and worked for more than three years to reopen the Indian Community School, which closed in 1983. The group held Indian fests beginning in 1984 at the Bartlett Avenue School grounds as a way to remind the community that they were still viable. Ford and the board fought to win the deed to Bartlett in order to use its sale to fund a new school site. After securing the deed in 1986, the board used the proceeds to purchase the site of the former Concordia College. In January 1987, the Indian Community School reopened at the Concordia site but struggled with funds. Ford and the board searched for tribal partners interested in taking advantage of recent rulings that allowed high-stakes bingo on trust land. (Courtesy of Diane Porter.)

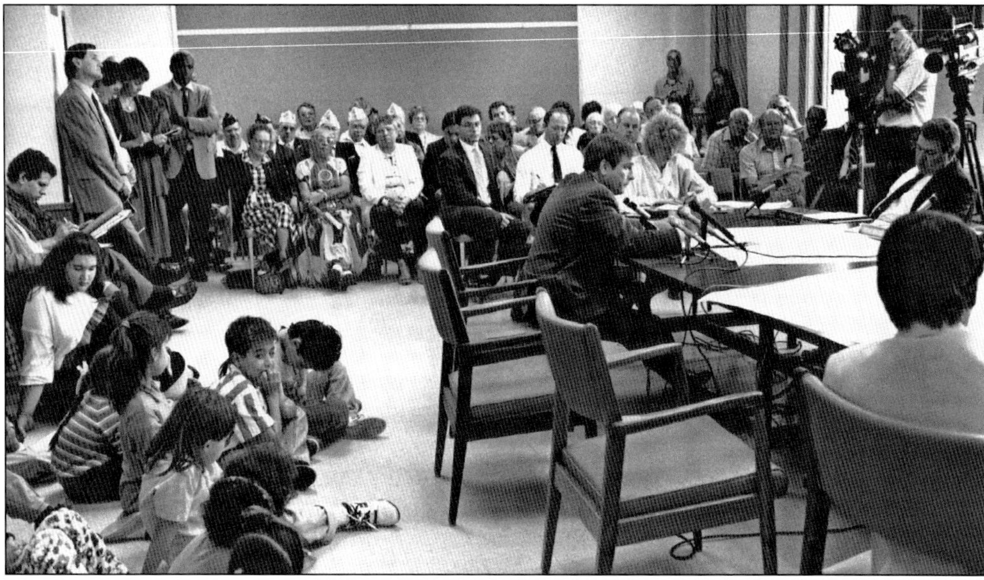

The Forest County Potawatomi's agreement to partner with the Indian Community School and secure trust status in Milwaukee faced considerable opposition. In this 1989 photograph, opponents led by US representative Jerry Kleczka and Indian Community School supporters square off at a tense public meeting. The Potawatomi were eventually granted trust land status on a site in the Menomonee Valley in Milwaukee, bringing back a portion of an area they had once occupied. (Courtesy of the *Milwaukee Journal Sentinel*.)

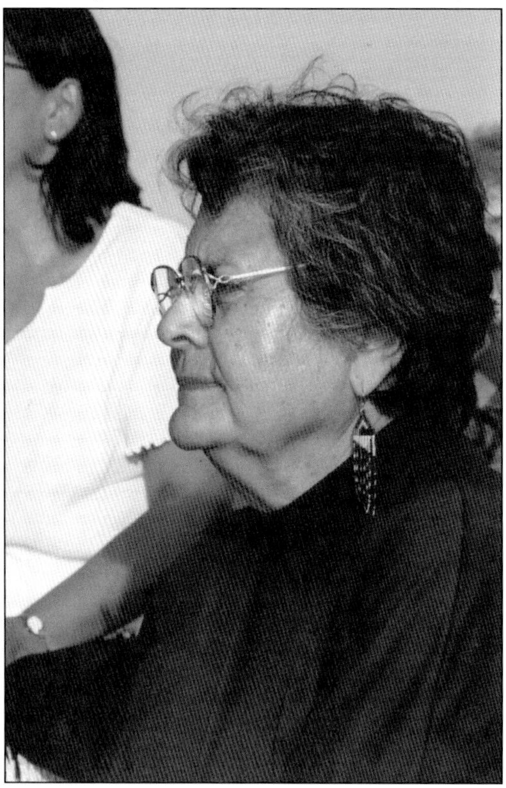

Ada Deer, Menominee, was instrumental in assisting the Indian Community School by providing support during the school's effort to partner with the Forest County Potawatomi. Deer, who was raised on the Menominee reservation, helped form a group that repealed the tribe's federal termination status. Deer was also the first woman to chair her tribe and run the Bureau of Indian Affairs. She retired in 2007 from the University of Wisconsin. (Courtesy of the UWM American Indian Student Services.)

While the Indian Community School was in the process of maintaining a separate school, the WE Indians Program was formed within the Milwaukee Public Schools system with federal funds in 1973. Children were pulled out of class to attend an Indian center once a week at the Allen-Field Elementary School on Lapham Avenue, and Indian aides visited other schools. Pictured from left to right are Mark Denning, Charlene Wheelock, Sarah Graffenberger (principal of Allen Field School), and Alfreda Young. (Courtesy of the Department of Special Collections and University Archives, Marquette University Libraries.)

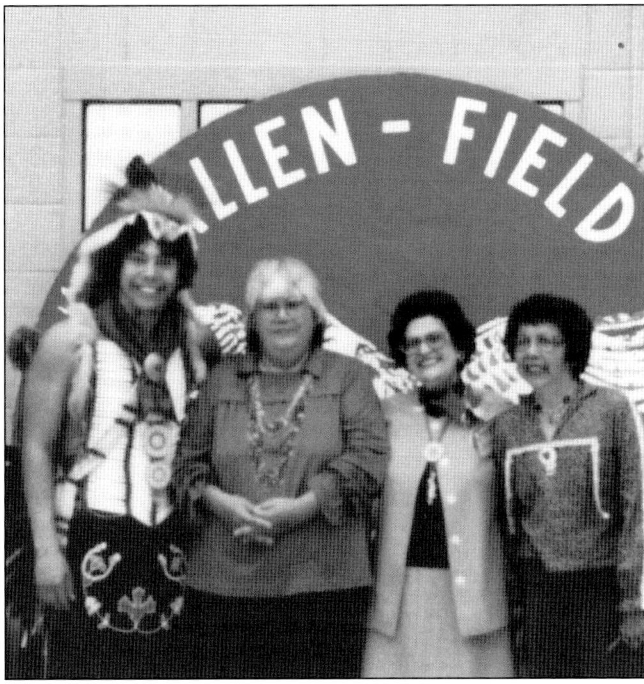

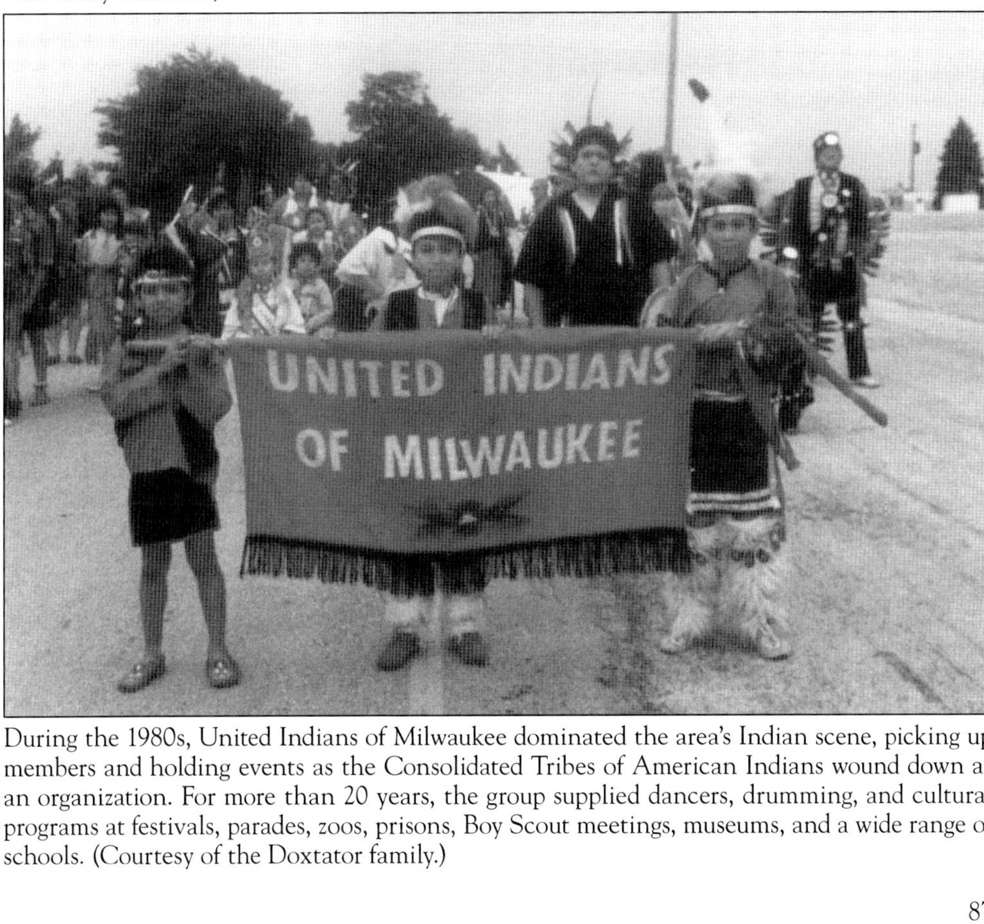

During the 1980s, United Indians of Milwaukee dominated the area's Indian scene, picking up members and holding events as the Consolidated Tribes of American Indians wound down as an organization. For more than 20 years, the group supplied dancers, drumming, and cultural programs at festivals, parades, zoos, prisons, Boy Scout meetings, museums, and a wide range of schools. (Courtesy of the Doxtator family.)

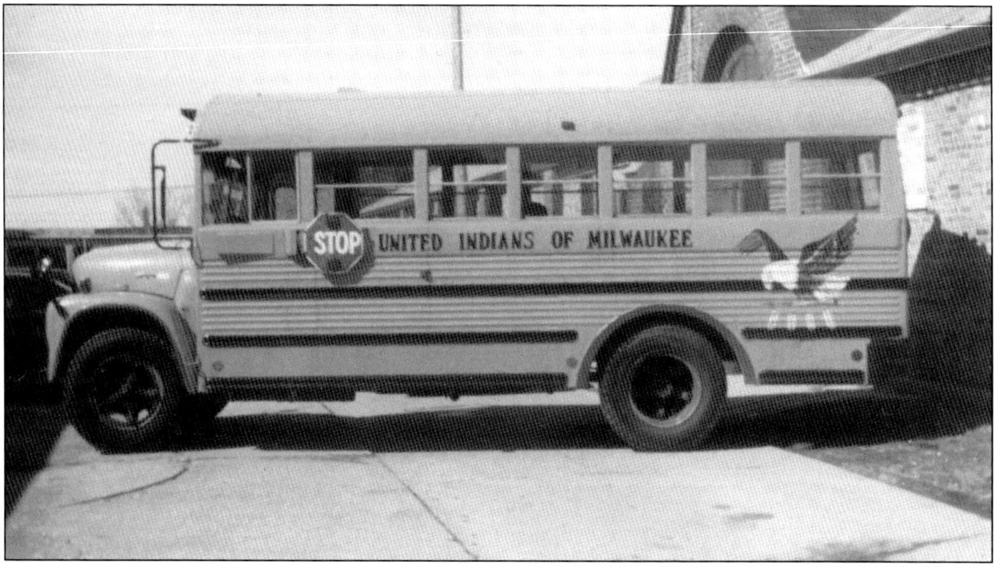

United Indians of Milwaukee's bus was a fixture at the old firehouse on Bruce Street, which housed the organization. Often broken down between uses, it carried the makings for a whole Indian village: tables, chairs, food, outfits, tarps, speakers, propane tanks, tepee poles, and of course people to events all over the state. Children painted the bus and played within it when it was parked. (Courtesy of the Doxtator family.)

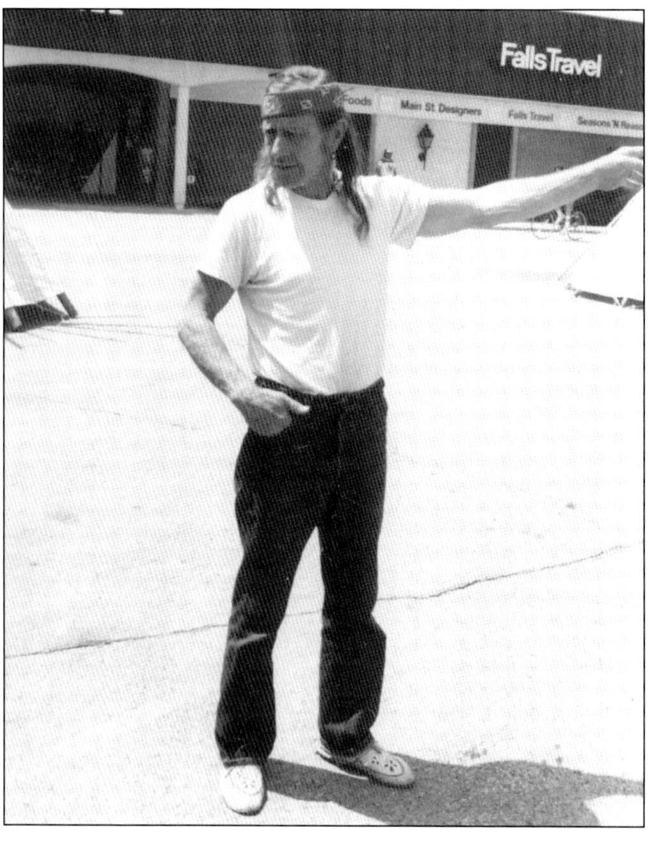

Shown left wearing his ever-present headband, Richard E. Watkins, Canadian Plains Cree, ran United Indians of Milwaukee for 20 years. Watkins served in Korea and later mentored under Ellis Chipps, Wallace Pyawasit, and Elmer Runnings in the study of Indian culture. He played bingo with the United Indians in the late 1970s and became president in 1980. He served as president until 1996 and remained involved as a treasurer. He continued leading sweat lodges until his death in 2005. (Courtesy of the Doxtator family.)

In 1984, Richard E. Watkins argued and won the right for the United Indians to receive the skeletons of two Indian people, plus an additional box of assorted bones, from the Hopewell period that were displayed in the Waukesha County Museum. The United Indians planned to rebury the bones in a suitable site in Wisconsin. (Courtesy of Peter Draves.)

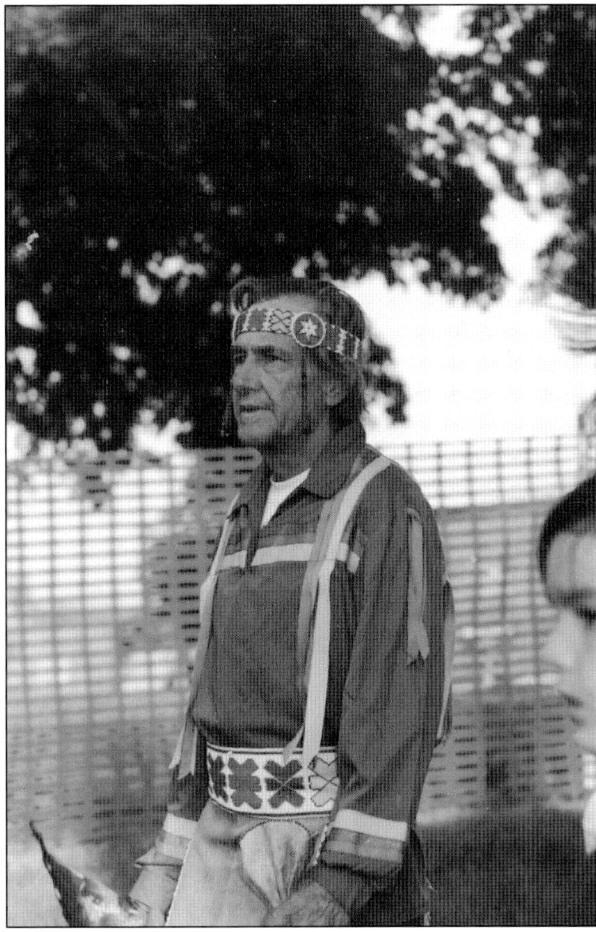

Seated right in the image below, Stella Watkins, Cherokee, takes a break during a program for the United Indians. To her left is Joyce Ninham, Oneida, the Indian Community School's first cook at the church site who also served as board president, the school's first truant officer, and home school coordinator at the Coast Guard station. The children are Amy Wade (left) and Philip Chipps (right). (Courtesy of the Doxtator family.)

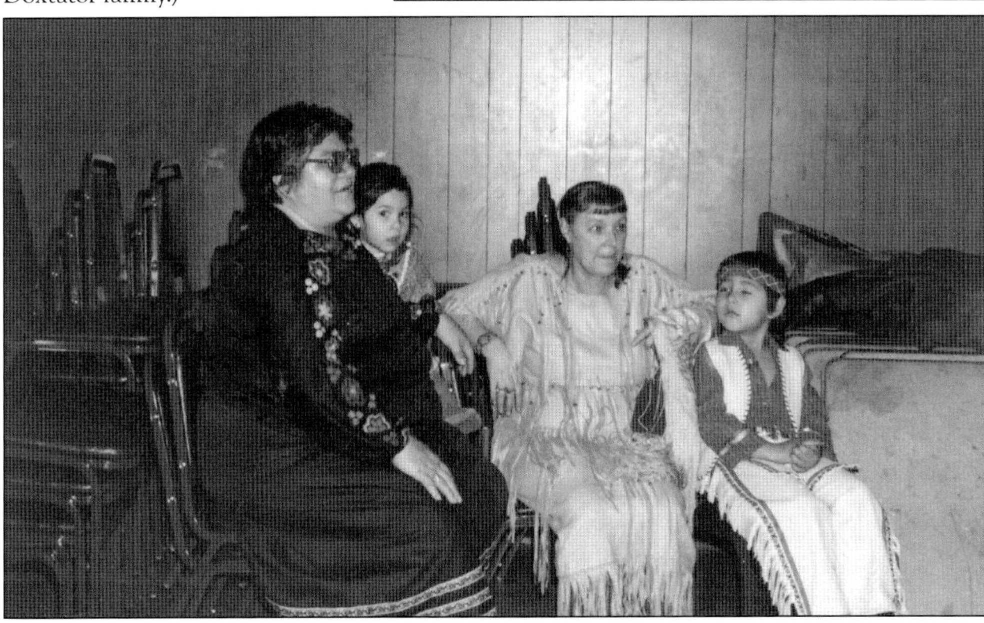

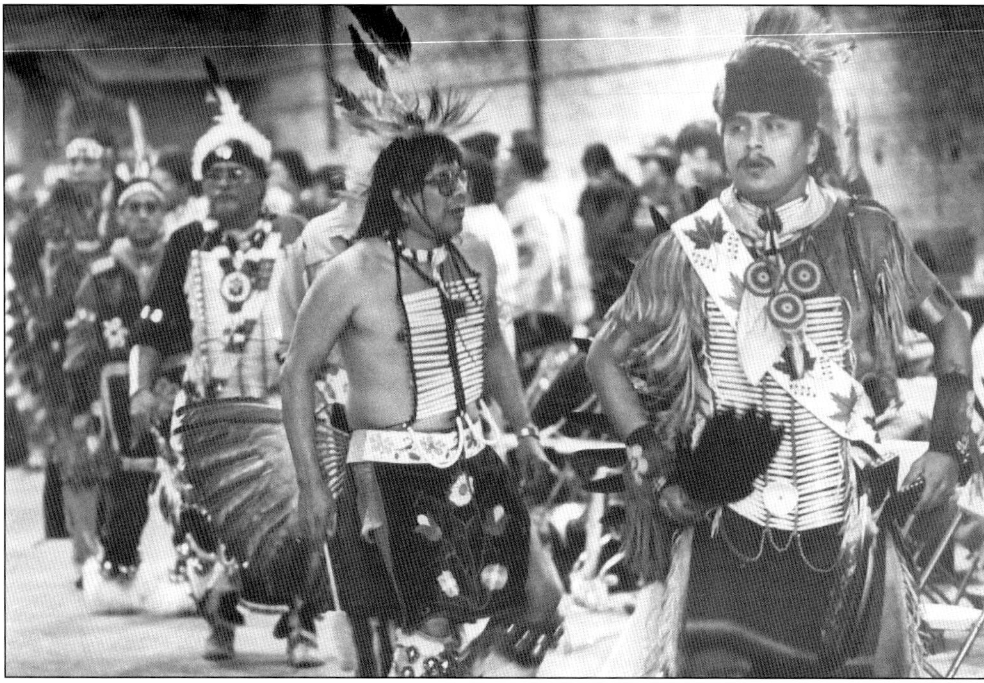

United Indians of Milwaukee held traditional powwows at the Richards Street National Guard Armory for nearly a decade. This photograph was taken on March 19, 1983. In the foreground is an unidentified man followed by Joseph Ackley, Mole Lake Chippewa. Behind Ackley is Huston Wheelock, Oneida. (Courtesy of the Historic Photo Collection/Milwaukee Public Library.)

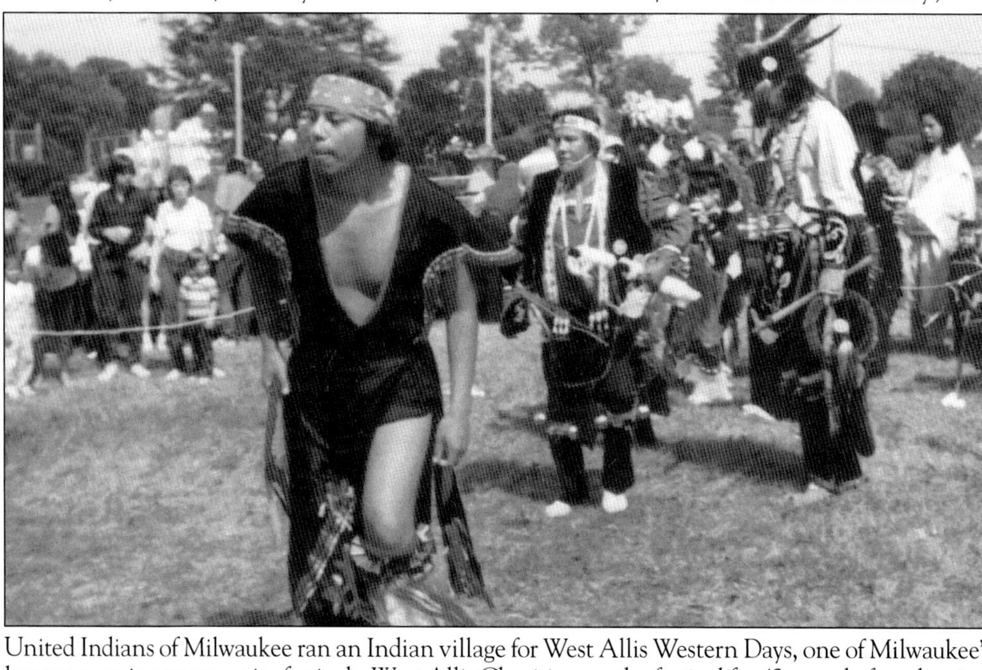

United Indians of Milwaukee ran an Indian village for West Allis Western Days, one of Milwaukee's longest-running community festivals. West Allis Charities ran the festival for 42 years before shutting down in 2007. Pictured in front is Mark Denning, who's mother, Shari Denning, coordinated the parade for more than 10 years. (Courtesy of Diane Porter.)

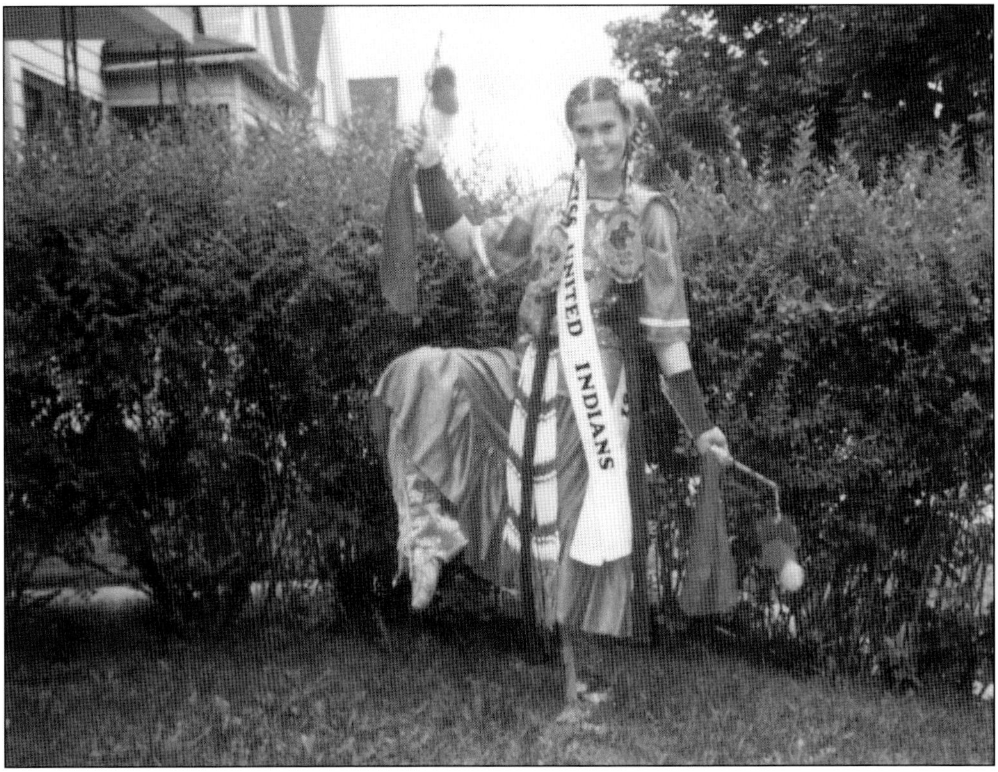

Deanna Porter, Ojibwa, daughter of Del Porter, is an award-winning dancer who traveled with her family to powwows around the country. She was also part of the United Indians dance troupe. Deanna and her mother, Diane Porter, have coordinated the Indian Summer Festival Pow Wow for the past 23 years. (Courtesy of Diane Porter.)

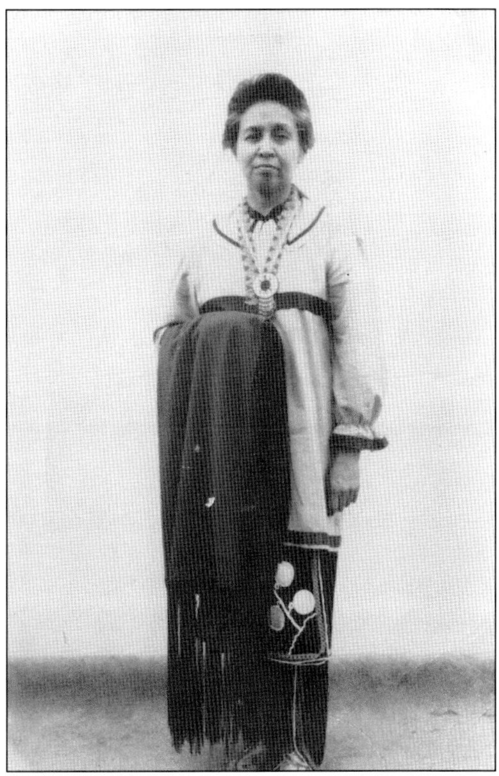

In 1951, Roberta Doxtator moved to Milwaukee from Oneida, Wisconsin. Roberta and her family were part of the United Indians dance troupe that toured the city and surrounding areas, performing nearly every week. Additionally, she served on the board of the Indian Community School from 1985 to 1994, was a founding member of the Lutheran Church of the Great Spirit, and is featured in the Milwaukee Public Museum's *Tribute to Survival* diorama. (Courtesy of the Doxtator family.)

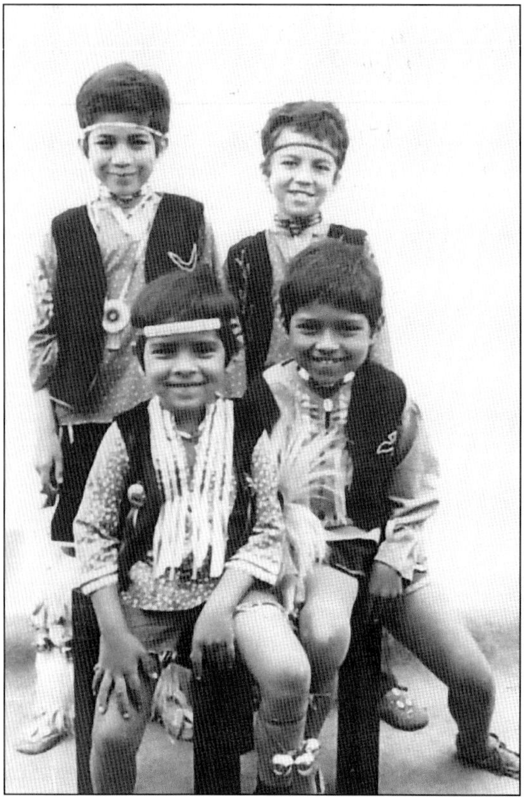

The Doxtator family's brothers and cousins are pictured at the Racine Zoo Festival in 1984. They are, from left to right, (sitting) Ahnoki and Ahano Doxtator; and (standing) Antonio and Armando Doxtator. The group danced and performed with United Indians of Milwaukee from 1984 through 1990. In the image below, Karin Doxtator dances at the United Indians of Milwaukee Center in 1985. Karin was the first United Indians Princess in 1986. The Doxtators were one of several families who were active in the United Indians at this time, and they participated in dance performances, dance practice nights, craft classes, fundraisers, and special holiday events. It was a very busy time at the center. (Both courtesy of the Doxtator family.)

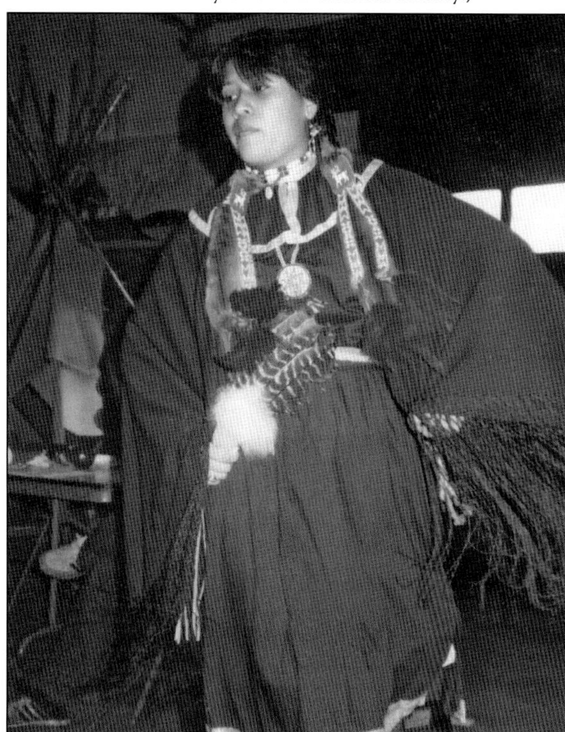

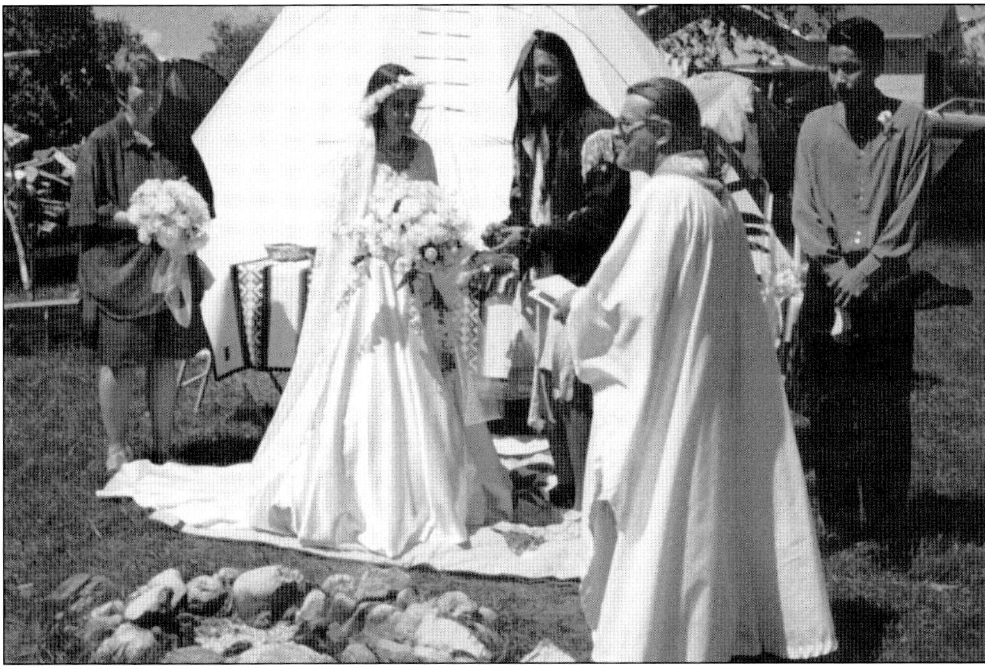

Milwaukee's Siggenauk Center was the outgrowth of an effort by the Catholic church to accommodate urban Indians who felt their needs were not met by traditional church sociability and practices. The Milwaukee Catholic Archdiocese recognized Indian people had a desire to blend their native traditions with Christian beliefs. Sr. Margaret Troy initially operated out of her apartment, and with encouragement and personal funds from Milwaukee archbishop Rembert G. Weakland, the group eventually founded the Siggenauk Center for Native American Ministry around 1980. Siggenauk welcomes all Christian denominations and traditional Indian religions under one roof. In 1987, the Catholic archdiocese established the Congregation of the Great Spirit at the Siggenauk Center with Fr. Ed Cook as pastor. Initially without a priest, the Siggenauk Center conducted baptisms, weddings, funerals, Bible classes, First Communion, and confirmation classes. Like many other Milwaukee Indian organizations, members of the Siggenauk Center marched in parades, such as the Mitchell Street parade seen below around 1980. Pictured above is Fr. Ed Cook officiating the wedding of Reuben Fast Horse, Lakota, from the Standing Rock Reservation. (Above, courtesy of the Doxtator family; below courtesy of the Department of Special Collections and University Archives, Marquette University Libraries.)

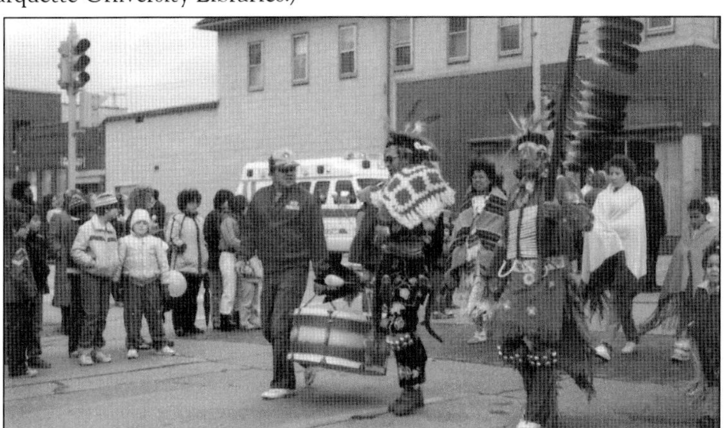

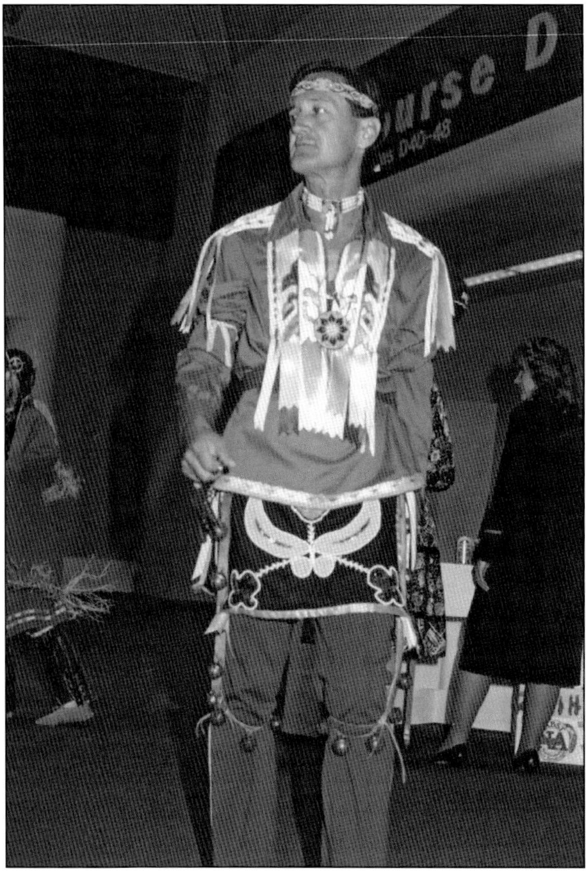

James DeNomie, Bad River Ojibwa, has participated in the Holiday Folk Fair for more than 20 years, including acting as chairman since 2005. DeNomie, an author and cultural consultant, also produces MPTV's *Outdoor Wisconsin* and hosts a radio program in Chicago. (Courtesy of Diane Porter.)

John Boatman, Ojibwa and Menominee (left), was the director of American Indian and ethnic studies at the University of Wisconsin–Milwaukee for 34 years, from 1973 to 2005. An outspoken and popular professor, his classes were some of the highest enrolled at UWM. Boatman was an accomplished author and researcher who specialized in Great Lakes Indian history. (Photograph by John Walley; courtesy of the American Indian Student Services.)

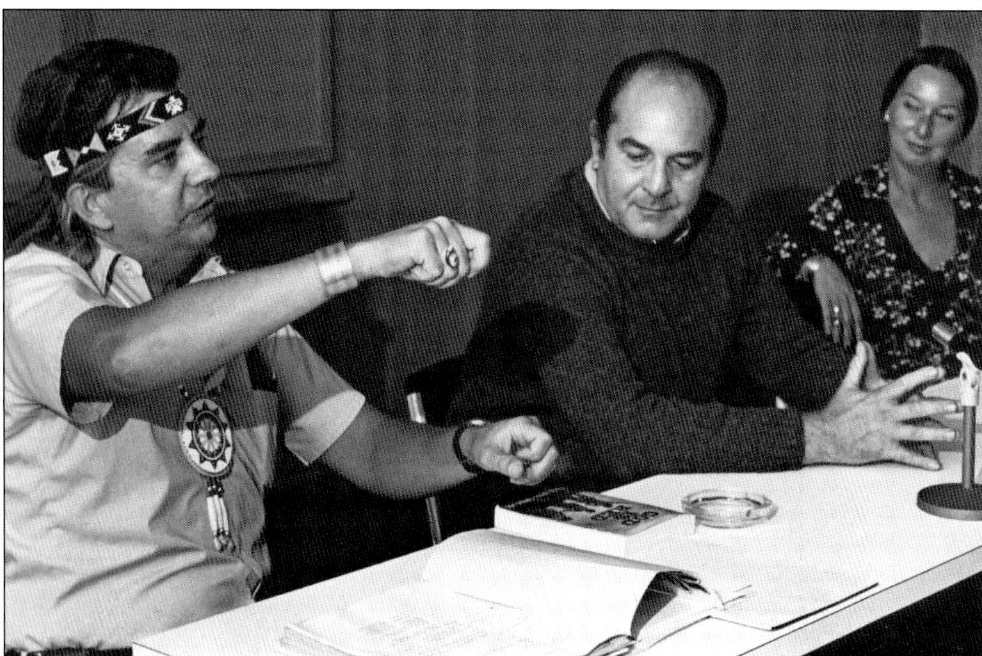

Seven

Onward

By the 1990s, the emerging voice and control of American Indians in Milwaukee solidified into long-running programming and institutions celebrating more than 20-year milestones all within a few years of each other. Indian Summer celebrates its 25th anniversary in September 2011, Potawatomi Bingo Casino's 20th anniversary is in 2011, the Congregation of the Great Spirit has been in existence for more than 22 years, and the Lutheran Church of the Great Spirit celebrated 20 years in 2011. With more-secure funding over 20 years ago from their partnership with the Potawatomi, the Indian Community School reorganized in 1990 and financed a move to Franklin, Wisconsin, but it remains an urban school through an extensive bussing program. Other entities, such as United Indians of Milwaukee, have lost membership, most likely due to more specialized organizations funded by specific tribes such as the Southeastern Oneida Tribal Services of Milwaukee, which began in the 1990s as an arm of the Oneida Nation. Both the University of Wisconsin–Milwaukee and the Milwaukee Area Technical College have had powwows, speakers, and programming for more than 30 years. There is drumming practice at the Gerald Ignace Indian Health Center, and hymn-singing groups in two different locations. Recently, the Potawatomi have rededicated their effort to meet the goal of providing an American Indian center, high school, and museum on the Concordia site vacated by the Indian Community School. There are now many options for Milwaukee Indian people in search of fellowship and assistance.

Although the efforts of people and organizations have turned into institutions, Indian action still remains traditional in that these organizations are family ventures rather than a loosely associated group of Indians with little in common other than living in Milwaukee. Leaders recruit family members and friends who provide membership, vitality, and endurance to an organization. Also, although Milwaukee Indian institutions and organizations have survived and grown over the past 25 years, none are immune to the economy, changing patterns and goals of Indian fellowship, or the political will and support of the city that surrounds them.

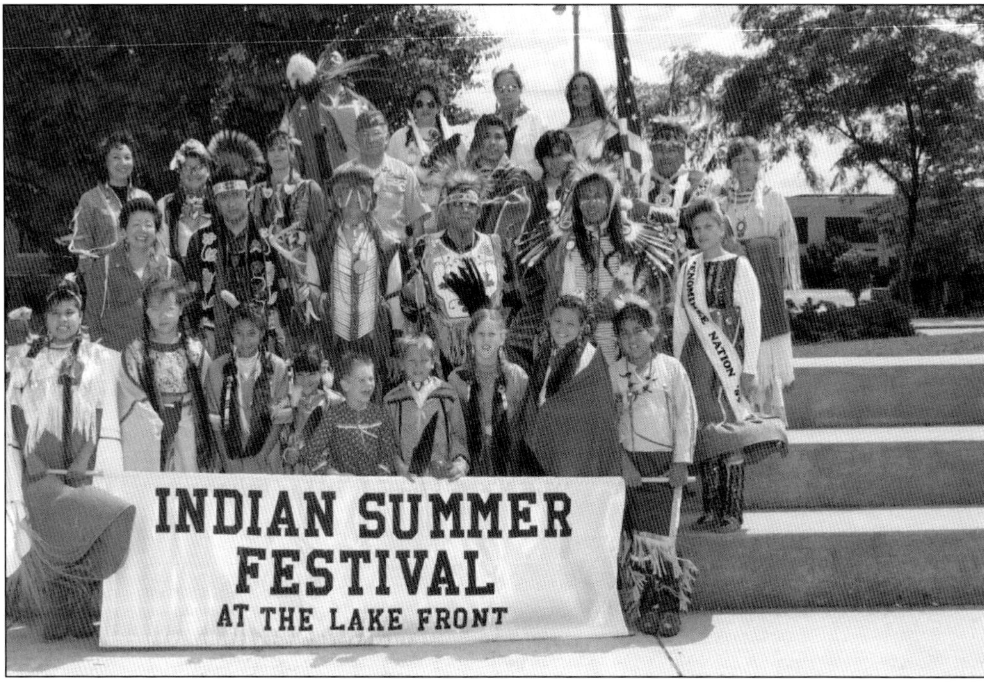

The American Indian Center took part in the City of Festivals Parade, a prelude to the first Indian Summer Festival in 1987. The American Indian Center also held a powwow in March 1987, prior to the debut of Indian Summer Festival. (Courtesy of Empire Studios of Madison.)

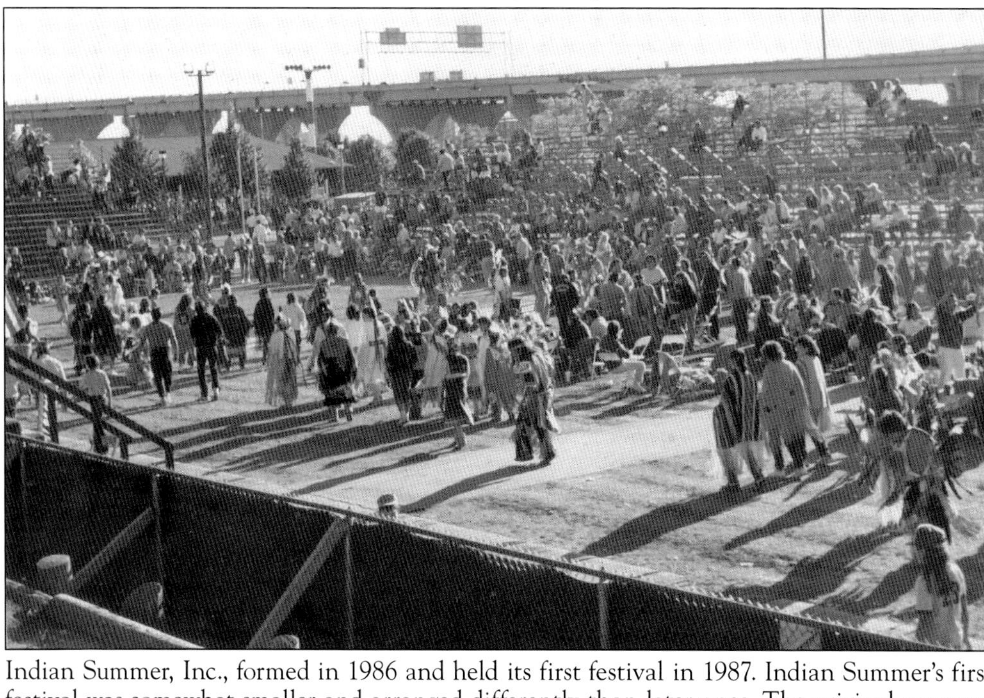

Indian Summer, Inc., formed in 1986 and held its first festival in 1987. Indian Summer's first festival was somewhat smaller and arranged differently than later ones. The original powwow grounds were more centrally located and featured a bit of grass. (Courtesy of the UWM Libraries Archives Department.)

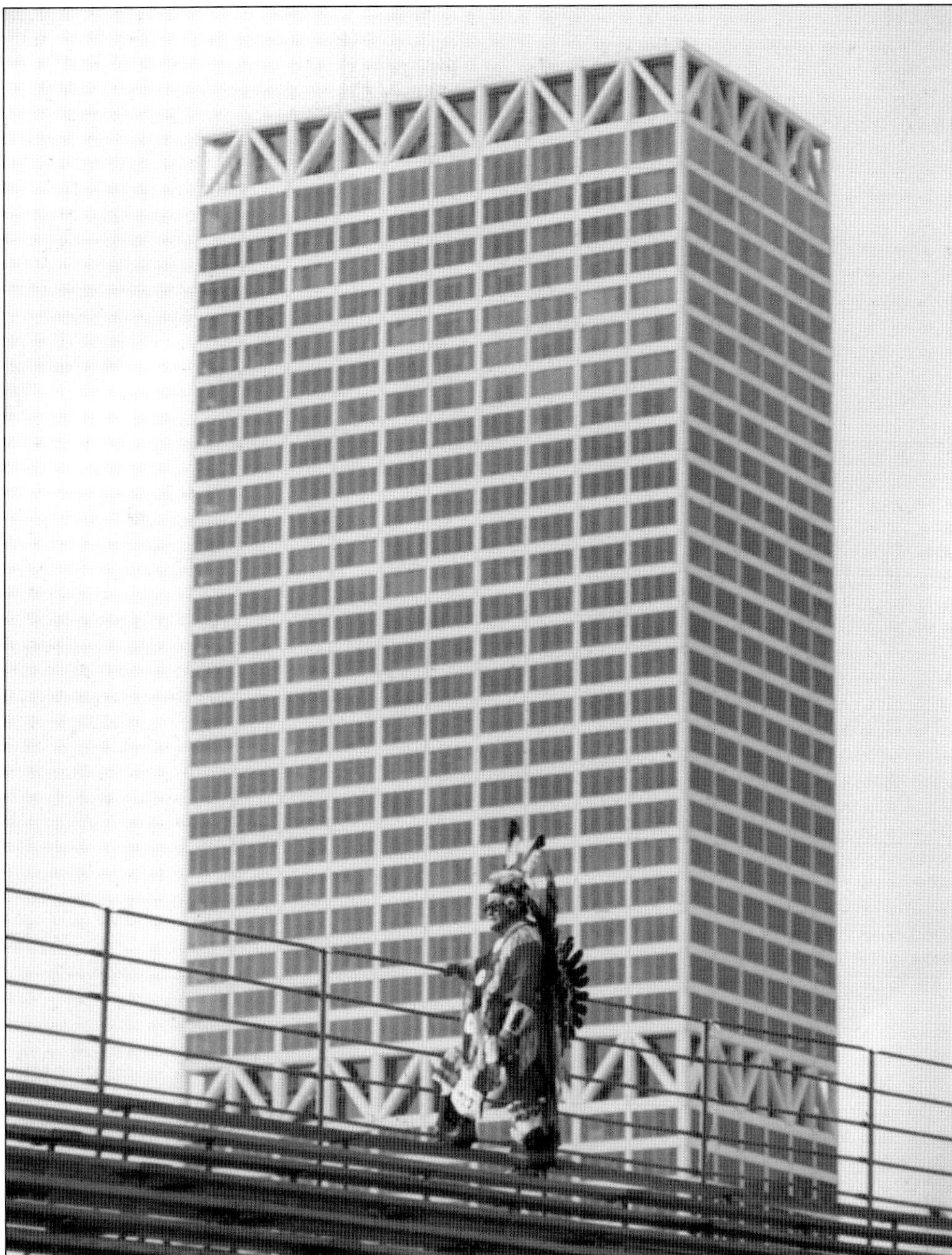

In Peter Draves's photograph "Looking West," Huston Wheelock, Oneida, gazes west—the direction of those who have passed, as did his wife, Charlene Wheelock, Menominee, during the opening of Indian Summer on the powwow grounds in 1987. Charlene, a recognized leader in the community, worked for the WE Indians Program, held offices for Untied Indians of Milwaukee, and made dozens of outfits and pieces for dancers in Milwaukee. (Courtesy of Peter Draves.)

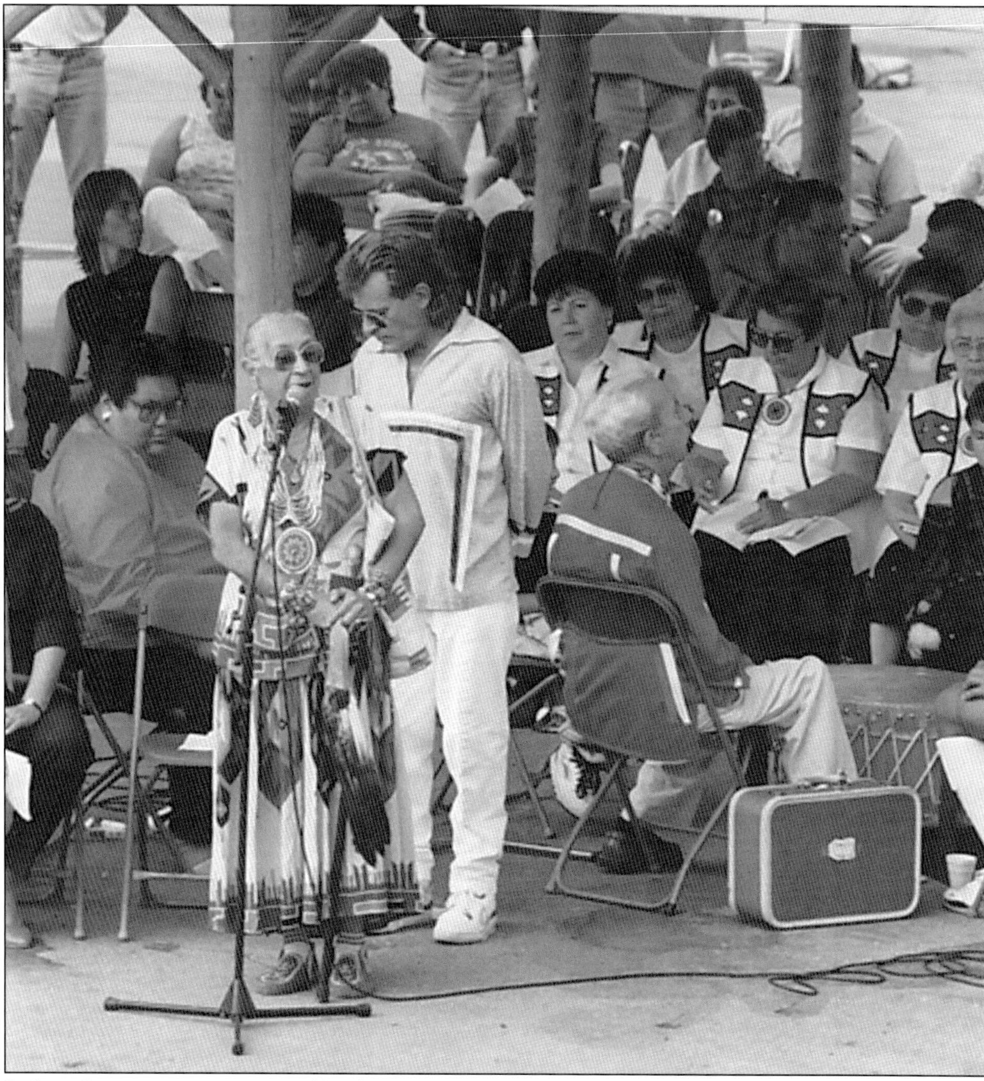

Indian Summer continues to offer the core of its first-year activities. Every year, there is a weekend-long competition powwow with a nonalcoholic zone including the children's area; four stages of music, comedy, or sports; food; Sunday morning services on the grounds; and a veteran's parade on opening day with organizational participation and fireworks. Pictured here, Fr. Edward Cook, Irene Mack, and hymn singers join for Sunday services. (Courtesy of Barb Jakopac.)

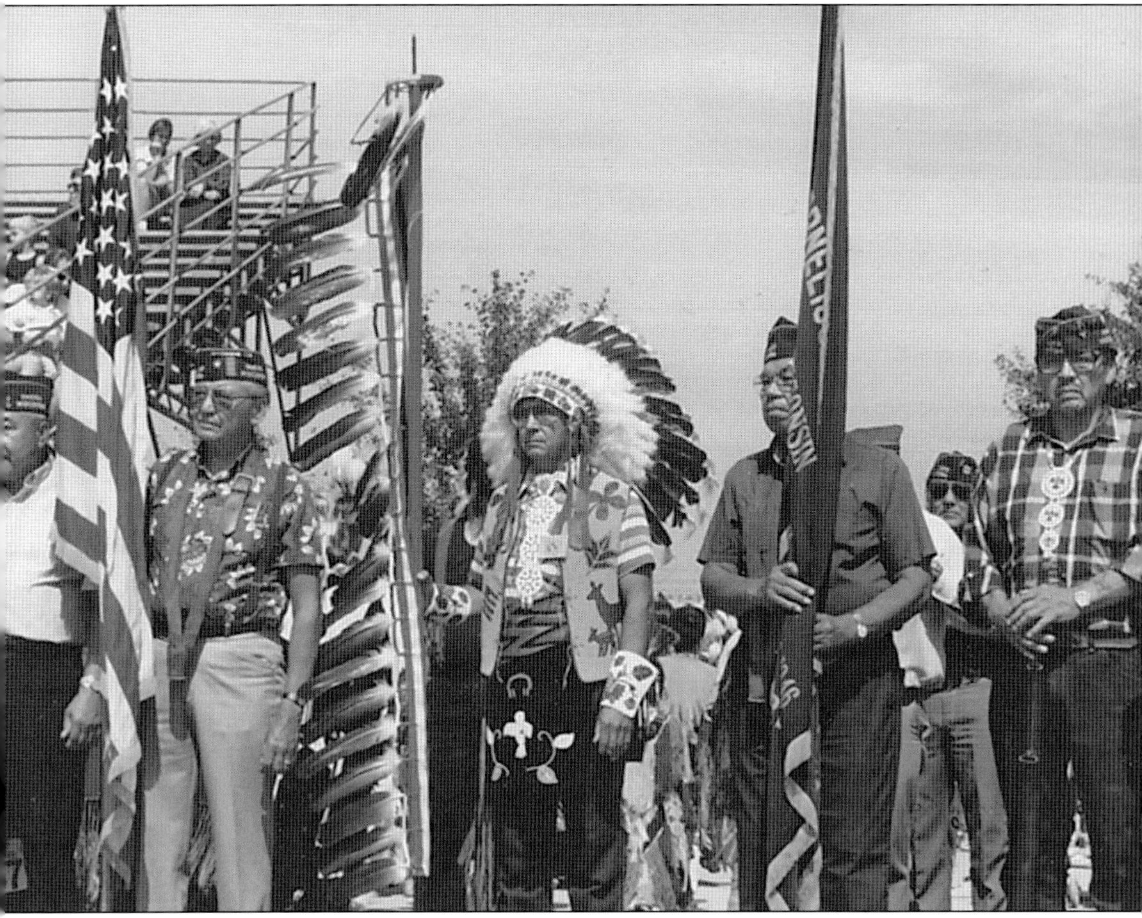

Native veterans line up for the grand entry at Indian Summer. Additionally, the festival has its own version of the Indian village within a cultural and historical framework—and no one has to live on the grounds. (Courtesy of Barb Jakopac.)

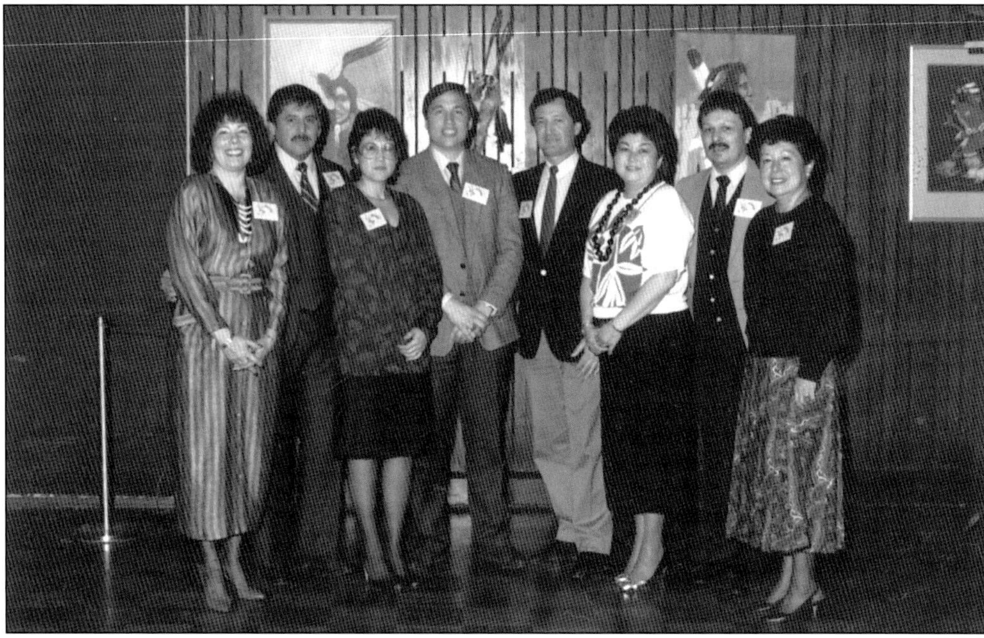

Pictured are the original founding members of Indian Summer, Inc. They are, from left to right, treasurer Jenelle Klumb, president Lawrence Roberts, secretary JoAnn Lenz, director James Warren, director James DeNomie, director Maxine Smallish, director Russell DeNomie, and vice president Donna Domencich. (Courtesy of the Indian Summer Festival.)

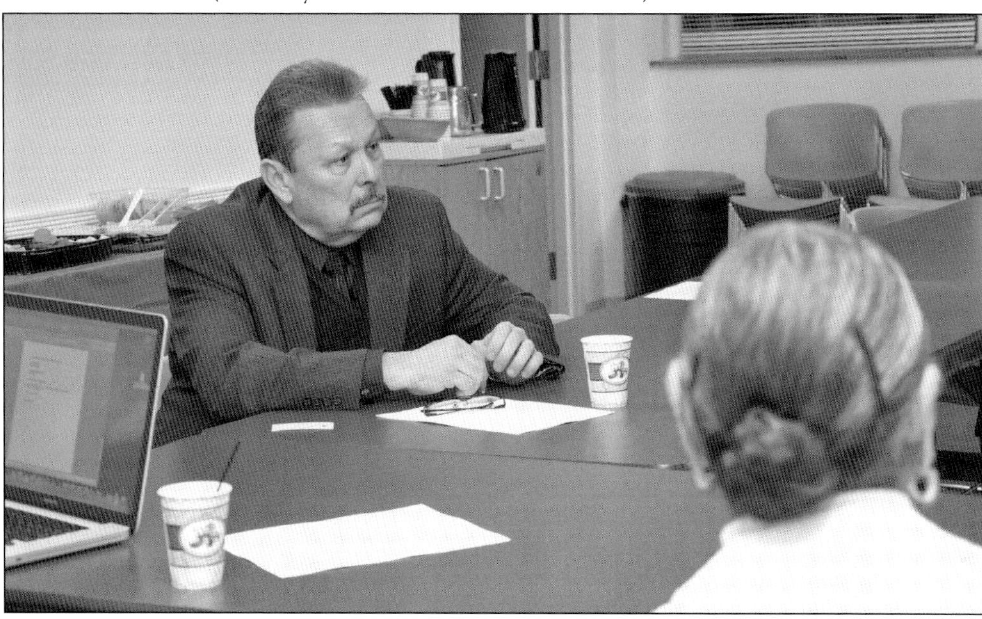

Lawrence "Butch" Roberts, Oneida, was the president of the founding board of Indian Summer. Roberts, a Milwaukee police officer, was part of the American Indian and Information Action Group, a Native American specialist for the Milwaukee Area Technical College (and formed its Indian education office), president of the National Indian Youth Council Board, and served on more than 10 other advisory boards and committees for the Milwaukee Indian community. (Courtesy of Sonsee-Array Creative.)

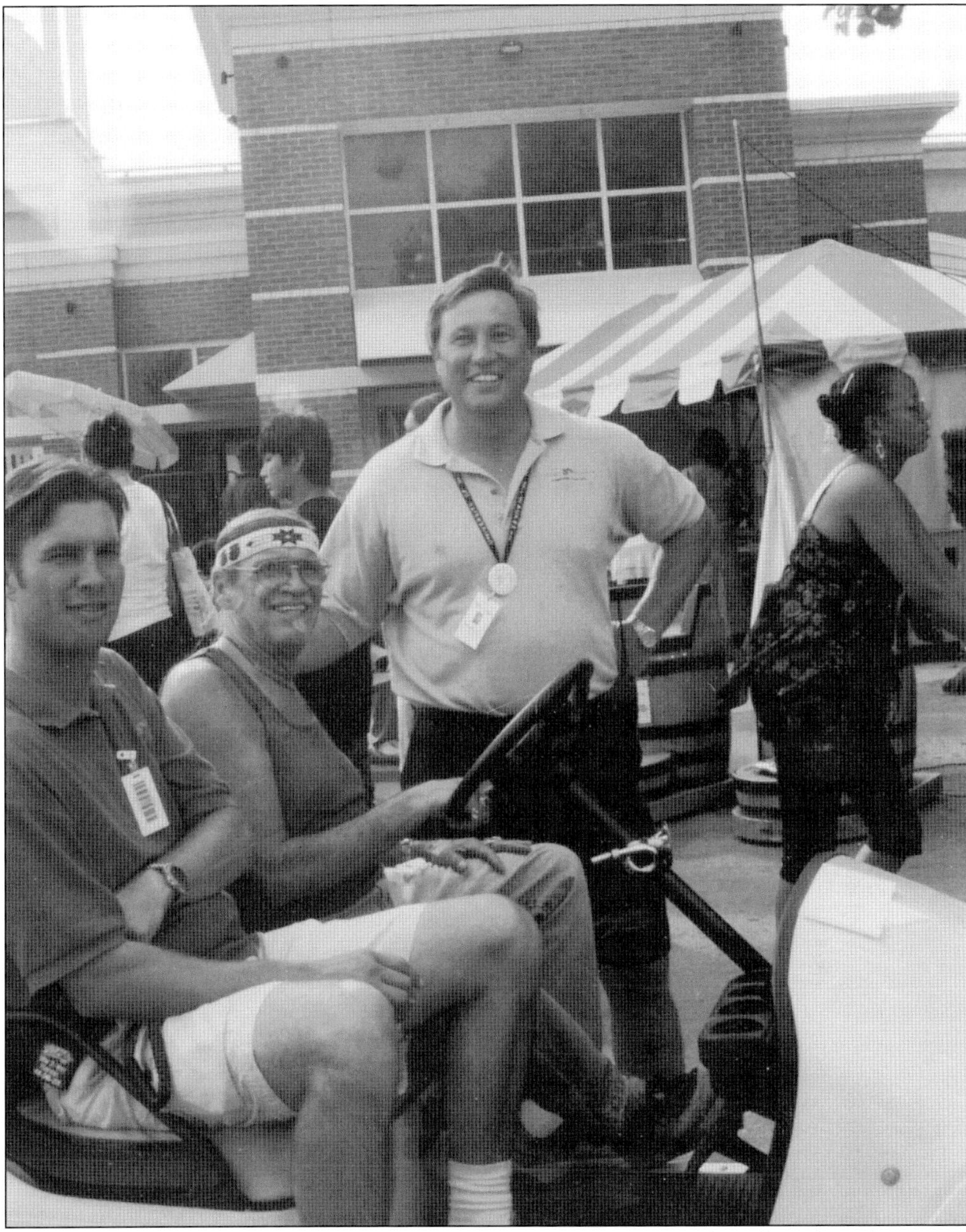

It was Lawrence Roberts's dream to add an American Indian festival to the ethnic lineup. He recruited fellow police officer James Warren (standing), White Earth Ojibwa, who brought in his sister Jenelle Klumb, who is also a White Earth Ojibwa. Jenelle and her husband, Kurtis Klumb, used their savings as start-up money for the festival. The organization also received a small grant from the Milwaukee Foundation. Indian Summer was in the planning for two years and incorporated in 1986 as Indian Summer, Inc. The group received help and encouragement from the Milwaukee Irish Fest organization. During the opening year, the Irish festival organization's financial officer was there to help organize the receipts. The Indian Summer Festival remains a family organization similar to many other Indian organizations in Milwaukee that tend to endure. (Courtesy of Diane Porter.)

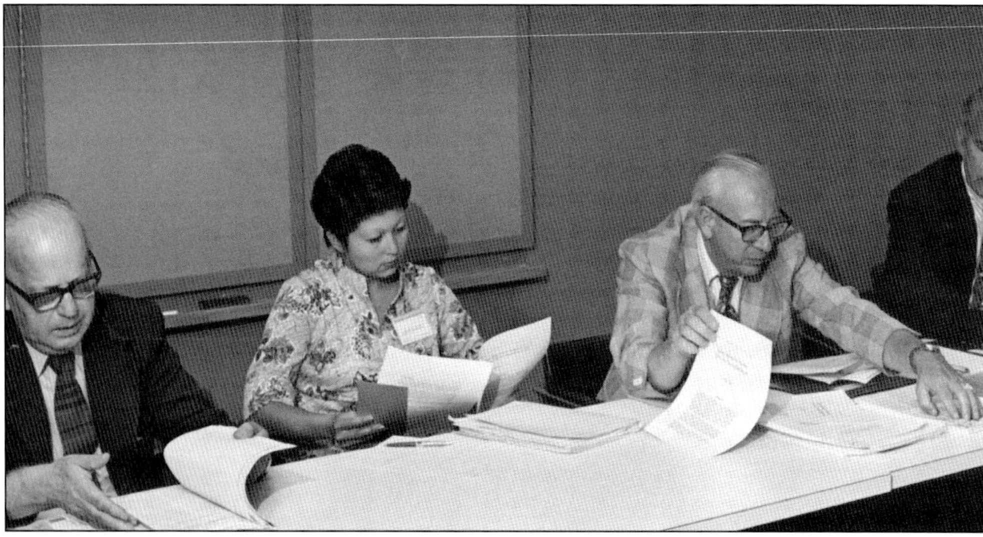

Donna L. Domencich (center), Oneida, was one of the original Indian Summer board members. She retired from the Wisconsin State Bureau of Apprenticeship Standard as a district representative. Domencich also worked as the Indian Manpower Council program head in the Milwaukee Jobs Initiative, is a past president of the board of directors of the YWCA, and served on the governor's committee on affirmative action. (Photograph by John Walley; courtesy of the American Indian Student Services.)

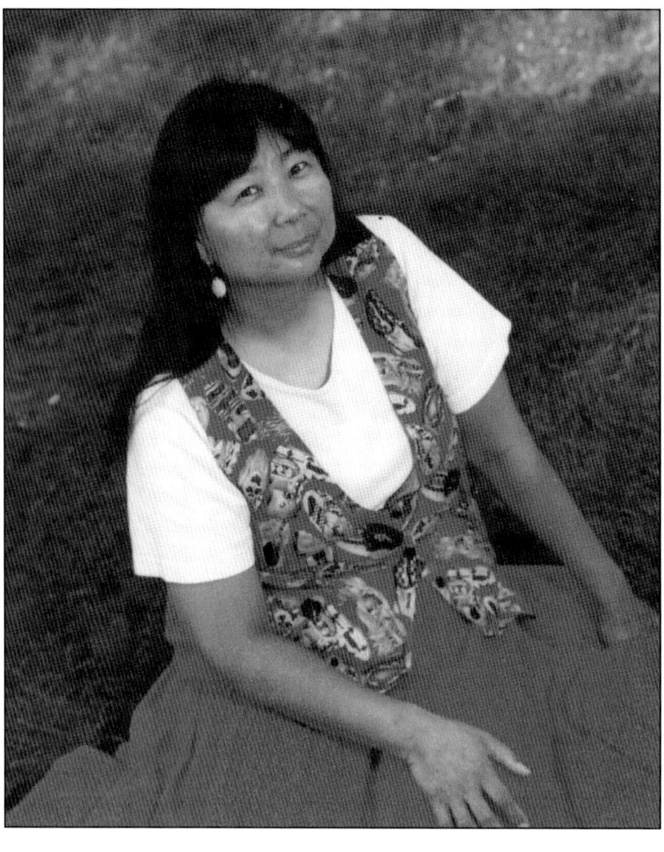

Diane Amour, Potawatomi, has been with the American Indian Student Services (AISS) at the University of Wisconsin–Milwaukee (UWM) for more than 30 years and led the program since John Boatman's retirement. Amour has been active in the education community for many years, serving on the Indian Community School board and as director on the Indian Summer Festival board. AISS staff coordinated the National Indian Education Conference in 2010. (Courtesy of the American Indian Student Services.)

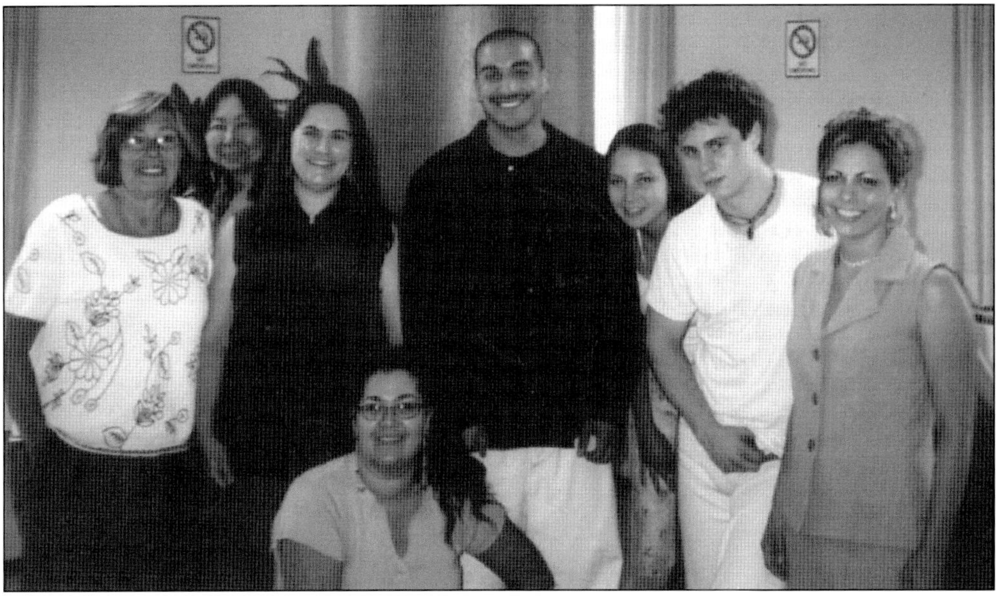

The American Indian Student Services has held a traditional powwow for more than 30 years and coordinates with UWM Indian staff and research programs, such as this one for the Ronald E. McNair Postbaccalaurete Achievement Program. From left to right are AISS staff Jenelle Klumb; Diane Amour; professor of American Indian history Cary Miller; Bradley Renfro; Angela Fernandez; Harrison Schultz; and Nicole Stroobants. Seated is AISS counselor Celeste Clark. (Courtesy of the American Indian Student Services.)

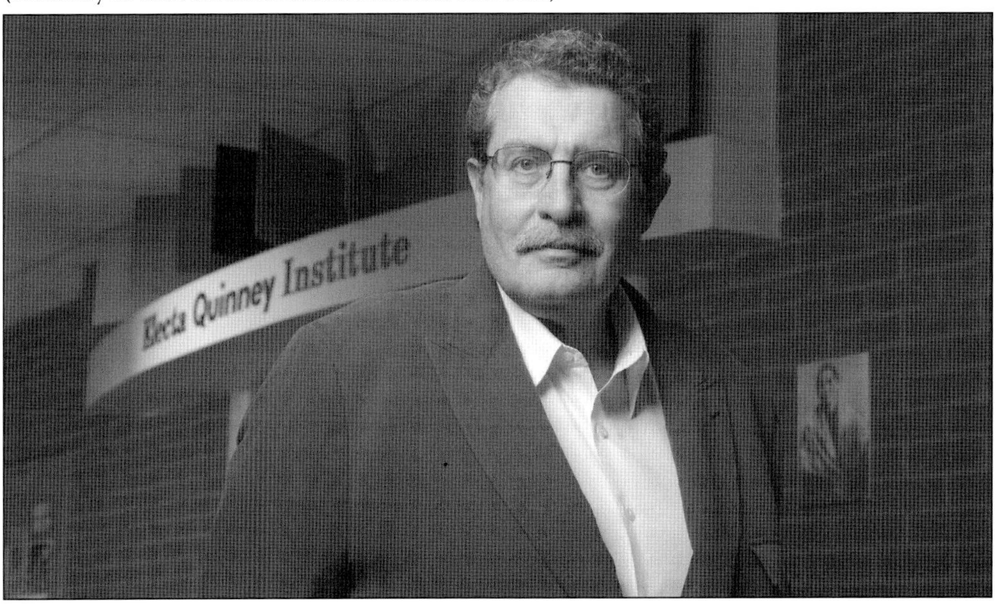

Prof. David Beaulieu, White Earth Chippewa, is the director of the Electa Quinney Institute for American Indian Education, which was established through an endowment from the Indian Community School at the University of Wisconsin–Milwaukee. In addition to a long career in government and education, Beaulieu has served on the board of directors and as president of the National Indian Education Association. From 1997 to 2001, he was the director of the US Department of Education's Office of Indian Education. (Photograph by Alan Magayne-Roshak; courtesy of UWM.)

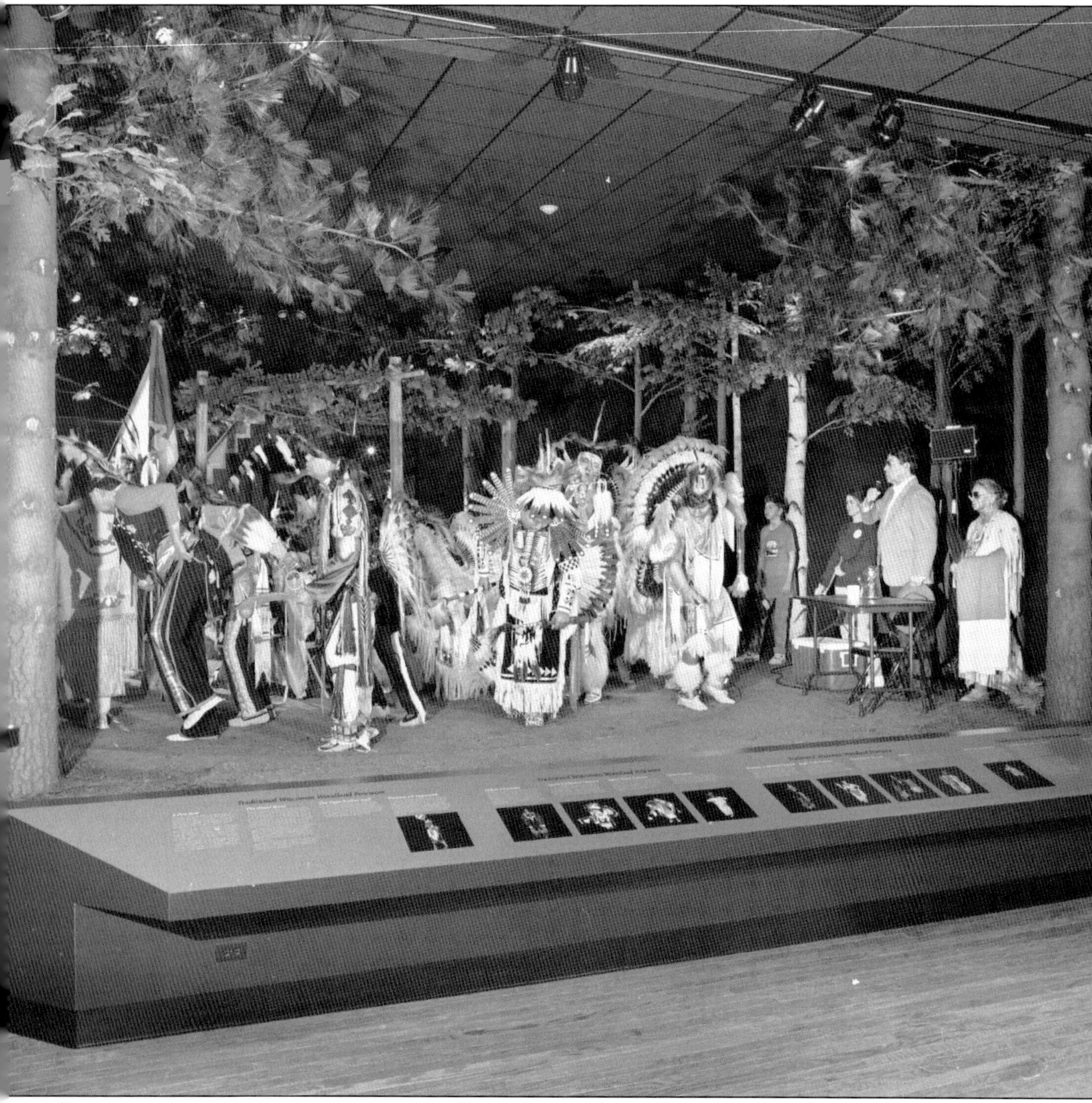

Indian Country, more commonly known as "*Tribute to Survival*," is a one-of-a-kind urban Indian exhibit that is a collaboration between the Milwaukee Indian community and the Milwaukee Public Museum. The exhibit opened in September 1993 after several years of planning with the Indian community who were models for the dancers. Their likenesses were molded in plaster, and outfits were made by participants. "Tribute" welcomes museum visitors at the entry of the American Indian collection area and is a counter to the older installations of the museum. The diorama recreates a modern powwow grand entry scene with 37 life-sized figures moving on an enormous turntable around singers at a drum, accompanied by the sounds of American Indian music. (Courtesy of the Milwaukee Public Museum.)

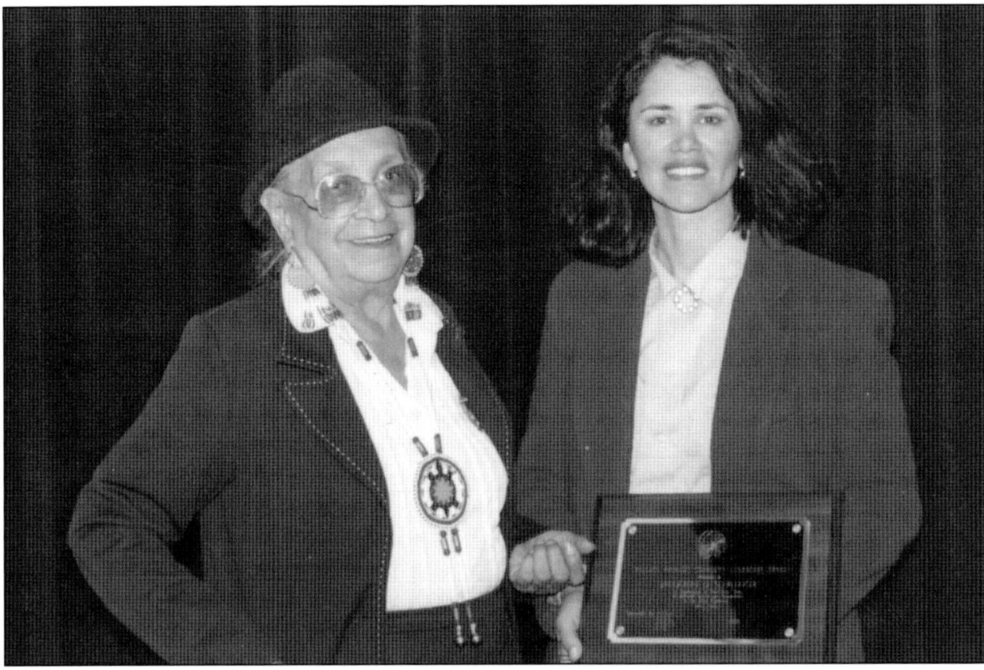

In this photograph, Jacqueline Schellinger, right, receives the Wallace Pyawasit Award from Irene Mack. Schellinger was a circuit court judge in Milwaukee from 1992 through 2003. She joined the Indian Community School board in 1996 and now serves as general counsel for the school. She oversaw the school through its move to Franklin, Wisconsin, and the construction of a multimillion-dollar building that has won awards for its unique design. (Courtesy of the American Indian Student Services.)

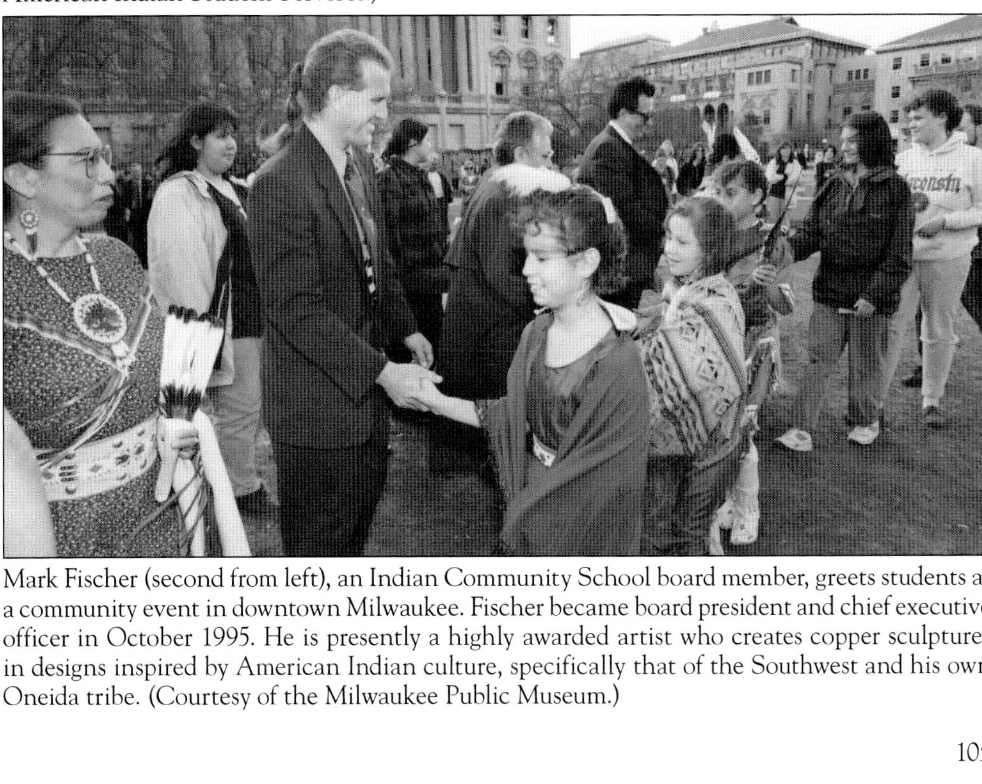

Mark Fischer (second from left), an Indian Community School board member, greets students at a community event in downtown Milwaukee. Fischer became board president and chief executive officer in October 1995. He is presently a highly awarded artist who creates copper sculptures in designs inspired by American Indian culture, specifically that of the Southwest and his own Oneida tribe. (Courtesy of the Milwaukee Public Museum.)

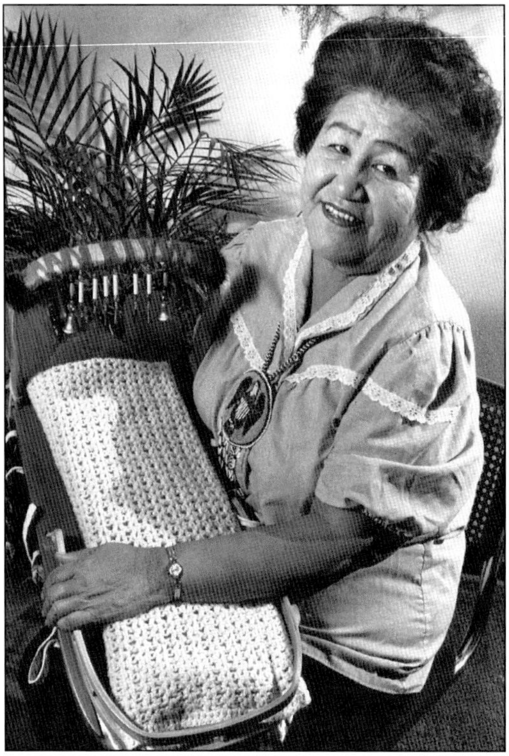

Mary Daniels, Forest County Potawatomi, joined the Wisconsin Native American Languages Project at the University of Wisconsin–Milwaukee from 1973 through 1976. She worked as a Potawatomi language consultant. She later taught Potawatomi language and American Indian culture at the Indian Community School State Street site from 1986 to 1988. She is pictured here at age 62 with an Indian cradleboard on January 11, 1988. (Courtesy of the *Milwaukee Journal Sentinel* Archives.)

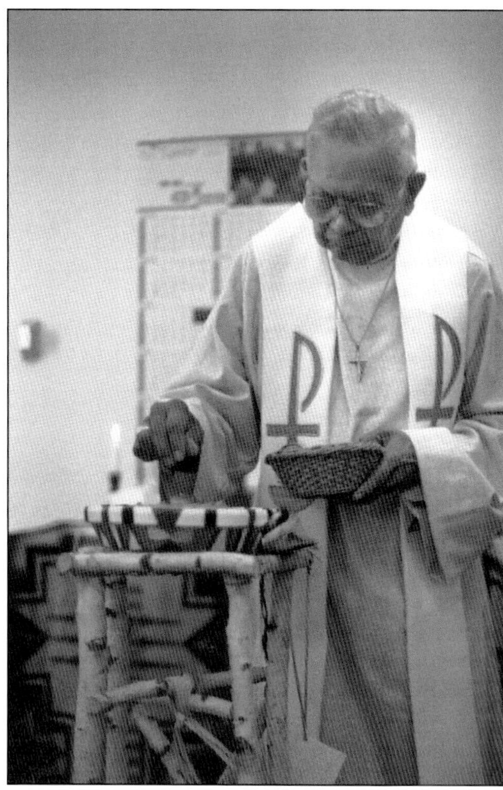

Lawrence Jacobs, Stockbridge-Munsee, is seen here sprinkling sacred herbs on the flame while asking for prayers in 1992. Jacobs, 76 years old at the time this photograph was taken, was ordained and installed as pastor of the Lutheran Church of the Great Spirit in 1990. The church, located at 3127 South Howell Avenue in Milwaukee, incorporates elements of American Indian culture and spirituality into its Sunday church services. This includes music, herbs, and prayers. (Courtesy of the Doxtator family.)

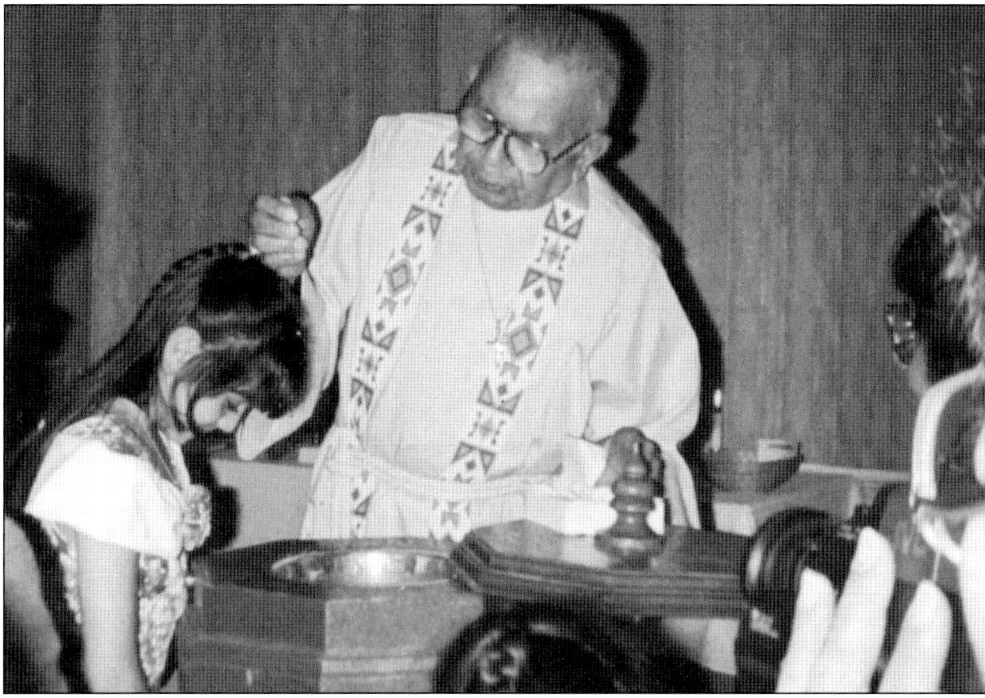

In this April 1991 image, Lawrence Jacobs of the Lutheran Church of the Great Spirit baptizes Claudia Rodriguez, Oneida. Jacobs moved to Milwaukee in the 1940s and worked in the carpentry trade for about 20 years before becoming a crane operator at A.O. Smith. He worked there until his retirement in 1982. Jacobs, the first chairman of United Indians of Milwaukee in 1970, was also a founding member in 1968. (Courtesy of the Doxtator family.)

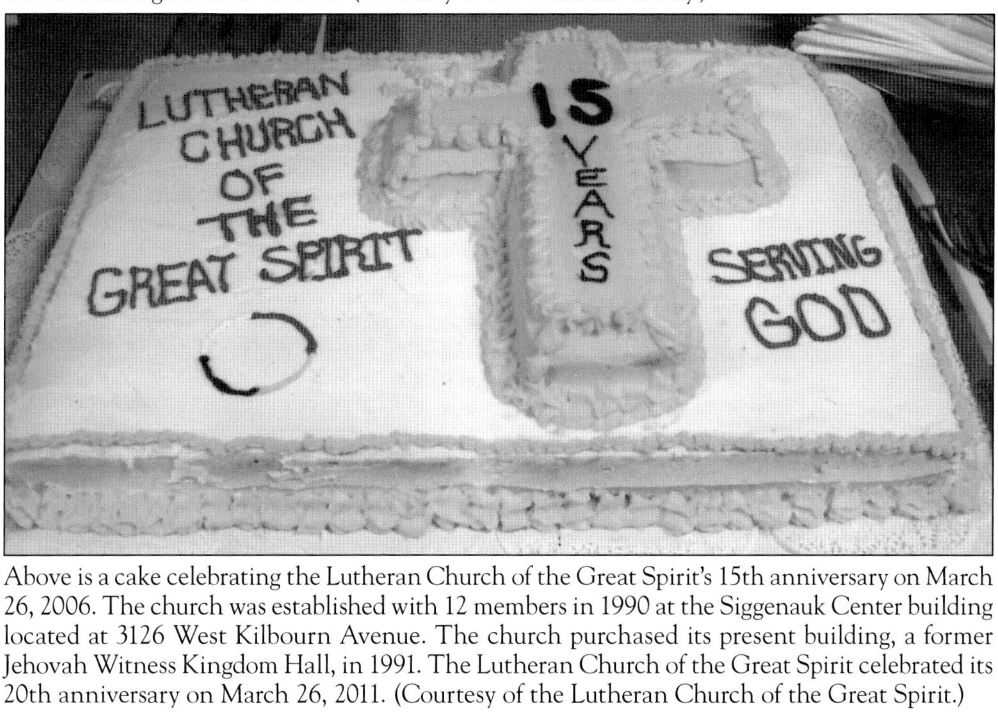

Above is a cake celebrating the Lutheran Church of the Great Spirit's 15th anniversary on March 26, 2006. The church was established with 12 members in 1990 at the Siggenauk Center building located at 3126 West Kilbourn Avenue. The church purchased its present building, a former Jehovah Witness Kingdom Hall, in 1991. The Lutheran Church of the Great Spirit celebrated its 20th anniversary on March 26, 2011. (Courtesy of the Lutheran Church of the Great Spirit.)

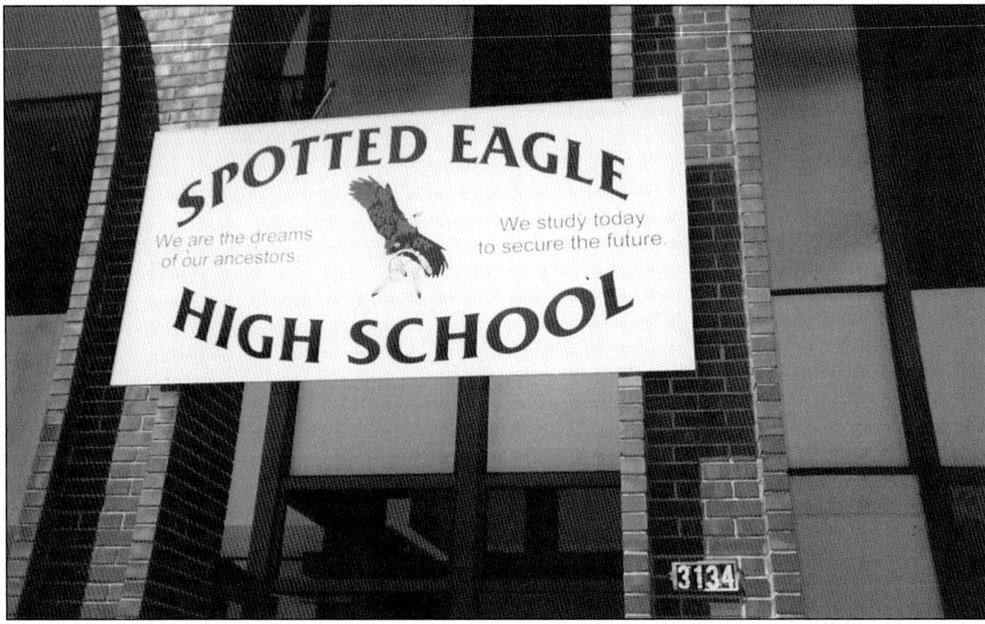

Spotted Eagle High School, located at 3134 West State Street in Milwaukee, is an alternative Milwaukee Public school that serves up to 100 students each school year. The student body hovers around 50 percent American Indian. The school was founded in 1994 on the knowledge that American Indian students in Milwaukee have the highest dropout rates of any group. Its mission was based on teaching American Indian principles, values, and culture. (Courtesy of the Doxtator family.)

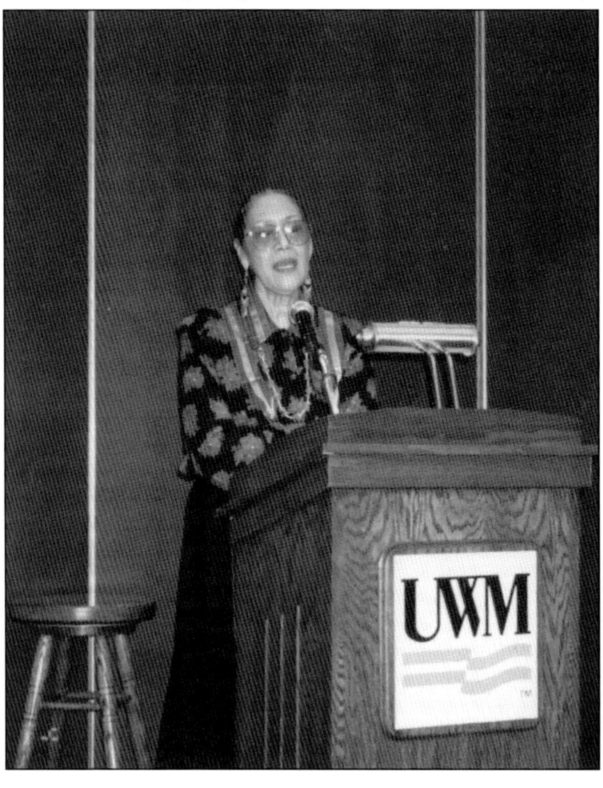

In 1992, Carol Sample, Turtle Mountain Ojibwa, became executive director of the Milwaukee Area Indian Manpower Council, which is now Spotted Eagle, Inc. She later founded Spotted Eagle High School in 1994. Sample served as principal of the school and executive director of the parent organization until she retired in 2008. She holds a master's degree in social welfare. (Courtesy of Diane Amour.)

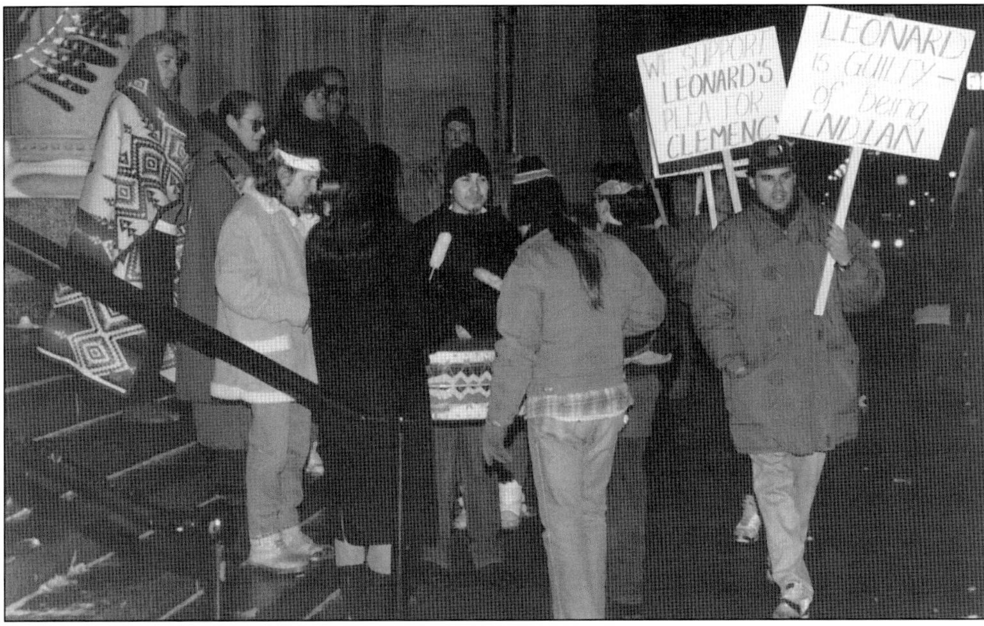

Members of United Indians of Milwaukee protest in front of the federal courthouse in downtown Milwaukee on Wisconsin Avenue in this 1994 photograph. The group is also rallying in support for executive clemency for Leonard Peltier. The president of the United Indians, Richard E. Watkins, (wearing a headband on the far left) leads a song on the drum. Dale Kindness (far right), Oneida, leads a group carrying signs in support of Peltier. (Courtesy of Richard Watkins Jr.)

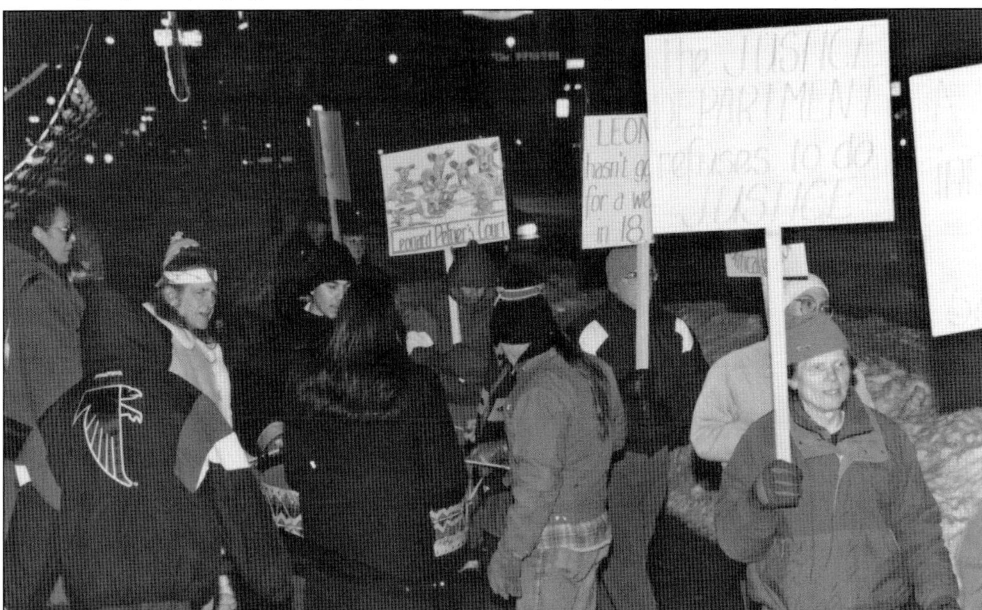

Robert Ulrich, holding a sign in the far right, lends his support to the Peltier rally. Leonard Peltier was a member of the American Indian Movement who was found guilty in 1977 for the June 26, 1975, murder of two Federal Bureau of Investigation agents on the Pine Ridge reservation. Many American Indians and their supporters feel Peltier was unjustly convicted and view him as a political prisoner. (Courtesy of Richard Watkins Jr.)

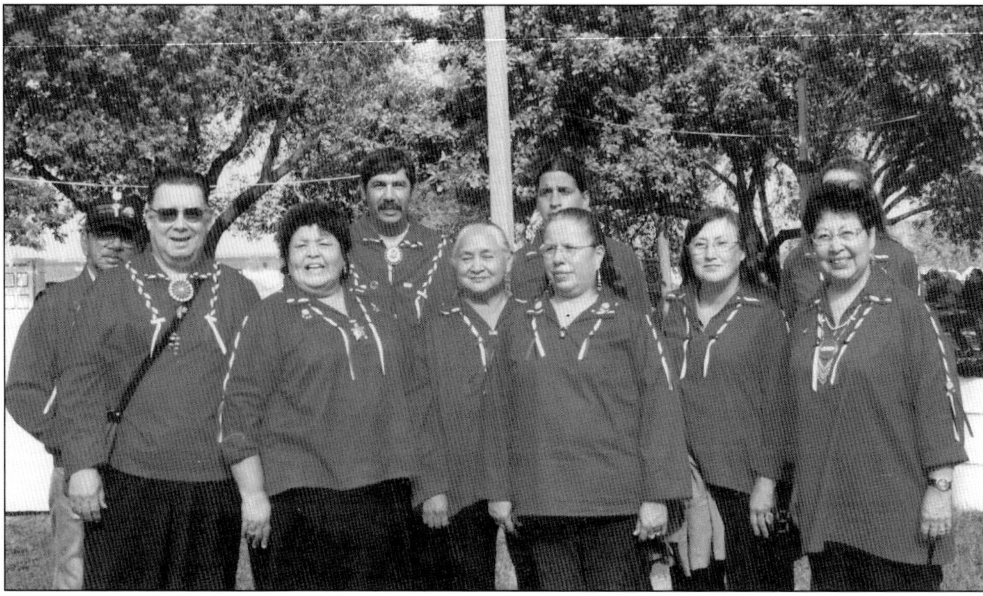

Above are the Oneida Hymn Singers of Milwaukee. From left to right are (first row) Orin Johns, Charlene Smith, Roberta Doxtator, Mary Elm, Clara Ayala, and Opal Skenandore; (second row) John Thunder, John House, Daniel Preston, and Mamie Arrellano. The group, established by James Cooper in 1990, follows a long tradition going back to almost 200 years of Oneidas singing Christian hymns in their own language. (Courtesy of the Doxtator family.)

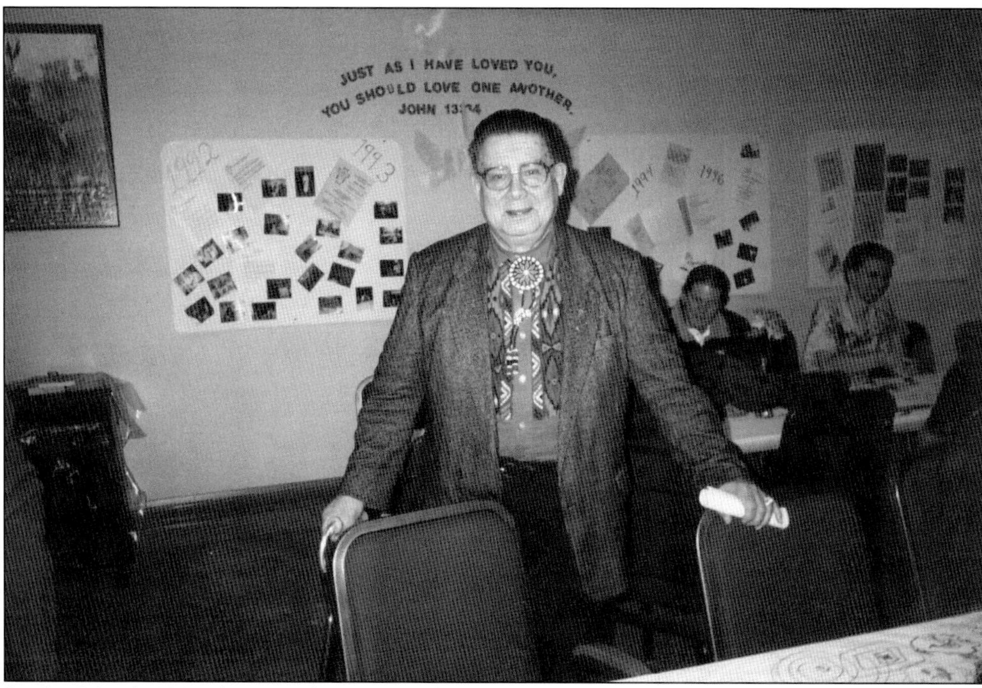

In this March 2001 photograph is Orin Johns, Oneida and Chickasaw, at the Lutheran Church of the Great Spirit, of which he was a member. Johns, a Korean War veteran who served in the Army artillery, worked at the Falk Corporation for 35 years before retiring. He is also a founding member of the Oneida Hymn Singers of Milwaukee. (Courtesy of the Doxtator family.)

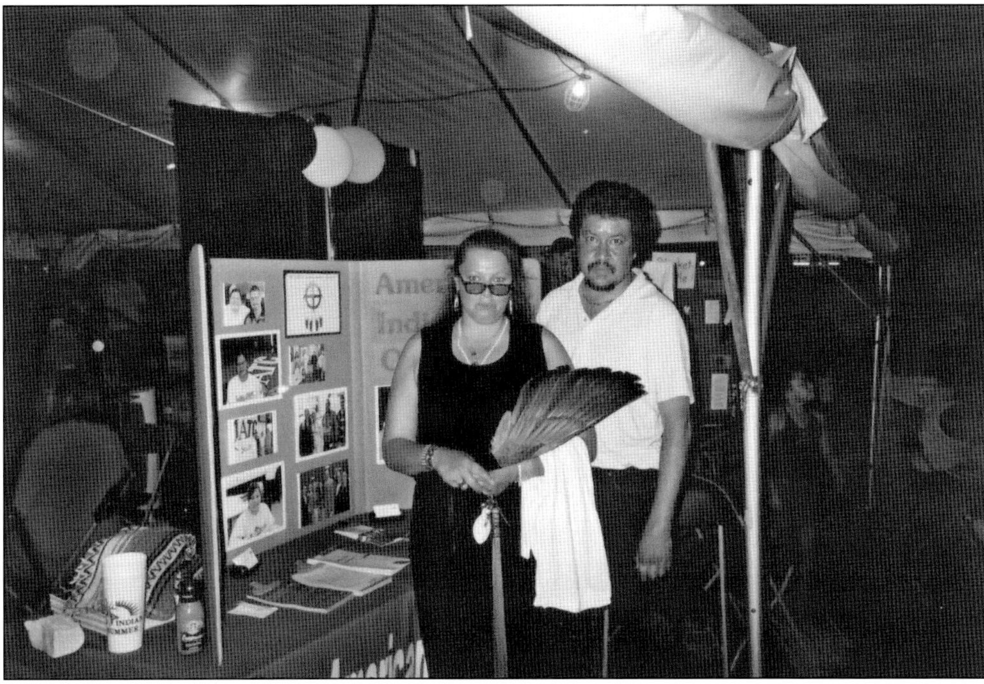

In the image above are Mamie Arrellano (left), Oneida, and an unidentified man at the Indian Summer Festival in Milwaukee. Arrellano was one of the first members of the Oneida Hymn Singers of Milwaukee, having joined through her uncle James Cooper, who started the group in 1990. The group is asked to sing at wakes, funerals, and community events, including the Indian Summer Festival's Oneida village. (Courtesy of the Milwaukee Area Technical College.)

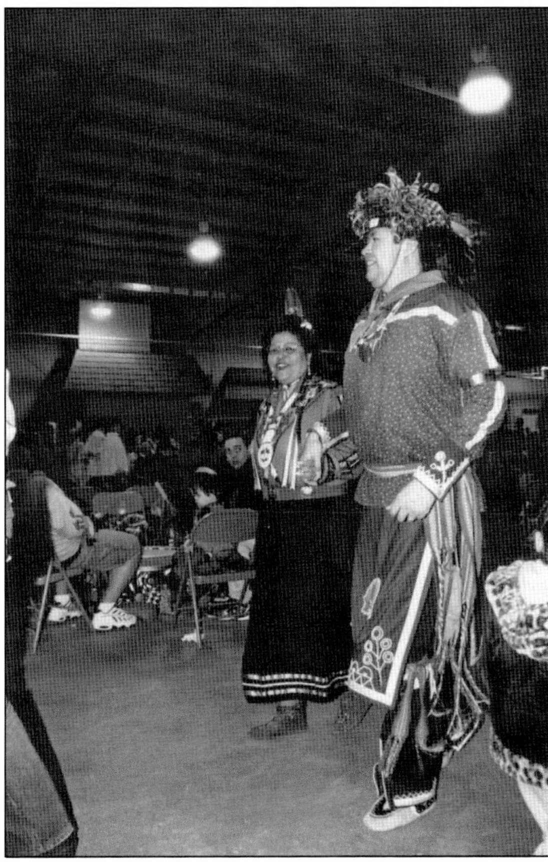

John Padron, Oneida, dances a two-step at the March 2001 Indian Summer Mid-Winter Pow Wow. Padron, the oldest of 15 siblings, was a member of United Indians of Milwaukee in the late 1980s. He is one of the first Oneidas in the Milwaukee area to wear traditional Oneida regalia, which is all made by his wife, Maria. (Courtesy of the Doxtator family.)

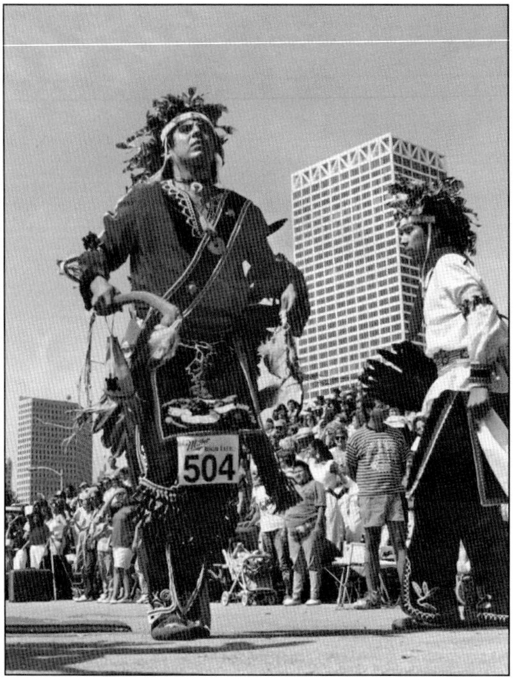

Ken Metoxen (left) and Kirby Metoxen (right), Oneidas, dance at the 1990 Indian Summer Festival at Milwaukee's lakefront. Both dancers wear traditional Oneida regalia, which differs from the other Woodlands tribes in Wisconsin. Historically, Oneidas have not incorporated their traditional culture into the powwow scene, but at the annual Oneida powwow, they do offer smoke dancing competitions, which is a version of the Oneida war dance and social dance. (Courtesy of Barb Jakopac.)

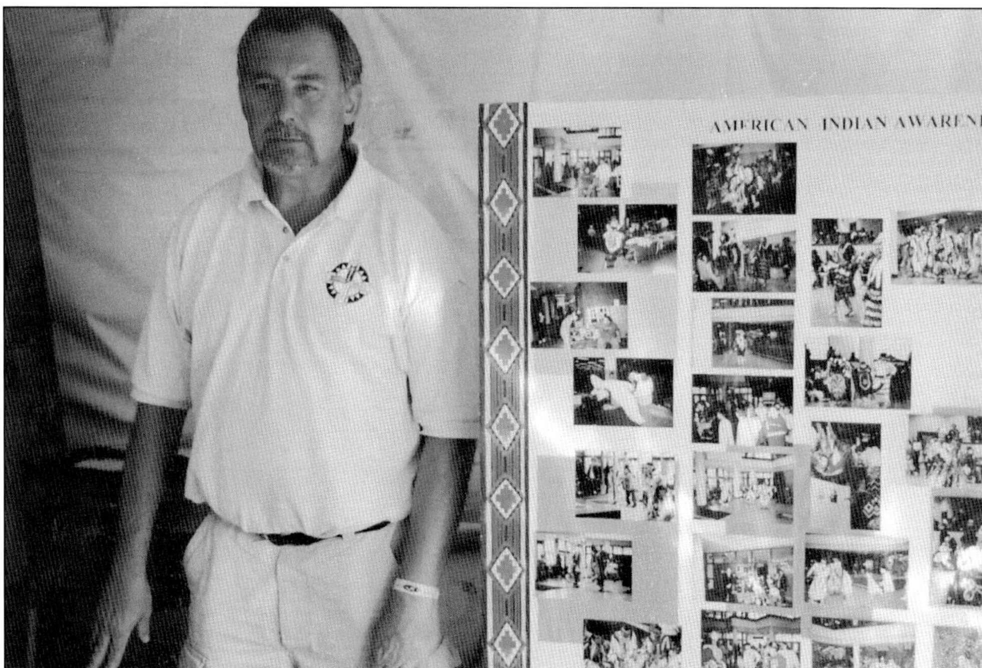

Gregory Johns, Oneida, has worked as a Native American student advisor at the Milwaukee Area Technical College's downtown campus since 1999. He serves American Indian students through recruitment and retention services that lead to graduation. Those services include admission assistance and program selection, career exploration, academic advising and class scheduling, and financial-aid assistance including tribal benefits. Many American Indian students have graduated as a result of Johns's assistance. (Courtesy of the Milwaukee Area Technical College.)

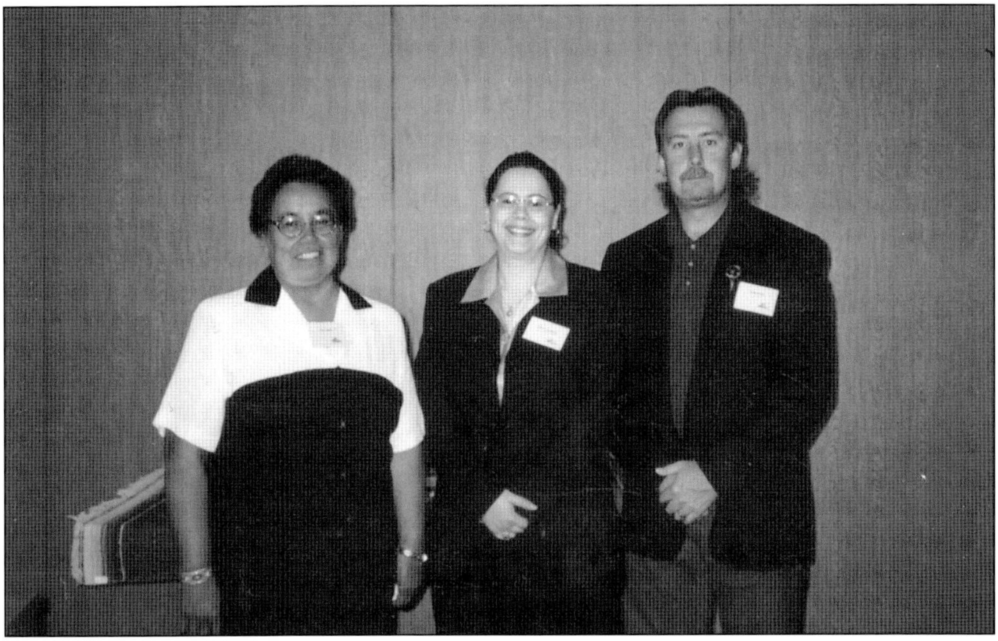

Pictured above are staff members of the Milwaukee Area Technical College. They are, from left to right, Patricia Logan, an unidentified woman, and Gregory Johns. Both Logan and Johns are Native American student advisors. Patricia Logan, Ho-Chunk, has been working at the Milwaukee Area Technical College since 1978. She started out as a Native American student recruiter and worked as an advisor at the college's south campus. Logan is also a nationally recognized championship dancer in the women's traditional style. (Courtesy of the Milwaukee Area Technical College.)

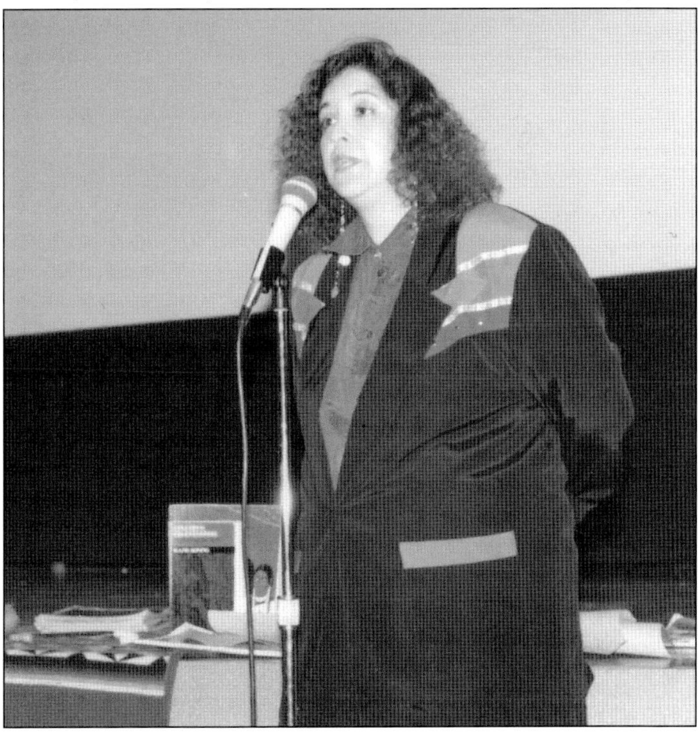

Donna Beckstrom, Minnesota Ojibwa, worked hard to educate and advocate for American Indians in Milwaukee. She served on an Indian health board in 1993. She worked as a Native American student advisor at Milwaukee Area Technical College's downtown campus in the 1990s. Milwaukee Area Technical College's history department later hired her to teach classes in American Indian studies and women's history. (Courtesy of the American Indian Student Services.)

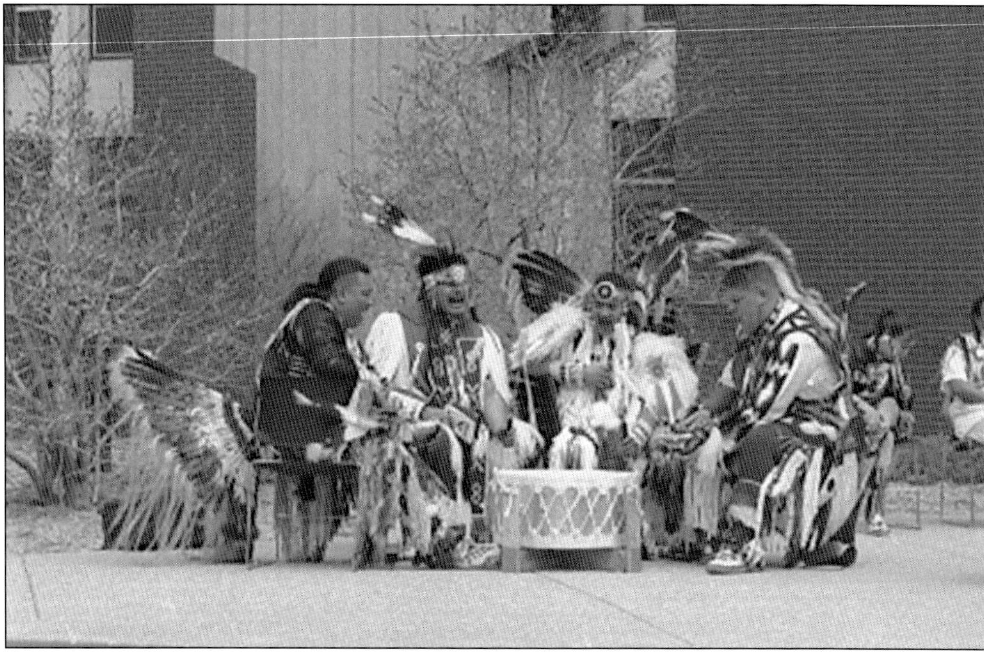

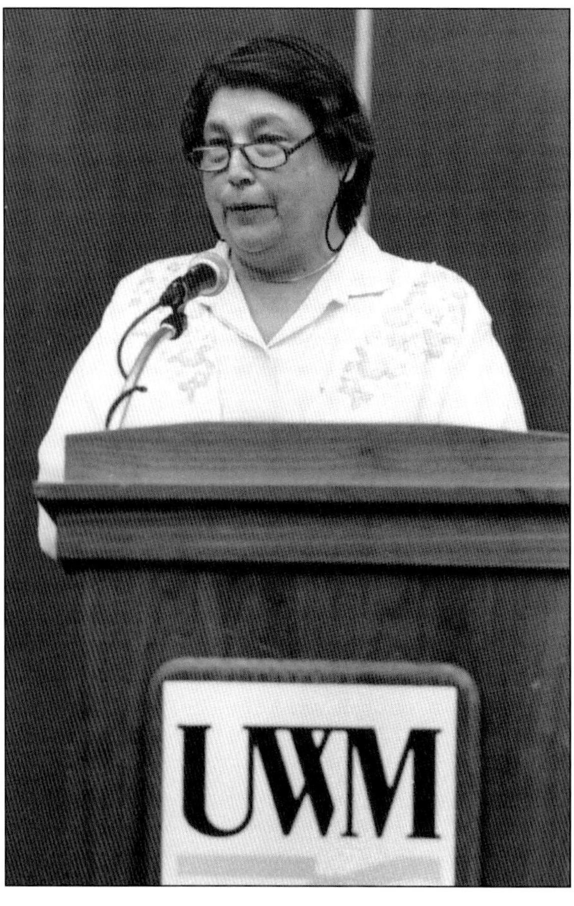

Above is the Bucks drum, formerly the Milwaukee Bucks, a northern singing intertribal group from the city. Kelly Logan presently leads the Bucks, a third-generation singing group started by Kelly's father, Herman Logan, and grandfather, both Ho-Chunks, in 1963. They named the group after the wildlife in the area. The group travels throughout the country and Canada, participating in powwows. They have released several compact discs. (Courtesy of the Milwaukee Area Technical College.)

Sandi Cornelius, Oneida, worked as a former Milwaukee Public Schools bilingual teacher. She started working with the Indian Community School in 1992 and was named principal in 1996. Cornelius also served as president of the board of the directors for the school. She held a third-degree black belt in judo and competed and won awards for judo nationally and internationally for more than 32 years. (Courtesy of the American Indian Student Services.)

Joseph Ackley, Mole Lake Chippewa, is seen in his traditional regalia. Ackley taught American dancing class at the Indian Community School on the Bartlett Avenue site. He was also a longtime member of United Indians of Milwaukee and a well-known men's traditional dancer at powwows in Wisconsin. (Courtesy of the *Milwaukee Area Technical College Times.*)

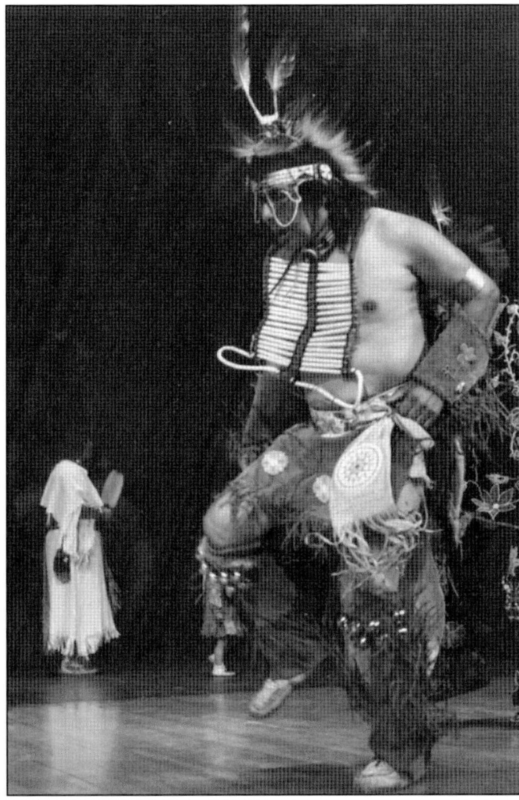

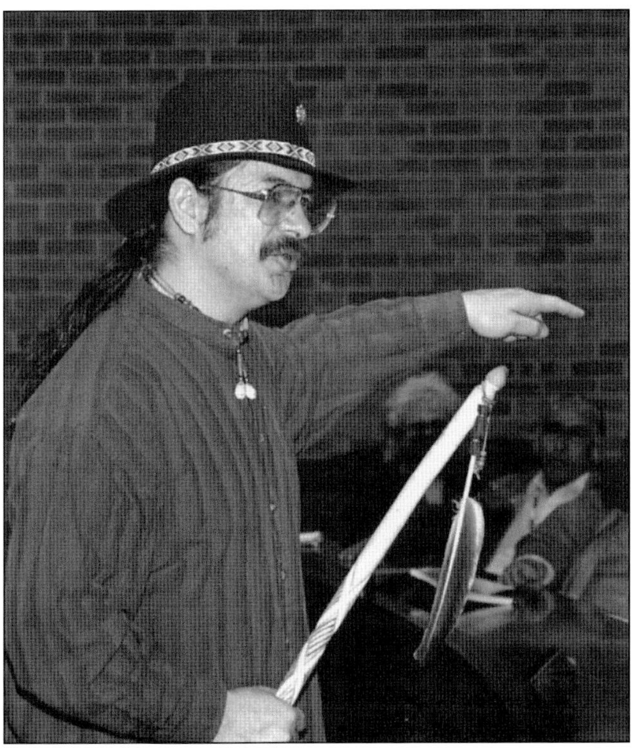

Andrew Connors, Bad River Chippewa, was the theater director at the Indian Community School and editor of the school newsletter, the *Migizi Express*. He is also a published writer and musician in the Acoustic Warriors band, which performs at many local events. Additionally, Connors is a storyteller and playwright who has written and performed many plays through the Wind Whisper American Indian Dance Theatre. (Courtesy of the *Milwaukee Area Technical College Times.*)

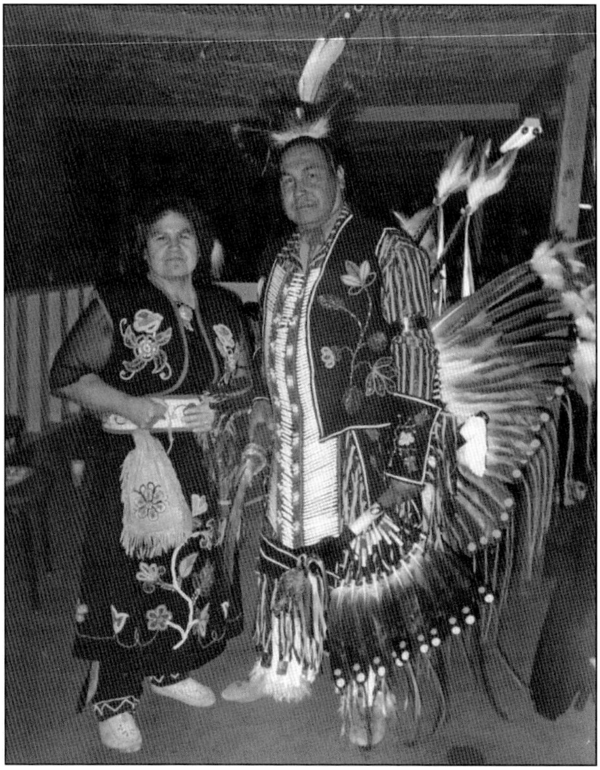

Marie Estelle Gilane, Oneida and Chippewa, is pictured at left with an unidentified man. She was raised in Milwaukee and was a member of the Consolidated Tribes of American Indians organization, as was the rest of her family. She performed and danced in the group's dance troupe. She was also active in sports and joined the Bravettes, an all-female American Indian softball team. Gilane is also a veteran of the US Marine Corps and a trustee of the Congregation of the Great Spirit Catholic Ministry. (Courtesy of Dona Yahola.)

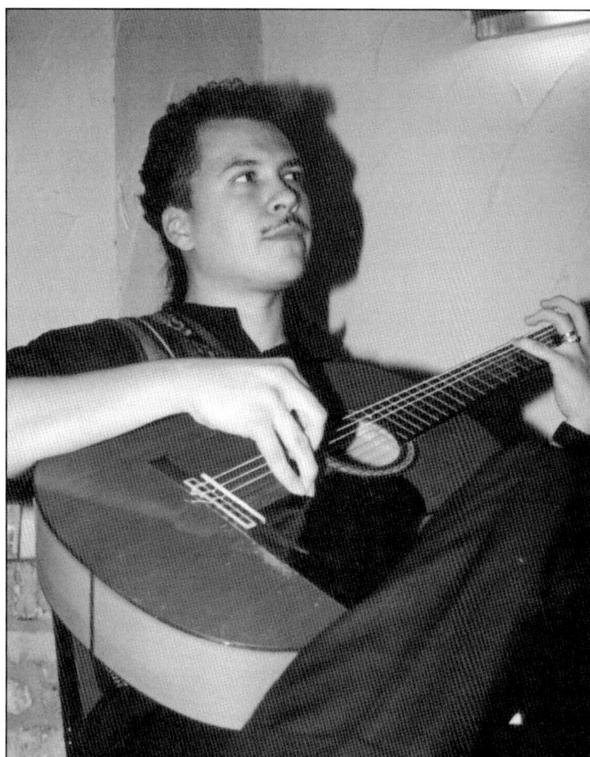

Wade Fernandez, Menominee, is a talented singer, songwriter, guitarist, and flute player. He attended the University of Wisconsin–Milwaukee and worked in the music department at the Indian Community School's State Street location. He performs nationally and locally at all forms of venues and has released several albums of his original music, as well as a music video. He has won several Native American Music Awards and Indian Summer Music Awards. (Courtesy of the *Milwaukee Area Technical College Times*.)

The Southeastern Oneida Tribal Services is located at 6820 West Wedgewood Drive in Milwaukee, the second location of the office, which was founded in 1992. It was formed to serve a population of more than 2,000 Oneida tribal members in southeast Wisconsin. It offers prescription medication service, culture and language classes, youth and elder recreation events, and social services assistance. Its former office was located at 2778 South Thirty-fifth Street. (Courtesy of SEOTS.)

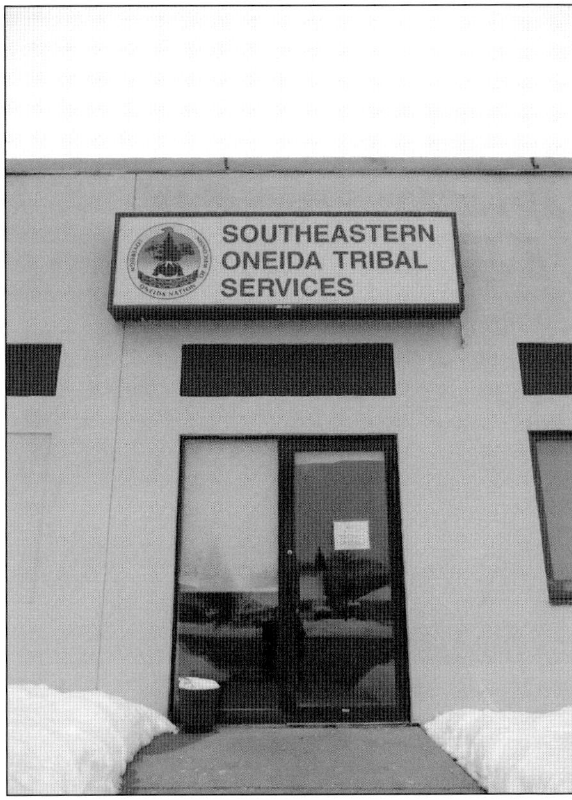

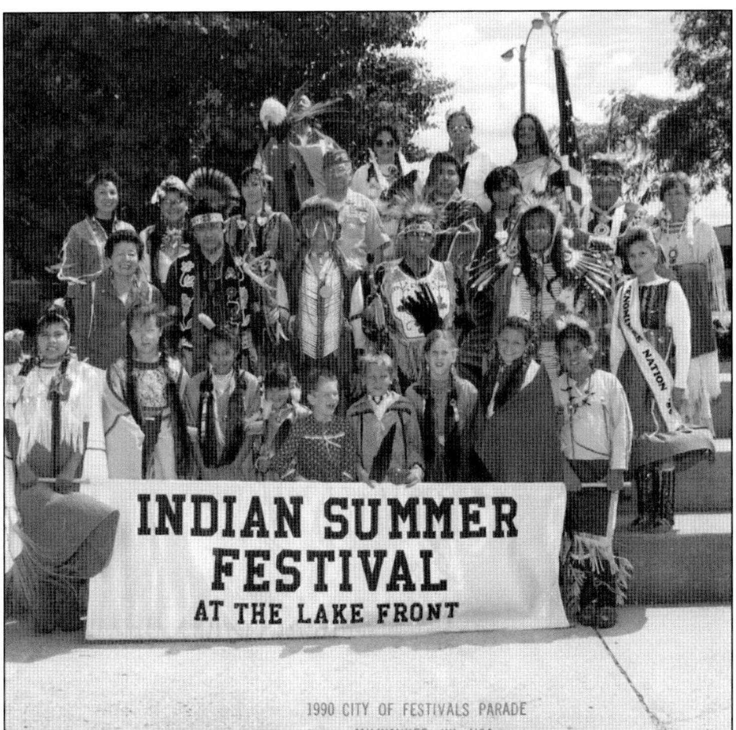

The Indian Summer Festival group is pictured at left in the 1990 City of Festivals Parade in Milwaukee. Many American Indian groups participated in the parade since it began, and the former host organization was United Indians of Milwaukee. Former Milwaukee mayor Henry Maier started the parade in 1983 as a way to highlight the city's ethnic festivals at the lakefront Henry Maier Festival Park. (Courtesy of Empire Studios of Madison.)

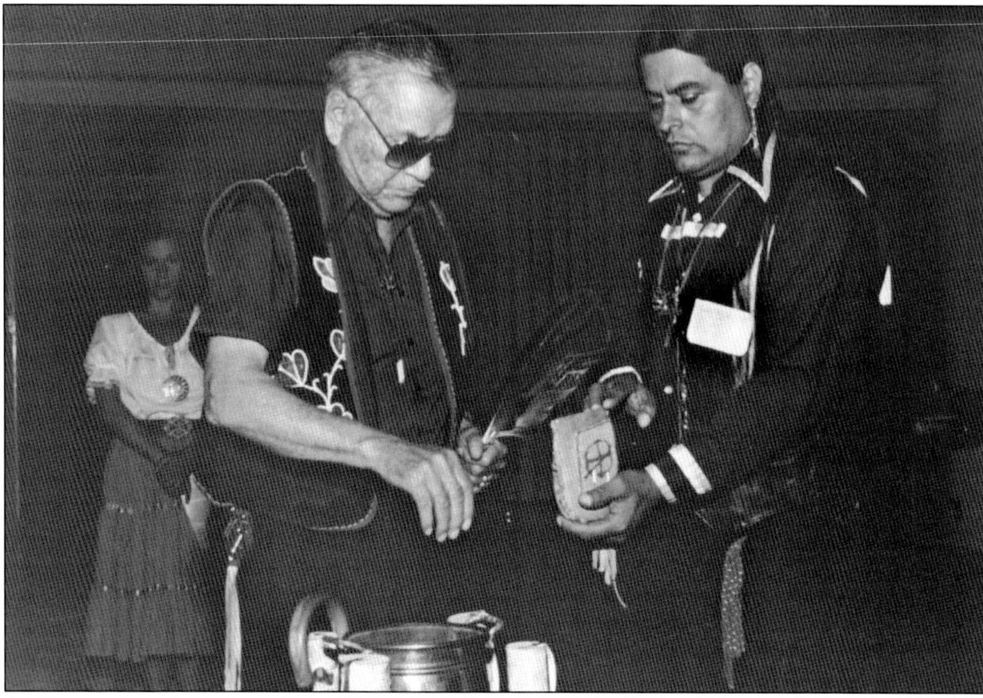

Al Skenandore (left), Oneida, and Edwin Poulin (right), Apache, both from the Siggenauk Center, take part in a ceremony at Marquette University in 1986. Skenandore holds an eagle feather in his left hand as he reaches for medicines in a leather pouch to burn as prayer offerings for the event. Poulin serves as a consultant for the Milwaukee Archdiocese Multicultural Services's Native American Ministry. (Courtesy of Todd Dacquisto.)

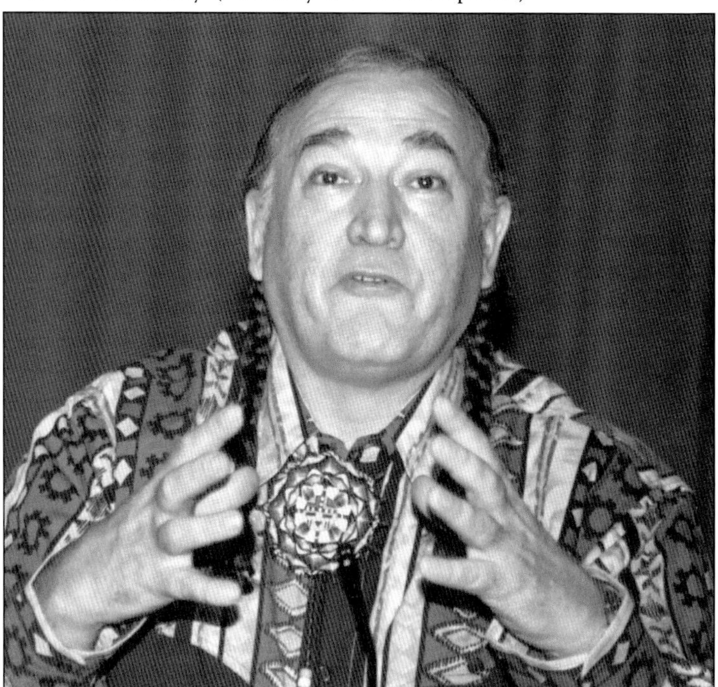

In the image at left, John Clifford, Lakota, speaks at the Milwaukee Area Technical College about Lakota beliefs. Clifford is a longtime member of the Congregation of the Great Spirit and serves as spiritual advisor to them and many other American Indian organizations in Milwaukee. He is often asked to say prayers and offer invocations. (Courtesy of the *Milwaukee Area Technical College Times*.)

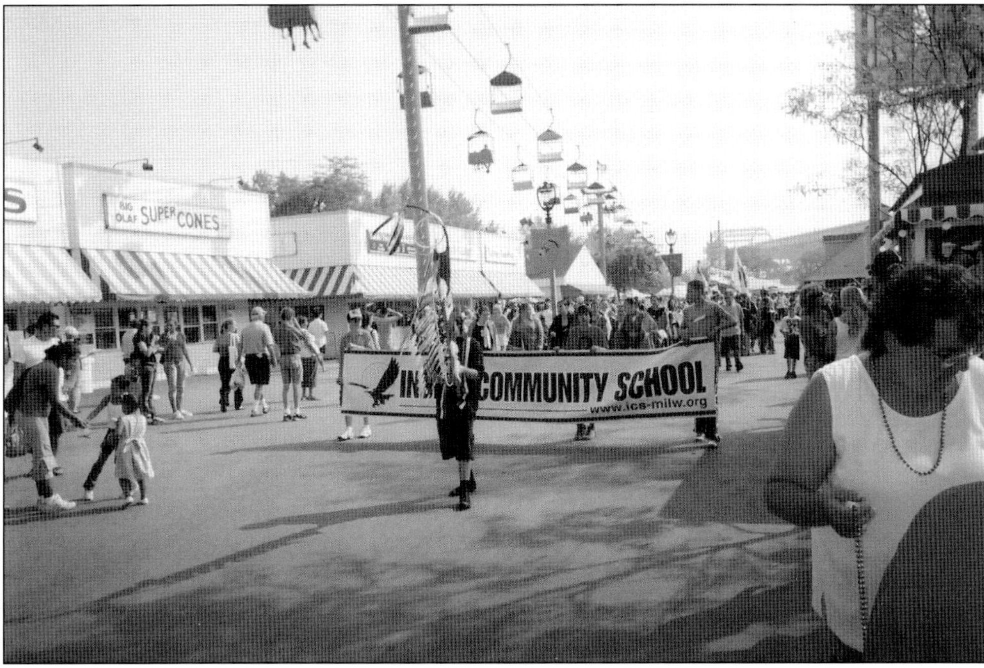

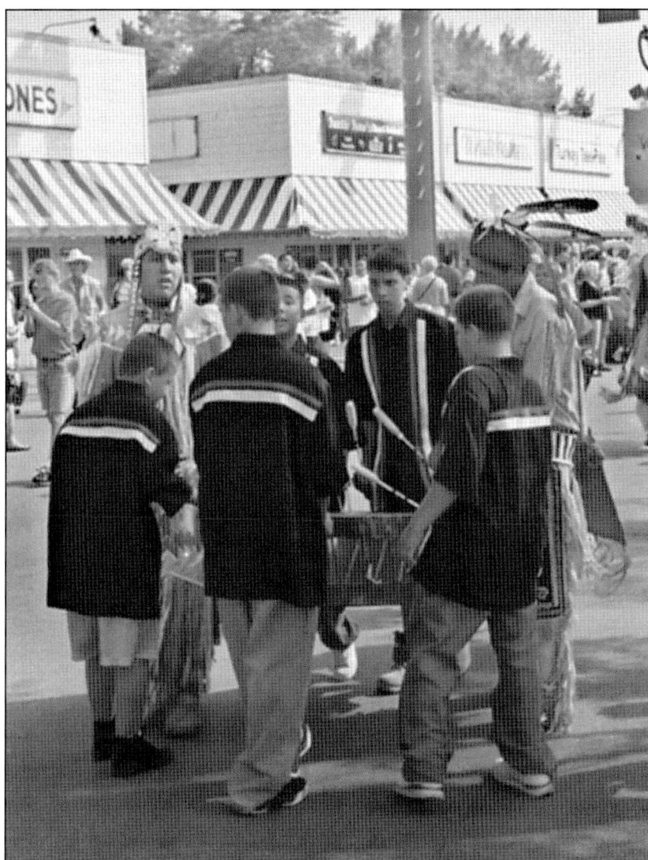

In these photographs, Indian Community School students participate in the Indian Summer Festival parade. Above, they are led by an eagle staff carrier and hold a banner with the Indian Community School logo and website on it. They are followed by the Indian Community School Eagle Singers' drum, seen at right. There have been several different compositions of students in the drum group, which has been around since 2001. The students have also had several different drum instructors since they started, each one adding to their knowledge and song base. They have performed at many local powwows and events and have also produced and released an album with the accompanying Canary Singer girls. (Courtesy of the Milwaukee Area Technical College.)

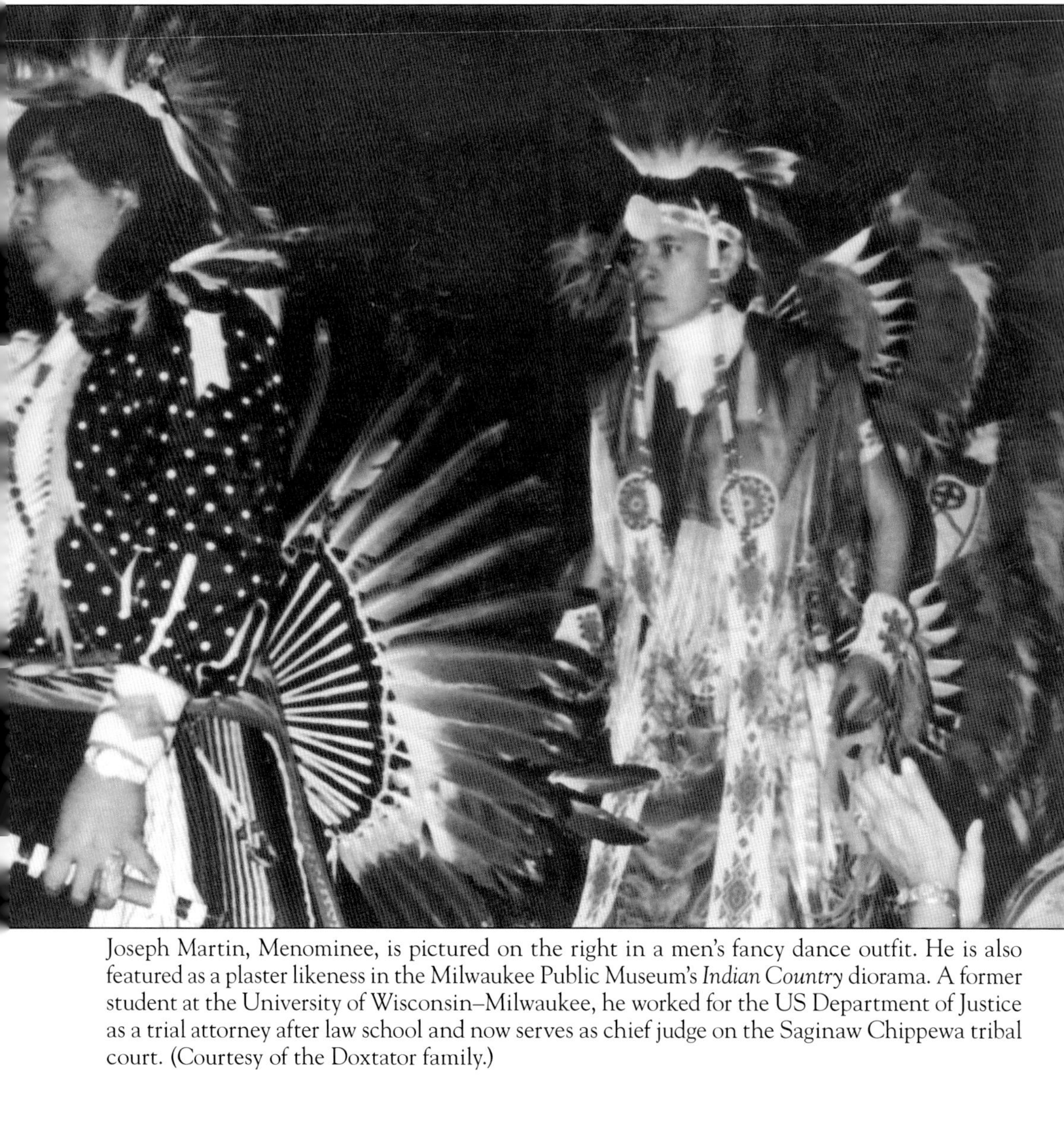

Joseph Martin, Menominee, is pictured on the right in a men's fancy dance outfit. He is also featured as a plaster likeness in the Milwaukee Public Museum's *Indian Country* diorama. A former student at the University of Wisconsin–Milwaukee, he worked for the US Department of Justice as a trial attorney after law school and now serves as chief judge on the Saginaw Chippewa tribal court. (Courtesy of the Doxtator family.)

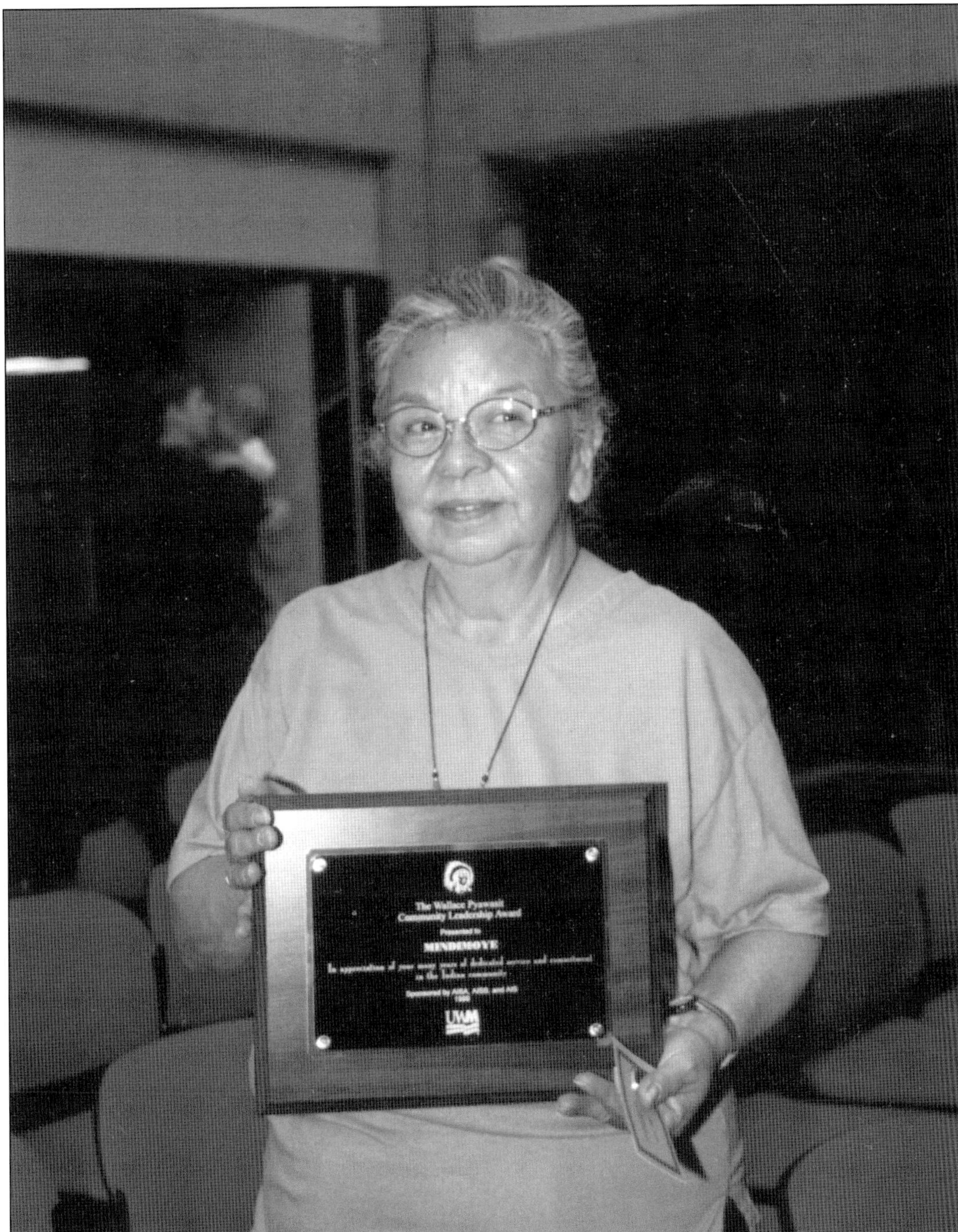

Mindimoye, Oneida, received the Wallace Pyawasit Community Leadership Award in 1999. "Mindi" was active in the Milwaukee Indian community for many years. She was the coordinator of the North American Indian Women's Council on Chemical Dependency, a developer of the Milwaukee Area American Indian Manpower Council, a counselor at the Milwaukee Indian Health Center, the community education liaison for Southeastern Oneida Tribal Services, and she received the Women of Influence Award from Oneida Social Services. (Courtesy of Mindimoye.)

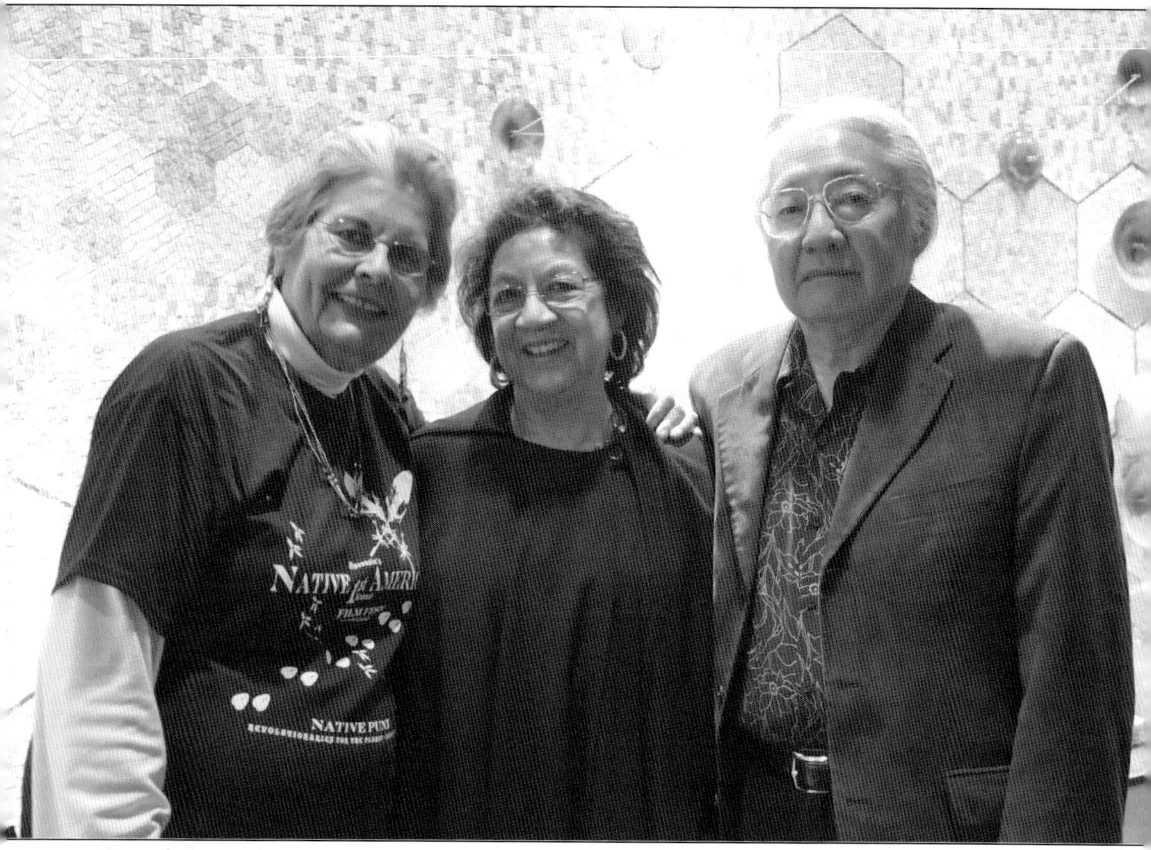

From left to right are Ada Deer; Georgianna Ignace, Menominee; and her husband, Dr. Gerald L. Ignace, at a Milwaukee community event. Gerald is from the Coeur d' Alene tribe and was born on their reservation in Idaho. He earned his medical degree from Marquette University School of Medicine in 1965. He founded and served as chairman of the Milwaukee Indian Health Board in 1973. He also founded the Indian Health Clinic, which carries his name. It opened in 1999. (Courtesy of Sonsee-Array Creative.)

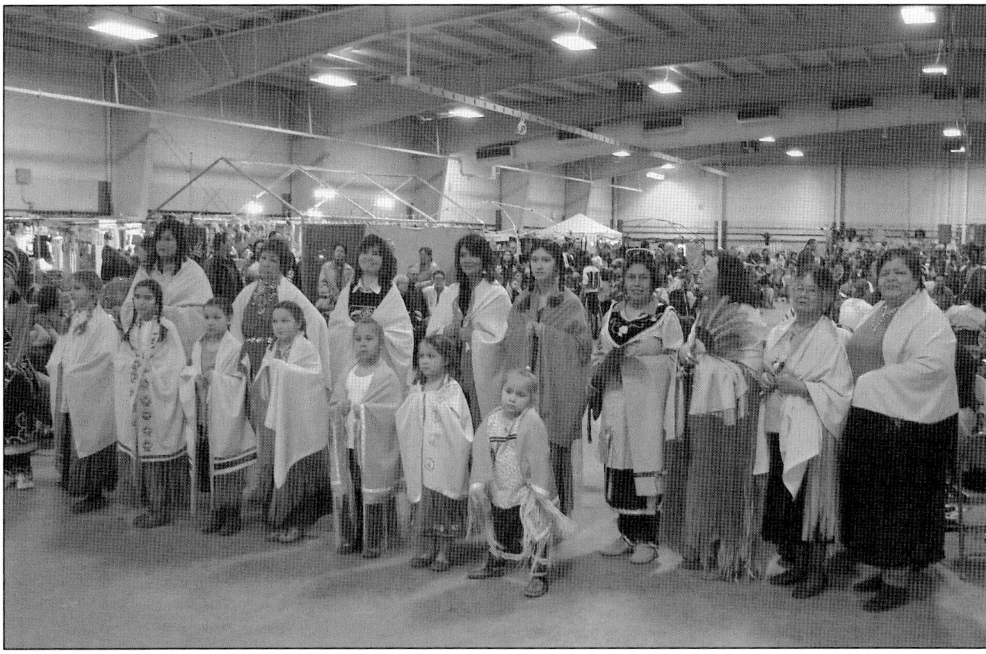

Debra Ushakow (third from left, second row), of Southeastern Oneida Tribal Services, is the chair of the local branch of the Pink Shawl Project in Milwaukee. The group holds monthly meetings for mothers and their daughters, and members make pink shawls that are worn at the grand entry to raise awareness of breast cancer detection, health, and nutrition. (Courtesy of Sonsee-Array Creative.)

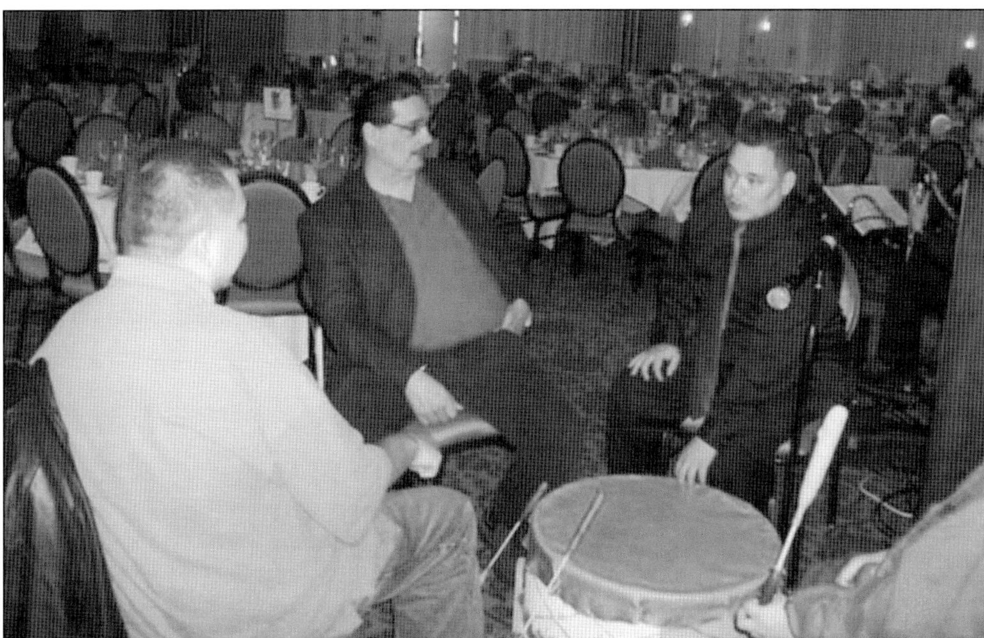

The Red Shawl Gala is a yearly event hosted by the Gerald L. Ignace Indian Health Center since 2006. The fundraiser is held with the goal of building a larger facility for the health center. Pictured from left to right are the Tradition Keepers drummers, Antonio Doxtator, James Marino, and Ignace volunteer Joshua Arvelo. (Courtesy of the Doxtator family.)

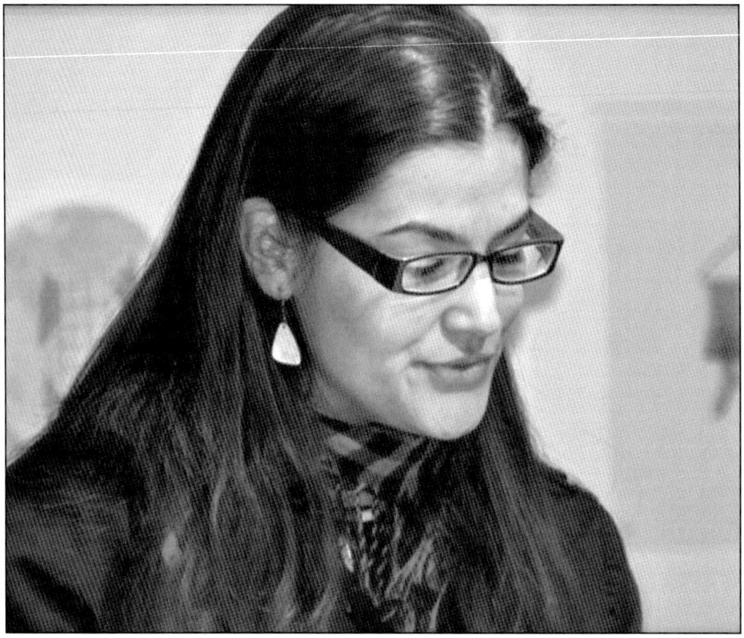

Thirza Defoe, left, is a member and organizer of Native Punx, a new cultural organization in Milwaukee featuring performances, movie screenings, and panel discussions to raise awareness through artistic expression rooted in Native American philosophies. Defoe, a hoop dancer and actress, also won a Grammy for Best Native American Music in 2009. (Courtesy of Sonsee-Array Creative.)

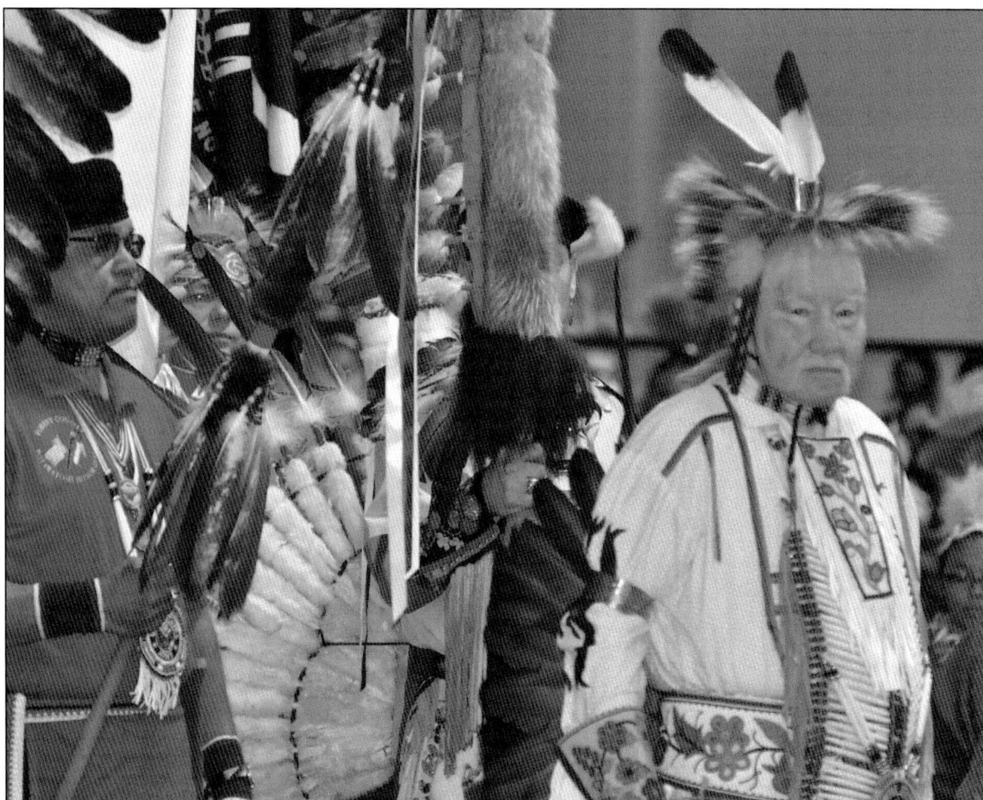

Powwows are still going strong in Milwaukee. Potawatomi Bingo and Casino holds a competition powwow every fall and the Hunting Moon Pow-Wow attracts dancers from all over the Midwest. Pictured on the right is Forest County Potawatomi elder Billy Daniels. (Courtesy of Sonsee-Array Creative.)

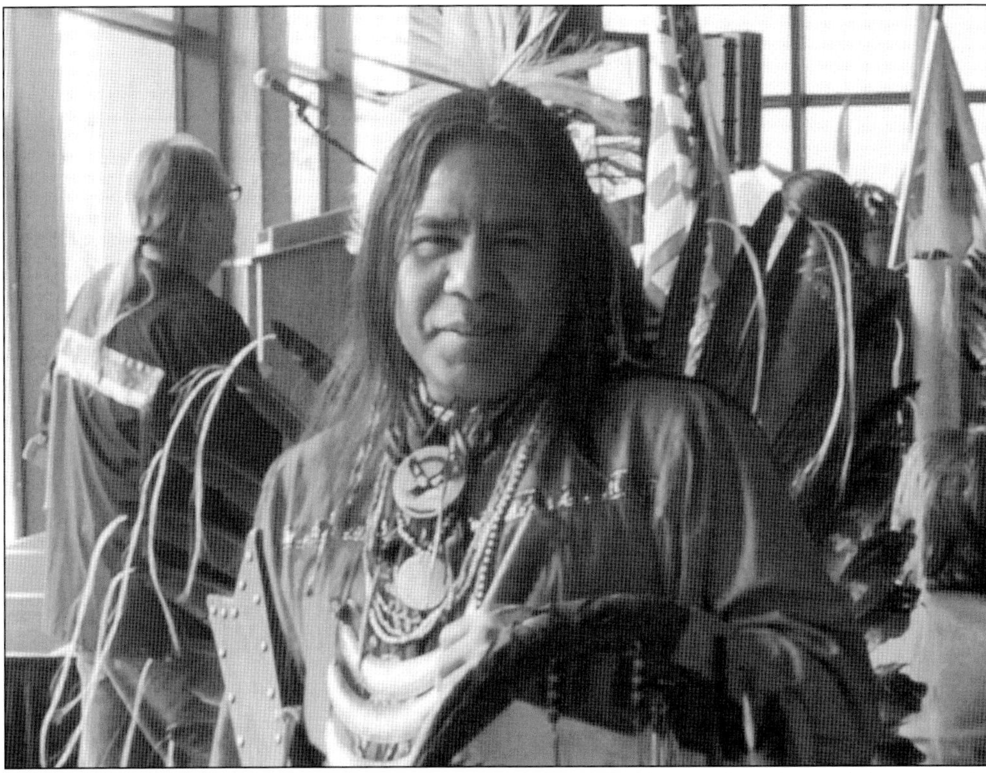

Ben Yahola, Muskogee Creek Indian, in seen above dressed in his men's traditional dance regalia at the University of Parkside. He is the founder of Earth Keepers Voices of Native American, Inc., and the Sacred Sites Run, which began in 2006. Yahola does a lot of work with food sovereignty issues, healthy eating, and workers' rights. He is also a writer and musician and has released an album. (Courtesy of the Doxtator family.)

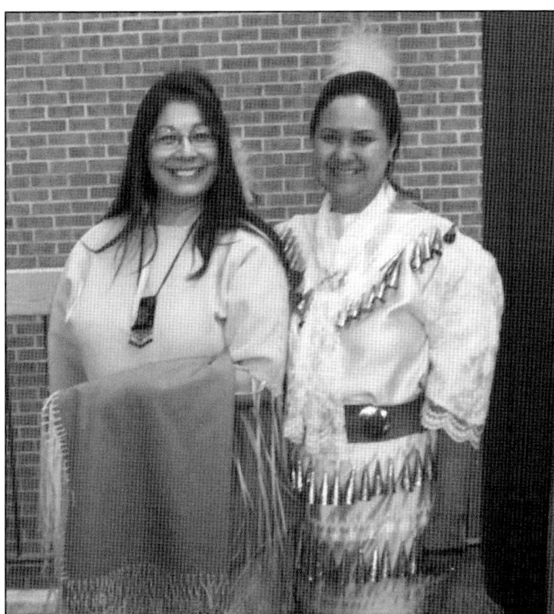

Dona Yahola, Ojibwa, is pictured on the right in her women's jingle dress outfit, and to her left is Kathy Lichterman, also Ojibwa. Yahola is very active in education and has worked as a teacher since the 1990s at Spotted Eagle High School, the Indian Community School, and the WE Indians Program. Yahola recently published a book, *Mino-Bimaadiziiwin*, or "*The Good Life*." (Courtesy of the Doxtator family.)

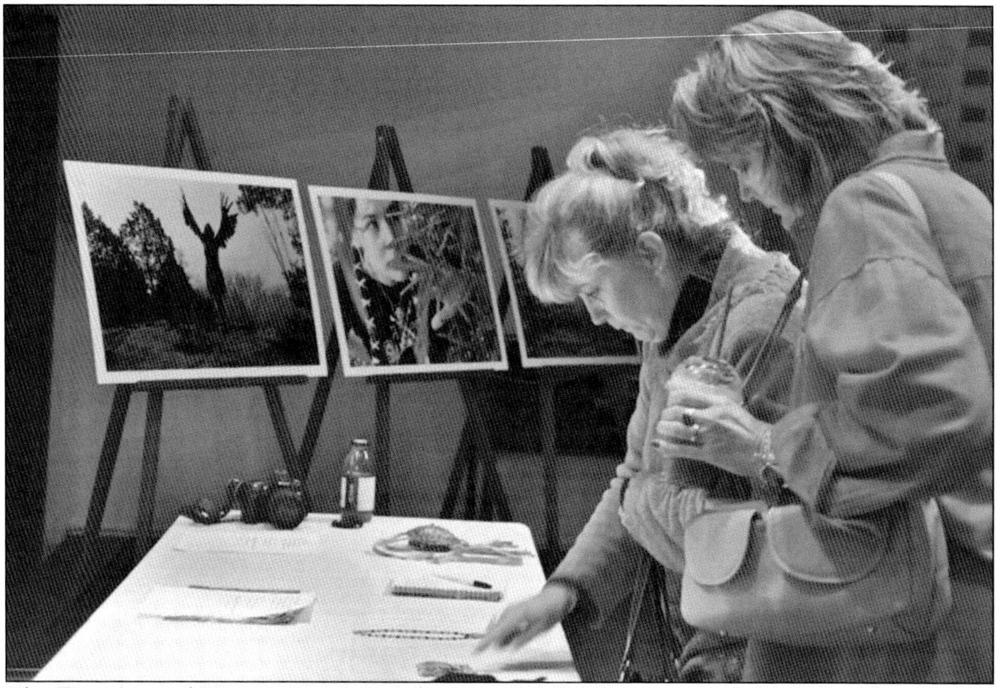

The First Annual Native American Film Fest and Celebration was held in October 2010 in Milwaukee. The event featured work created and acted by American Indians around the nation and included in-depth discussions about the native experience, issues of stereotyping, and mascots of Indian people. (Courtesy of Sonsee-Array Creative.)

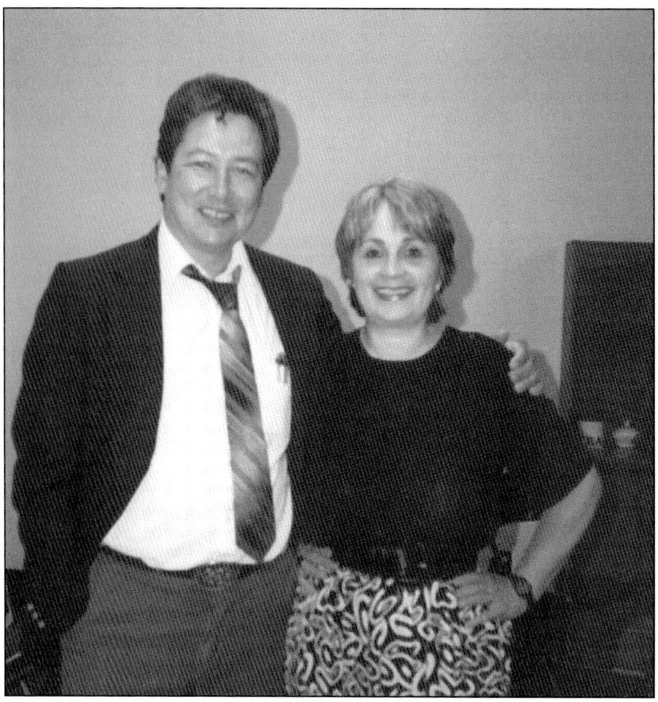

In 1989, Dr. Arlene Zakhar (shown standing with John Beaudein), director of the Milwaukee Indian Economic Development Agency, identified and conducted the first survey of 140 Wisconsin Indian-owned businesses. The agency then established the American Indian Chamber of Commerce of Wisconsin as a separate entity, modeled after the Minnesota American Indian Chamber of Commerce. Assistant director Kitty Hill, Oneida, provided research assistance and attorney Jeffrey DeCora, Ho-Chunk, provided legal expertise. (Courtesy of Arlene Zakhar.)

BIBLIOGRAPHY

The majority of the information used in the captions was found in articles from the *Milwaukee Journal Sentinel* newspaper archives, which are too numerous to list here. No less important were notes from discussions with Milwaukee Indian community members, specifically Opal Skenandore, Diane Amour, Jenelle Klumb, Mark Denning, and Roberta Doxtator. Mark Thiel helped conceptualize the interpretation of the museum's *Felicity* diorama.

Barrett Papers at the Milwaukee Public Museum.

Buss, Fran Leeper. *Dignity: Lower Income Women Tell of Their Lives and Struggles: Oral Histories*. Ann Arbor, MI: University of Michigan Press, 1984.

Hoan Papers at the Milwaukee Public Museum.

Fox, Isabella. *Solomon Juneau: A Biography with Sketches of the Juneau Family*. Milwaukee, WI: Evening Wisconsin Printing Company, 1916.

Krouse, Susan Applegate. "What Came Out of the Takeovers: Women's Activism and the Indian Community School of Milwaukee." *American Indian Quarterly*, Vol. 27, 2003: 533–547.

McLester III, Gordon, and Laurence M. Hauptman. *Nation within a Nation: Voices of the Oneida of Wisconsin*. Madison, WI: Wisconsin Historical Society Press, 2010.

Hauptman, Laurence M. *The Iroquois Struggle for Survival: World War II to Red Power*. Syracuse, NY: Syracuse University Press, 1986.

McBride, Genevieve G., ed. *Women's Wisconsin: From Native Matriarchies to the New Millennium*. Madison, WI: Wisconsin Historical Society Press, 2005.

Milwaukee Area Technical College Times Archives.

Milwaukee Indian News. American Indian Files, 1973–1977. Milwaukee Public Museum.

Milwaukee Journal Sentinel Archives.

Papers of Nancy O. Lurie. University of Wisconsin–Milwaukee Libraries Archives Department.

Ritzenthaler Collection at the Milwaukee Public Museum.

Servais, Stephen P. *At Trail's Edge: American Indian Occupation of Milwaukee to 1850*. Master's thesis from the University of Wisconsin–Milwaukee, 1998.

Thiel. Mark G. "The Indian Way." *Whispering Winds: American Indians Past and Present*. Vol. 6–8, 1973.

Discover Thousands of Local History Books Featuring Millions of Vintage Images

Arcadia Publishing, the leading local history publisher in the United States, is committed to making history accessible and meaningful through publishing books that celebrate and preserve the heritage of America's people and places.

Find more books like this at
www.arcadiapublishing.com

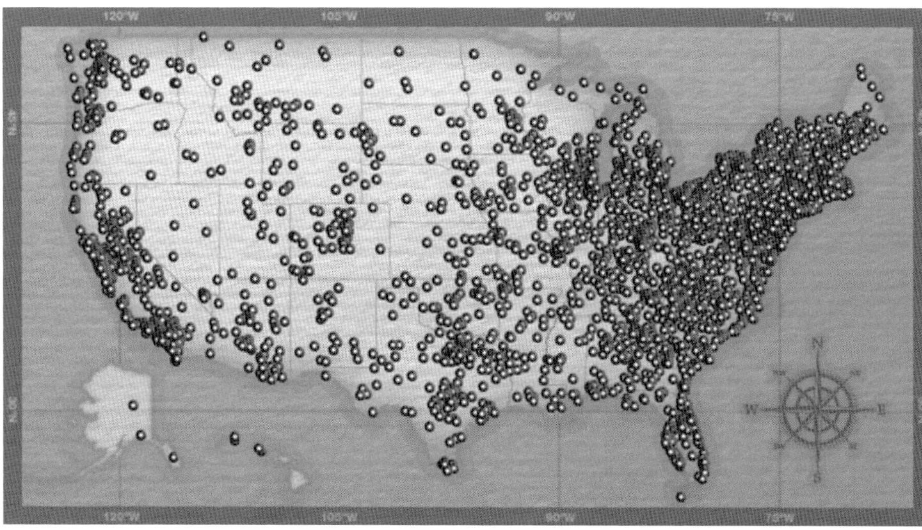

Search for your hometown history, your old stomping grounds, and even your favorite sports team.

Consistent with our mission to preserve history on a local level, this book was printed in South Carolina on American-made paper and manufactured entirely in the United States. Products carrying the accredited Forest Stewardship Council (FSC) label are printed on 100 percent FSC-certified paper.

MADE IN THE USA